D1823241

New Perspectives in German Political Studies

Series Editors
William E. Paterson
Aston University
Birmingham, UK

Thomas Saalfeld
Universität Bamberg
Bamberg, Bayern, Germany

Far reaching changes are now taking place in Germany. Stability lay at the core of the German model and much of the writing from Peter Katzenstein and Manfred Schmidt onwards sought to explain this enviable stability. Changes in the external environment have created a number of fundamental challenges which pose a threat to that stability. Germany is now Europe's central power but this has generated controversy about how it is to exercise this new power. Although attention is often centred on German power the migration crisis demonstrates its limits. *New Perspectives in German Political Studies* aims to engage with these new challenges and to cater for the heightened interest in Germany. The Editors would welcome proposals for single-authored monographs, edited collections and Pivots, from junior as well as well-established scholars working on contemporary German Politics.

More information about this series at
http://www.palgrave.com/gp/series/14735

Liana Fix

Germany's Role in European Russia Policy

A New German Power?

Liana Fix
Gießener Dissertation im Fachbereich Sozial- und Kulturwissenschaften
Justus Liebig University
Giessen, Germany

New Perspectives in German Political Studies
ISBN 978-3-030-68225-5   ISBN 978-3-030-68226-2   (eBook)
https://doi.org/10.1007/978-3-030-68226-2

© The Editor(s) (if applicable) and The Author(s), under exclusive licence to Springer Nature Switzerland AG 2021
This work is subject to copyright. All rights are solely and exclusively licensed by the Publisher, whether the whole or part of the material is concerned, specifically the rights of translation, reprinting, reuse of illustrations, recitation, broadcasting, reproduction on microfilms or in any other physical way, and transmission or information storage and retrieval, electronic adaptation, computer software, or by similar or dissimilar methodology now known or hereafter developed.
The use of general descriptive names, registered names, trademarks, service marks, etc. in this publication does not imply, even in the absence of a specific statement, that such names are exempt from the relevant protective laws and regulations and therefore free for general use. The publisher, the authors and the editors are safe to assume that the advice and information in this book are believed to be true and accurate at the date of publication. Neither the publisher nor the authors or the editors give a warranty, expressed or implied, with respect to the material contained herein or for any errors or omissions that may have been made. The publisher remains neutral with regard to jurisdictional claims in published maps and institutional affiliations.

Cover credit © mbbirdy, gettyimages

This Palgrave Macmillan imprint is published by the registered company Springer Nature Switzerland AG.
The registered company address is: Gewerbestrasse 11, 6330 Cham, Switzerland

To my grandparents

Foreword

When Germany was reunified three decades ago, there was both confidence and concern about what role it might play both in Europe and globally going forward. Would it persist as an "economic giant and political dwarf", would it aspire to recreate a great power role, would the new, larger Germany remain as committed to the European Union? Thirty years later these questions have been answered. Germany remains committed to the European Union, it has become both an economic and political leader in Europe, and it persists as a resolute civilian power.

Germany has also become, as Liana Fix shows in this informative study, the key country in fashioning the EU's Ostpolitik and seeking to reconcile the divergent attitudes toward Russia that have emerged since the EU enlargement in 2004. Germany has for the past century had a complex and fluctuating relationship with the Soviet Union and post-Soviet Russia, and has been Russia's most important European interlocutor since Chancellor Willy Brandt's Ostpolitik and the Moscow Treaty of 1970. Germany's current policies toward Russia are shaped by the legacy of gratitude for permitting Germany to unify peacefully, a longstanding mutually beneficial economic and energy relationship, and a belief that engagement with Vladimir Putin's Russia is necessary, however challenging it is to deal with the Kremlin.

While much of Europe shares the German commitment to engagement with Russia, new EU members Poland and the Baltic states are far more wary of dealing with Moscow, given their own negative historical experiences with Russia. Since 2004, it has been challenging to forge an EU consensus on how to deal with Russia on a number of different levels. This book explains clearly how and why Germany has gradually emerged as the leader of the EU's Ostpolitik by examining four case studies.

The first case study is the Russia-Georgia War of 2008. Dmitry Medvedev had become president just prior to the outbreak of hostilities, yet Putin was driving the negotiations that led to a ceasefire. This time, French president Nicolas Sarkozy led the talks, because France had the presidency of the European Council, and Germany was supportive of the mediation efforts.

Germany did, however, take the lead in conceptualising the 2010 EU-Russia Partnership for Modernisation, which began as a bilateral German-Russian Partnership for Modernisation, the brainchild of then Foreign Minister Frank-Walter Steinmeier. The idea was to pursue programs that would encourage Russia to modernise its economy and promote the Rule of Law. In 2008, Medvedev had proposed a new Euro-Atlantic security architecture at a speech in Berlin, but little was done to follow up his ideas.

Chancellor Merkel was determined to engage Medvedev on issues which directly affected Europe's security, and in 2010 she initiated the Meseberg process with him, designed to resolve the conflict in Moldova's breakaway statelet of Transnistria, in return for which the EU would establish a joint Security Committee with Russia, thereby giving it a greater stake in the established Euro-Atlantic security architecture. This was largely a German, as opposed to an EU, project, but it was ultimately unsuccessful. The same can be said for the Partnership for Modernisation. Both initiatives were based on the premise that President Medvedev was empowered to deliver a more cooperative policy toward the EU, which, in retrospect, was misplaced.

Liana Fix explains how Germany came to dominate and fashion the EU's Ostpolitik through Berlin's actions following Russia's 2014 annexation of Crimea and launch of a war in Southeastern Ukraine. Chancellor Merkel's government took the lead in crafting EU sanctions against Russian individuals and also the financial sanctions following the downing of the MH17 plane in July 2014. Germany has ensured that sanctions are renewed every six months, as Russia has failed to honour the commitments it made in the February 2015 Minsk agreements designed to end the war in Ukraine. Although some EU members are ready to end the sanctions despite Russian non-compliance, Germany has managed to impose discipline and unity on the EU so far.

Since 2014, Europe's relations with Russia have sharply deteriorated and Germany's role in guiding the EU's relations with Russia has become more challenging. Merkel understands Putin better than any other world leader because she and Putin literally speak the same language and her GDR background has given her insights into the mindset of the former Soviet KGB agent who leads Russia. As she reportedly told President Obama after a conversation with the Russian leader following the outbreak of the Ukraine war, Putin "lives in his own world". Events since then, including the hacking by Russian state agents of the Bundestag's computers, the assassination of a Chechen dissident in Berlin's Tiergarten by agents of the Russian state, and the poisoning of opposition leader Alexei Navalny who was diagnosed and treated in Berlin, have further strained the relationship. Nevertheless, Merkel continues to argue for the need for the EU to engage Russia.

Liana Fix's analysis leaves the reader wondering how both German-Russian and EU-Russia relations will evolve after Chancellor Merkel has left the political scene. Will France take over leading Europe's Ostpolitik, as President Macron has signaled he would like to? Will other EU countries agree to this? Will a future European leader continue to be able to reconcile the contrasting views of Russia that persist in different parts of Europe? *Germany's Role in European Russia Policy—A New German Power?* illuminates the background to these important questions and provides an innovative framework for analysing how EU-Russia relations might develop well into the twenty-first century.

Washington, DC, USA   Angela E. Stent

(Author of *Putin's World: Russia Against the West and with the Rest*)

Acknowledgements

This book has travelled a long way from Berlin, Moscow and Tbilisi to Brussels, Paris, Warsaw, Washington, DC, and back to Berlin. The first idea emerged during my time as Mercator Fellow on International Affairs at the German Federal Foreign Office in discussions with German diplomats working on Russia. The following stays at the Carnegie Moscow Office and the European Union Delegation in Georgia were a further inspiration. This was still before the outbreak of the Ukraine conflict in 2014, which has changed the parameters not only of Germany's role in Europe, but also of our understanding of relations with Russia.

The publication of this book would not have been possible without the support of numerous individuals and institutions that have accompanied me professionally and personally in the last years. First and foremost, I would like to thank Professor Andrea Gawrich for the continuous support, generous advice and enduring patience throughout this endeavour, as well as Professor Simon Bulmer for inspiring some of the main ideas of this book. I am grateful to the following institutions for having hosted me as associate and doctoral fellow during my research: The German Council on Foreign Relations (DGAP), the German Institute for International and Security Affairs (SWP), in particular Sabine Fischer and the Eastern Europe/Eurasia Division, as well as the SWP Brussels office, the Institute for German Studies at the University of Birmingham and the American Institute for Contemporary German Studies (AICGS) in Washington, DC.

I am indebted to the Friedrich Ebert Foundation for having funded not only my research at the University of Giessen, but also my master and bachelor studies at the London School of Economics and Political Science (LSE) as well as the Ruhr-University Bochum and the Université François Rabelais in Tours. A warm thank you goes to the colleagues and fellow researchers at these institutions for the inspiration and burden-sharing. I would also like to thank Körber-Stiftung, in particular my colleagues at the Berlin office and Nora Müller, for the support in concluding this book while working as Programme Director in the International Affairs department.

Furthermore, my most profound thank you goes to all interlocutors in different capitals, including numerous officials and experts, that have taken the time to share their insights and discuss the ideas of this book. I have benefitted immensely from the feedback of colleagues at conferences and workshops in Bilbao, Cambridge, Helsinki, Bremen, Leipzig and Tartu, and I would like to thank Nicu Popescu, Stefan Meister, and Susan Stewart for giving feedback on chapters of this book, as well as Patricia Daehnhardt and Vladimír Handl for the opportunity to contribute to a Special Issue of German Politics. My heartfelt thank you goes to Fabian Schöppner for improving my English and to my friends Jan Steinbach for diligently and patiently editing the references and Sarah Schmid for reading the first draft. I assume responsibility for any remaining errors and shortcomings of this book.

Along the way, I had the privilege to count on the support of many friends from near and far. My dearest thanks belongs to Christina Denhard for being there from the start, Marcia Schenck for the constant inspiration and long evenings in co-working mode, Lis Wey for her wisdom, David Maier for keeping up spirits during difficult times, Laura Söllner for the companionship, my Mercator friends and all those I could not mention for lending an ear whenever necessary. Thank you, Tobias Martens, for bringing joy. Most importantly, I would like to thank my family—my parents Eugen Fix and Nadja Fix as well as my sister Xenia Fix—for their continuous support throughout these years. This book is dedicated to my grandparents, who experienced German-Russian relations in a very different time and under different circumstances.

CONTENTS

ABOUT THE AUTHOR

Liana Fix is a historian and political scientist. In her work, she focuses on European security, Russia and Eastern Europe, as well as German foreign policy. She has commented and published widely on these topics in academia, think tanks and national and international media.

She works as Programme Director for International Affairs at Körber-Stiftung's Berlin Office and was an associate and doctoral fellow at the German Council on Foreign Relations (DGAP) as well as the German Institute for International and Security Affairs (SWP). Liana Fix holds a PhD degree from the Justus Liebig University of Giessen and a master's degree in Theory and History of International Relations from the London School of Economics and Political Science (LSE). She has also studied at the Ruhr-University Bochum and the Université François Rabelais in Tours. In 2015, she held a DAAD/AICGS Fellowship in Washington, DC, and in 2012/2013, a Mercator Fellowship with postings at the German Foreign Office, the Carnegie Moscow Center and the EU Delegation in Georgia. She also was a fellow of the Global Governance Futures—Robert Bosch Foundation Multilateral Dialogue. Liana Fix is member of the extended board of Women in International Security Germany.

ABBREVIATIONS

AA   Association Agreement
CFSP   Common Foreign and Security Policy
CSDP   Common Security and Defence Policy
EaP   Eastern Partnership
EC   European Commission
EU   European Union
EUMM   European Union Monitoring Mission
MAP   Membership Action Plan
NATO   North Atlantic Treaty Organization
NRC   NATO-Russia Council
OSCE   Organization for Security and Co-operation in Europe
PCA   Partnership and Cooperation Agreement
P4M   Partnership for Modernisation
SMM   Special Monitoring Mission
TACIS   Technical Assistance to the Commonwealth of Independent States
UN   United Nations

LIST OF TABLES

CHAPTER 1

Introduction

In 1985, historian Hans-Peter Schwarz observed that Germany has developed from a country obsessed with power, in terms of a Wilhelminian craving for status, to forgetfulness of power in the West German Federal Republic, which felt comfortable in its own perceived impotence. Schwarz recommended the German public develop more self-confidence, which it seemed to have forgotten along with power politics. Almost thirty-five years later, Schwarz' observation deserves to be restated, yet in reverse order: Is Germany at the beginning of a change from "Machtvergessenheit" to "Machtbesessenheit", meaning a return from forgetfulness of power to power politics—not in a Wilhelminian sense, but rather understood as greater assertiveness?[1] Has Germany relearned only too well how to exercise power and therefore become too dominant an actor in Europe?

Especially since reunification, Germany has been under continuous scrutiny and suspicion of harbouring hegemonic impulses.[2] As one of the

---

[1] Cf. Simon Bulmer and William E. Paterson, 'Germany and the European Union: From 'Tamed Power' to Normalized Power?', *International Affairs*, 86.5 (2010), 1051–73, 1052.

[2] Cf. Arnulf Baring (ed.), *Germany's New Position in Europe: Problems and Perspectives*, German Historical Perspectives Series, 8 (Oxford, Providence, RI: Berg, 1994); Christian Hacke, *Weltmacht wider Willen: Die Aussenpolitik der Bundesrepublik Deutschland* (*Stuttgart: Klett-Cotta*, 1988); Kenneth N. Waltz, 'The Emerging Structure of International Politics', *International Security* 18.2 (1993); John J. Mearsheimer, 'Back to the Future: Instability in Europe after the Cold War', *International Security* 15.1 (1990),

© The Author(s), under exclusive license to Springer Nature Switzerland AG 2021
L. Fix, *Germany's Role in European Russia Policy*, New Perspectives in German Political Studies,
https://doi.org/10.1007/978-3-030-68226-2_1

most important member states keenly aware of its burdened past, Germany's enlarged role in Europe has become a topic of ardent debate in academia and politics. Even before the "Munich Consensus" of 2014, when the German Federal President as well as the German foreign and defence ministers advocated for a stronger role in international relations, Germany's increased engagement in the EU has raised questions about a new German power in Europe.[3] Furthermore, Germany's prominent leadership in the handling of numerous crises in Europe has reignited concerns about German hegemony. For instance, former German diplomat Wolfgang Ischinger argued Germany will be caught in a "hegemony trap"[4] if it does not give way to a more powerful European foreign policy. The historian Anne Applebaum warned against "putting Germany front and center in Europe's crises".[5] At the same time, leadership expectations towards Germany have increased inversely proportional to fears about Germany's role. After the election of US President Donald Trump, and against the backdrop of a deteriorating transatlantic relationship, German Chancellor Angela Merkel was praised as the new "leader of the free world". During the Eurozone crisis, Former Polish Foreign Minister Sikorski famously warned that he fears German power less than he is beginning to fear German inactivity.[6] Most recently, during the COVID-19 crisis, Germany together with France paved the way for an unprecedented EU economic recovery fund through collectively issued debt. According to *The Economist*, Germany is "doomed to lead Europe".[7]

While Germany has become significantly more influential within the EU, the conceptual terms to explain Germany's new role are still under debate. Is Germany a hegemon, an embedded hegemon or just a semi-hegemon? A geo-economic power or a tamed power? A reflective, reluctant or civilian power? This book seeks to contribute to the "puzzle of

5–56; Hans-Peter Schwarz, *Die Zentralmacht Europas: Deutschlands Rückkehr auf die Weltbühne*, 1st edn (Berlin: Siedler, 1994).

[3] Bastian Giegerich and Maximilian Terhalle, 'The Munich Consensus and the Purpose of German Power', *Survival*, 58.2 (2016), 155–66. Beverly Crawford, *Power and German Foreign Policy: Embedded Hegemony in Europe*, New Perspectives in German Studies (Basingstoke, New York: Palgrave Macmillan, 2007).

[4] Wolfgang Ischinger, 'Deutschland in der Hegemonie-Falle by Wolfgang Ischinger', *Project Syndicate*, 14 September 2015.

[5] Cf. Anne Applebaum, 'The Risks of Putting Germany Front and Center in Europe's Crises', *The Washington Post*, 20 February 2015.

[6] Cf. Radosław Sikorski, 'I Fear Germany's Power Less than Her Inactivity', *Financial Times*, 28 November 2008.

[7] 'Germany is doomed to lead Europe', *The Economist*, 25 June 2020.

German power"[8] through an analysis of Germany's role in European Russia policy.

Russia policy is an ideal test case for assessing Germany's role in Europe. Russia ranks for many reasons—historical, geopolitical, economic, energy-related and cultural—among Germany's top foreign policy priorities.[9] Both countries had long been key geostrategic actors in the European political landscape.[10] A change in Germany's role in Europe can likely be observed in this area of special importance: Russia policy touches upon core German interests, which suggests that if Germany is heading towards greater assertiveness in European policy, this should leave traces in this important policy field. Furthermore, since the EU's Eastern enlargement in 2004, Russia policy has become a contentious policy field in EU foreign policy, with competition between member states as well as EU institutions and representatives for control over policy outcomes.[11] How has Germany influenced Russia policy since the EU's Eastern enlargement in 2004— along or against the preferences of the new Eastern member states? What does it tell us about the way Germany exerts power in the European Union? With Russia policy as a test case, this book aims to contribute to the broader debate about Germany's power in Europe. Furthermore, it provides a comprehensive account of Germany's "Ostpolitik" and detailed analyses of how Germany addressed major crisis situations in the EU-Russia relationship, such as the Ukraine conflict and the Russian-Georgian War, and how it introduced policy initiatives, such as the EU-Russia Partnership for Modernisation and the Meseberg initiative. The analysis draws upon detailed document analysis and over forty interviews with senior officials and experts in Berlin, Brussels, Paris, Warsaw and Washington. Does Germany's influence on the EU's Russia policy provide evidence for

---

[8] Hanns W. Maull, 'Reflective, Hegemonic, Geo-Economic, Civilian…?: The Puzzle of German Power', *German Politics*, 27.4 (2018), 1–19.

[9] Christopher S. Chivvis and Thomas Rid, 'The Roots of Germany's Russia Policy', *Survival*, 51.2 (2009), 105–22.

[10] Cf. Angela Stent, *Russia and Germany Reborn: Unification, the Soviet Collapse, and the New Europe* (Princeton, NJ: Princeton University Press, 2001).

[11] Cf. Tuomas Forsberg and Hiski Haukkala, *The European Union and Russia*, The European Union Series, 1st edn (London, New York, NY: Macmillan Education; Palgrave, 2016), 44–75; Anke Schmidt-Felzmann, 'All for One?: EU Member States and the Union's Common Policy Towards the Russian Federation', *Journal of Contemporary European Studies*, 16.2 (2008), 169–87; Jackie Gower, 'The European Union's Policy on Russia: Rhetoric or Reality?', *Russia and Europe in the Twenty-First Century*, ed. by Gower and Timmins (2009), pp. 111–32.

German embeddedness in Europe (a European Germany) or, to the contrary, for its dominance within the EU (a German Europe)?[12]

The empirical analysis of Russia policy is combined with a theory-based perspective on Germany's exercise of power in the EU. By applying a comprehensive taxonomy of power, this book aims to bring back power as a category into the analysis of member states' influence within the EU and to untangle the different "shades" and conceptualisations of power underlying Germany's policy. The results demonstrate that German "Machtpolitik" (power politics) is much more nuanced and complex than previous conceptualisations and theoretical schools would suggest. By combining and applying different instruments of power, Germany engaged to become the central axis of policy making between the EU and Russia, decisively shaping the paradigm and outcome of EU policy towards Russia. The book argues that instead of hegemony, Germany's influence on Russia policy can be more adequately described by the term "policy dominance", designating a continuous engagement over a longer period of time in a certain policy field with the aim to set policies (or oppose others) and to shape the policy paradigm. This term is situated between leadership and hegemony as an "in-between" mode of long-term power exertion within the EU. The book concludes that despite Germany's central role in the EU's Russia policy, the exercise of power within the EU is crucially dependent on legitimacy and followership by other member states. Overall, the synthesis of theoretical and policy analysis in this book adds to our understanding of the nature of German power in the EU and how it is exercised in policy towards Russia.

Despite its relevance, Russia policy has rarely been systematically analysed to reveal how Germany exerts power within the EU.[13] This is surprising, given that the case of Russia policy promises useful insights into changes or continuities in Germany's European policy. On the one hand, many general contributions on EU-Russia relations only touch upon the specific role and influence that Germany has played and exercised. On the other hand, analyses on Germany's role in Europe often focus on select cases of Russia policy, such as the Ukraine conflict, to prove the thesis of

---

[12] Cf. Ulrich Beck, *Das deutsche Europa: Neue Machtlandschaften im Zeichen der Krise*, Edition Suhrkamp digital, 1st edn (Berlin: Suhrkamp, 2012).

[13] A notable exception is Stephen Szabo's geo-economic interpretation of Russia policy. Cf. Stephen F. Szabo, *Germany, Russia and the Rise of Geo-Economics*, 1st edn (London: Bloomsbury, 2015). Furthermore, Marco Siddi analysed German leadership in EU relations with Russia through the lenses of hegemony literature. Cf. Marco Siddi, 'A Contested Hegemon?: Germany's Leadership in EU Relations with Russia', *German Politics*, 94 (2018), 1–18.

German hegemony in Europe or a new German responsibility in Europe. The aim of this book is to bring these two perspectives together to understand the full picture of how Germany exerts influence in EU Russia policy. While there are certainly other cases that are similarly relevant to the debate about Germany's role in Europe, such as European economic and financial policy, Russia policy is an important piece in the puzzle of German power with much potential for generalisation. Therefore, it is all the more important to get this piece right.

Furthermore, there are important lessons to be learned by looking back at the period of EU-Russia relations after the EU's Eastern enlargement in 2004. After the "romantic" era of the 1990s, this era of EU-Russia relations was more sober, yet there was still enough room for manoeuvre and opportunities to shape policy—in contrast to the stalled relations after 2014. At the same time, Russia policy was more disputed among member states after the accession of Eastern European countries than before. In this new, more competitive and diverse playing field of actors, how was Germany able to retain its influence? How were coalitions built, initiatives advanced and crises managed? This decade after the EU's Eastern enlargement—marked by tensions, but with plenty of "oxygen" in the relationship—provides important lessons in order to avoid the same mistakes for a time when EU-Russia relations might return to more flexibility and room for manoeuvre: Why have some attempts, often driven by Germany, to improve relations with Russia during this period succeeded, and others failed?

FRAMING THE CONTEXT

Since the signing of the EU-Russia Partnership and Cooperation Agreement (PCA) in 1994, Germany assumed a preeminent role in shaping the EU's policy towards Russia. Germany was not only more active than other member states in proposing initiatives, but in many cases saw a successful implementation of its proposals at the EU level. Of the six major EU policy initiatives towards and on Russia since 1994, Germany was involved as primary actor in four proposals—at times in collaboration with other partners, particularly France and the European Commission (EC). Three of the four policy proposals were accepted and implemented by the EU, with the sole exception of the Meseberg initiative from 2010, which was neither implemented by the EU nor by Russia. On the other hand, Germany implemented only on one occasion a policy proposal initiated by another member state: The Finnish Northern Dimension, a policy framework for the EU, Russia, Norway and Iceland.

Table 1.1   Main EU policy initiatives towards/on Russia, 1994–2019

Initiative	Year	Primary actors	Outcome
EU-Russia Partnership and Cooperation Agreement	1994	European Commission	Implemented by EU and Russia
EU Common Strategy on Russia	1999	Germany/France	Implemented by EU (internal document)
Northern Dimension	1999/ renewed 2006	Finland	Implemented by EU, Russia, Norway and Iceland
EU-Russia Four Common Spaces	2003	Germany/France	Implemented by EU and Russia
EU-Russia Partnership for Modernisation	2010	European Commission/ Germany	Implemented by EU and Russia
Meseberg initiative	2010	Germany	Not implemented by EU and Russia

Source: Author's table, based on literature overview: Jackie Gower and Graham Timmins (eds), *Russia and Europe in the Twenty-First Century: An Uneasy Partnership* (London, New York, NY: Anthem Press, 2009); Hiski Haukkala, *The EU-Russia Strategic Partnership: The Limits of Post-Sovereignty in International Relations*, Routledge Advances in International Relations and Global Politics, 85 (London, New York, NY: Routledge, 2010); Maxine David, Jackie Gower and Hiski Haukkala (eds), *National Perspectives on Russia: European Foreign Policy in the Making?*, Routledge Advances in European Politics, 94 (London, New York, NY: Routledge, 2013); Tuomas Forsberg and Hiski Haukkala, *The European Union and Russia*, The European Union Series, 1st edn (London, New York, NY: Macmillan Education; Palgrave, 2016); Katrin Bastian, *Die Europäische Union und Russland*, 1st edn (Wiesbaden: VS Verlag für Sozialwissenschaften, 2006); Reinhard Krumm, Sergei Medvedev and Hans-Henning Schröder (eds), *Constructing Identities in Europe: German and Russian Perspectives*, Internationale Politik und Sicherheit, 66, 1st edn (Baden-Baden: Nomos, 2012); Hans-Joachim Spanger, 'Die deutsche Russlandpolitik', in *Deutsche Außenpolitik: Sicherheit, Wohlfahrt, Institutionen und Normen*, ed. by Thomas Jäger, Alexander Höse and Kai Oppermann, 2nd edn (Wiesbaden: VS Verlag für Sozialwissenschaften, 2011), pp. 648–72; Maxine David and Tatiana Romanova, 'Modernisation in EU–Russian Relations: Past, Present, and Future', *European Politics and Society*, 16.1 (2015), 1–10; Stefan Meister, *A New Start for Russian-EU Security Policy?: The Weimar Triangle, Russia and the EU's Eastern Neighbourhood*, Genshagener Papiere 7 (2011) <https://www.robert-schuman.eu/en/doc/actualites/genshagener-papiere-2011-7-eng.pdf> [accessed 27 September 2017]; Hiski Haukkala, 'Russian Reactions to the European Neighborhood Policy', *Problems of Post-Communism*, 55.5 (2014), 40–48.

A similar picture emerges when taking a look at the main EU crisis situations with Russia. Here, it is Germany and France that were most often involved as primary actors (Table 1.2). For instance, during the Second Chechen War in 1999/2000, both countries took a critical stance towards the human rights situation in Chechnya and supported six months of

Table 1.2   Main EU crisis situations with Russia, 1994–2019

Crisis situation	Year	Primary actors	Outcome
1st Chechen War	1994	European Commission	Postponement of Partnership and Cooperation Agreement ratification
2nd Chechen War	1999/2000	France/ Germany	Limited sanctions on TACIS funding (January–June 2000)
Russian-Georgian War	2008	France/ Germany	Temporary suspension of new Partnership and Cooperation Agreement negotiations
Russia-Ukraine Conflict	2014	Germany/ France	Political and economic sanctions

Source: Author's table, based on literature overview: Raimo Lintonen, 'Understanding EU Crisis Decision-Making: The Case of Chechnya and the Finnish Presidency', *Journal of Contingencies and Crisis Management*, 12.1 (2004), 29–38; Tuomas Forsberg and Graeme P. Herd, 'The EU, Human Rights, and the Russo-Chechen Conflict', *Political Science Quarterly*, 120.3 (2005), 455–78; Richard G. Whitman and Stefan Wolff, *The European Neighbourhood Policy in Perspective: Context, Implementation and Impact*, Palgrave Studies in European Union Politics (Basingstoke, New York, NY: Palgrave Macmillan, 2010); Richard G. Whitman and Stefan Wolff, 'The EU as a Conflict Manager?: The Case of Georgia and Its Implications', *International Affairs*, 86.1 (2010), 87–107; Teemu Sinkkonen, 'A Security Dilemma on the Boundary Line: An EU Perspective to Georgian–Russian Confrontation after the 2008 War', *Southeast European and Black Sea Studies*, 11.3 (2011), 265–78; Hans Mouritzen and Anders Wivel, *Explaining Foreign Policy: International Diplomacy and the Russo-Georgian War* (Boulder: L. Rienner, 2012); Svante E. Cornell and S. F. Starr (eds), *The Guns of August 2008: Russia's War in Georgia*, Studies of Central Asia and the Caucasus (Armonk, NY: M.E. Sharpe, 2015); Thomas de Waal, *The Caucasus: An Introduction* (Oxford, New York, NY: Oxford University Press, 2010); Richard Sakwa, *Frontline Ukraine* (London, New York, NY: I. B. Tauris, 2016); Anders Åslund, *Ukraine: What Went Wrong and How to Fix It* (Washington DC: Peterson Institute for International Economics, 2015); Andrew Wilson, *Ukraine Crisis: What it Means for the West* (New Haven, CT: Yale University Press, 2014).

limited sanctions on Technical Assistance to the Commonwealth of Independent States (TACIS) funding. During the Russian-Georgian War in August 2008, France took a leadership role in crisis management, supported by Germany. In reverse, during the Russia-Ukraine Conflict in 2014, Germany was primarily involved in crisis management and economic sanctions.

Germany's preeminent role in the EU's Russia policy, in particular after the EU's enlargement in 2004, seems puzzling. After all, the EU's policy towards Russia has become an ever more contentious policy field since the EU's Eastern enlargement in 2004. With the accession of the traditionally Russia-sceptic Poland and Baltic states, the power balance in the EU's foreign policy has shifted.[14] Germany has more than once been reproached for undermining EU policy and pursuing German economic interests without regard for Russia's democratic and human rights record.[15] Against this backdrop, one would expect a strong bilateral German-Russian relationship, but less avenues for Germany to influence the EU's policy towards Russia. Yet, a prominent German role is observable in shaping both policy initiatives and crisis situations.

STATE OF RESEARCH

How can Germany's influence in EU Russia policy be explained? This question is situated within a broader debate on Germany's evolving role and power in Europe. The state of research on Germany's European policy notes a more self-confident German approach since reunification towards the EU and more generally in foreign policy, with a stronger willingness to influence European policy in the pursuit of its national interests.[16]

[14] Cf. Bartosz Cichoki, 'Poland', in *National Perspectives on Russia*, ed. by David, Gower and Haukkala, pp. 89–100; Ainius Lašas and D. J. Galbreath, 'Estonia, Latvia and Lithuania: Baltic-Russian Relations in the Post-Enlargement Era', in *National Perspectives on Russia*, ed. by David, Gower and Haukkala, pp. 149–68.

[15] Cf. Anke Schmidt-Felzmann, 'All for One?: EU Member States and the Union's Common Policy Towards the Russian Federation', *Journal of Contemporary European Studies*, 16.2 (2008), 169–87; Jackie Gower, 'The European Union's Policy on Russia: Rhetoric or Reality?', in *Russia and Europe in the Twenty-First Century*, ed. by Gower and Timmins, pp. 111–32; Winfried Schneider-Deters, P. W. Schulze and H. Timmermann (eds), *Die Europäische Union, Russland und Eurasien: Die Rückkehr der Geopolitik* (Berlin, 2008).

[16] For an overview of recent literature on Germany's European policy, compare: Simon Bulmer and William E. Paterson (eds), *Germany and the European Union: Europe's Reluctant Hegemon?*, The European Union Series, 1st edn (Oxford: Macmillan Education, 2019); Katrin Böttger and Mathias Jopp, 'Grundlinien deutscher Europapolitik', in *Handbuch zur deutschen Europapolitik*, ed. by Katrin Böttger and Mathias Jopp, 1st edn (Baden-Baden: Nomos, 2016), pp. 13–28; Patricia Daehnhardt, 'Germany in the European Union', in *National and European Foreign Policies: Towards Europeanization*, ed. by Reuben Y.-P. Wong and Christopher Hill, Routledge Advances in European Politics, 74 (Abingdon, New York, NY: Routledge, 2011), pp. 35–56; Timm Beichelt, 'Germany: In Search of a New Balance', in *The Member States of the European Union*, ed. by Simon Bulmer and Christian Lequesne, The New European Union Series, 2nd edn (Oxford: Oxford University Press, 2013), pp. 85–107; Sebastian Harnisch, *Germany and EU Foreign Policy: Preliminary Chapter for Oxford Handbook of German Politics*, Universität Heidelberg (Heidelberg, 2018) https://www.uni-heidelberg.de/md/politik/harnisch/person/publikationen/harnisch_2018_germany_and_eu_foreign_policy_8.1.2018.pdf [accessed 13 March 2019]; Gunther Hellmann

After German reunification in 1990, the age-old discussion about the "German Question" has seen a revival in public debate.[17] Following the Cold War, Germany's neighbours feared its territorial gains would prompt Germany to once again become a destabilising factor in Europe. Traditional power centres grew anxious about Germany reclaiming a hegemonic position and even acquiring nuclear weapons.[18] German "Ostpolitik" and its long-standing close relationship with the Soviet Union/Russia further nurtured these fears. This political debate was mirrored by an academic dispute revolving around the theoretical approach most suited to explaining German foreign policy after reunification.[19] According to Gunther Hellmann, German reunification was used as a test case by International Relations theorists to validate their respective arguments:[20] Realist scholars predicted Germany would inevitably rise again as a great power, becoming more assertive and re-nationalised at the expense of multilateralism and European integration.[21] In contrast, constructivist

(ed.), *Germany's EU Policy on Asylum and Defence: De-Europeanization by Default?*, New Perspectives in German Studies (Basingstoke, New York, NY: Palgrave Macmillan, 2006).

[17] Cf. Rolf Steininger, 'The German Question, 1945–95', in *Germany since Unification: The Development of the Berlin Republic*, ed. by Klaus Larres, 2nd edn (Basingstoke, New York, NY: Palgrave, 2001), pp. 9–32.

[18] Cf. John J. Mearsheimer, 'Back to the Future: Instability in Europe after the Cold War', *International Security*, 15.1 (1990), 5–56 [accessed 24 February 2019]; Arnulf Baring (ed.), *Germany's New Position in Europe: Problems and Perspectives*, German Historical Perspectives Series, 8 (Oxford, Providence, RI: Berg, 1994); Christian Hacke, *Weltmacht wider Willen: Die Aussenpolitik der Bundesrepublik Deutschland* (Stuttgart: Klett-Cotta, 1988); Hans-Peter Schwarz, *Die Zentralmacht Europas: Deutschlands Rückkehr auf die Weltbühne*, 1st edn (Berlin: Siedler, 1994).

[19] Volker Rittberger, 'Deutschlands Außenpolitik nach der Vereinigung: Zur Anwendbarkeit theoretischer Modelle der Außenpolitik: Machtstaat, Handelsstaat oder Zivilstaat?', in *Friedenspolitik in und für Europa: Festschrift für Gerda Zellentin zum 65. Geburtstag*, ed. by Wolfgang Bergem, Volker Ronge and Georg Weißeno (Wiesbaden: VS Verlag für Sozialwissenschaften, 1999), pp. 83–108; Volker Rittberger (ed.), *German Foreign Policy since Unification: Theories and Case Studies*, Issues in German Politics (Manchester, New York, NY: Manchester University Press, 2001); Helga Haftendorn, *Deutsche Außenpolitik zwischen Selbstbeschränkung und Selbstbehauptung: 1945–2000* (Stuttgart, Munich: Deutsche Verlags-Anstalt, 2001).

[20] Gunther Hellmann, 'Fatal Attraction?: German Foreign Policy and IR/Foreign Policy Theory', *Journal of International Relations and Development*, 12.3 (2009), 257–92 (p. 258).

[21] These arguments were put forward most prominently by Kenneth N. Waltz, 'The Emerging Structure of International Politics', *International Security*, 18.2 (1993), 44; Mearsheimer, 'Back to the Future', 1990.

scholars supported by sociological/historical institutionalists argued there was little evidence to support this expectation. Given Germany's embed-dedness in international institutions, particularly the EU, German foreign policy would reinforce the continuity of multilateralism, non-military responses and a commitment to European integration.[22]

The assumptions of realist scholars have not demonstrated sufficient explanatory power in the following post-Cold War years when continuity prevailed in German European policy: According to Peter Katzenstein, Germany remained a "tamed power" in Europe.[23] Dyson and Goetz underlined that Europeanisation has put significant constraints on German politics.[24] Germany's influence in the EU was primarily explained as an exertion of "soft" or "indirect institutional power"[25] in the form of "shaping the regional milieu", one of the key facets of Germany's European diplomacy.[26] However, more recent interpretations have noticed a change in Germany's European policy: Some scholars detected a "new European policy" which has become "weaker, leaner and meaner",[27] while others

[22] Cf. Hanns W. Maull, 'Germany and Japan: The New Civilian Powers', *Foreign Affairs*, 69.5 (1990), 91–106 https://www.jstor.org/stable/20044603 [accessed 22 April 2019]; Beate Kohler-Koch, 'Deutsche Einigung im Spannungsfeld internationaler Umbrüche', *Politische Vierteljahresschrift*, 32.4 (1991), 605–20 https://www.jstor.org/stable/24196168; Sebastian Harnisch and Hanns W. Maull (eds), *Germany as a Civilian Power?: The Foreign Policy of the Berlin Republic*, Issues in German Politics (Manchester, New York, NY: Manchester University Press, 2001).

[23] Peter J. Katzenstein (ed.), *Tamed Power: Germany in Europe*, 1st edn (Ithaca, NY, London: Cornell University Press, 1997).

[24] Kenneth H. F. Dyson and Klaus Goetz (eds), *Germany, Europe and the Politics of Constraint*, Proceedings of the British Academy, 119 (Oxford: Oxford University Press, 2003).

[25] Cf. Peter J. Katzenstein, 'United Germany in an Integrating Europe', in *Tamed Power*, ed. by Katzenstein, pp. 1–48; Jeffrey J. Anderson, 'Hard Interests, Soft Power, and Germany's Changing Role in Europe', in *Tamed Power*, ed. by Katzenstein, pp. 80–107; Simon Bulmer, 'Shaping the Rules?: The Constitutive Politics of the European Union and German Power', in *Tamed Power*, ed. by Katzenstein, pp. 49–79.

[26] Simon Bulmer, Charlie Jeffery and William E. Paterson, *Germany's European Diplomacy: Shaping the Regional Milieu*, Issues in German Politics (Manchester: Manchester University Press, 2000)

[27] Cf. Sebastian Harnisch and Siegfried Schieder, 'Germany's New European Policy: Weaker, Leaner, Meaner', in *Germany's Uncertain Power: Foreign Policy of the Berlin Republic*, ed. by Hanns W. Maull (Basingstoke, New York, NY: Palgrave Macmillan, 2006), pp. 95–108; Heinrich Schneider, Mathias Jopp and Uwe Schmalz (eds), *Eine neue deutsche Europapolitik?: Rahmenbedingungen—Problemfelder—Optionen*, Europäische Schriften des Instituts für Europäische Politik, 77 (Bonn: Europa-Union, 2002); Michèle Knodt and

suggested a "de-Europeanization" in selected policy areas—yet more by default than for any strategic purpose.[28] In an attempt to explain the change in Germany's European policy, Simon Bulmer and William Paterson argued Germany moved from a "tamed" to a "normalized" power and behaved in a less inclusive manner within the EU.[29]

In the context of the Eurozone crisis, numerous scholars such as Hans Kundnani explained Germany's European policy as driven by geo-economic considerations and national preferences, and some even as hegemonic.[30] In contrast, others postulated German hegemony to be a "myth"[31] suggesting instead a role theoretical model of international leadership, defining leadership as a social role adopted under specific circumstances.[32]

Beate Kohler-Koch (eds), *Deutschland zwischen Europäisierung und Selbstbehauptung*, Mannheimer Jahrbuch für europäische Sozialforschung, 5 (Frankfurt a. M., New York, NY: Campus, 2000).

[28] Hellmann (ed.), *Germany's EU Policy on Asylum and Defence*, 2006.

[29] Simon Bulmer and William E. Paterson, 'Germany and the European Union: From 'Tamed Power' to Normalized Power?', *International Affairs*, 86.5 (2010), 1051–73. Rainer Baumann also observed changes in Germany's discourse on multilateralism. Cf. Rainer Baumann, 'The Transformation of German Multilateralism: Changes in the Foreign Policy Discourse since Unification', German Politics & Society, 20.4 (2002), 1–26 https://www.jstor.org/stable/23740512.

[30] Cf. Hans Kundnani, *The Paradox of German Power*, 1st edn (London: Hurst, 2014); Melanie Morisse-Schilbach, '"Ach Deutschland!"': Greece, the Euro Crisis, and the Costs and Benefits of Being a Benign Hegemon', *Internationale Politik und Gesellschaft*, 1 (2011), 26–41; Joachim Schild, 'Leadership in Hard Times: Germany, France, and the Management of the Eurozone Crisis', *German Politics and Society*, 31.1 (2013), 24–47; Simon Bulmer and William E. Paterson, 'Germany as the EU's Reluctant Hegemon?: Of Economic Strength and Political Constraints', *Journal of European Public Policy*, 20.10 (2013), 1387–405; Magnus G. Schoeller, 'Providing Political Leadership?: Three Case Studies on Germany's Ambiguous Role in the Eurozone Crisis', *Journal of European Public Policy*, 24.1 (2015), 1–20.

[31] Cf. Sebastian Harnisch, *The Myth of German Hegemony: Assessing International Leadership Roles of the Merkel Governments*, Paper presented at the 2017 Annual Conference of the International Studies Association, Baltimore, February 21–25th (2017) https://www.uni-heidelberg.de/md/politik/harnisch/person/publikationen/harnisch__isa_2017_german_and_leadership_roles_final.pdf [accessed 30 September 2018].

[32] Cf. Sebastian Harnisch and Joachim Schild (eds), *Deutsche Außenpolitik und internationale Führung: Ressourcen, Praktiken und Politiken in einer veränderten Europäischen Union*, Aussenpolitik und Internationale Ordnung, 1st edn (Baden-Baden: Nomos, 2014); Lisbeth Aggestam, *European Foreign Policy and the Quest for a Global Role: Britain, France and Germany*, Routledge Advances in European Politics (London: Routledge, 2017); Lisbeth

Germany's role in the EU's Common Foreign and Security Policy (CFSP) has also been described as increasingly that of a "shaper" rather than a "taker"[33] and Germany's policy during the monetary and refugee crisis in 2015 were considered examples for a more self-confident German foreign and European policy.[34]

With regard to Russia policy, Stephen Szabo used the test case of German-Russian relations to suggest a geo-economic interpretation of German foreign policy. This interpretation was to some extent put into question during the Ukraine conflict, when Germany used its economic power against Russia instead of prioritising its business relations.[35] The Ukraine conflict has since been used as a prominent test case to argue for Germany's new leadership role in European foreign policy.[36] According to

Aggestam and Markus Johansson, 'The Leadership Paradox in EU Foreign Policy', *Journal of Common Market Studies*, 55.6 (2017), 1203–20.

[33] Cf. Alister Miskimmon, *Germany and the Common Foreign and Security Policy of the European Union: Between Europeanisation and National Adaptation*, New Perspectives in German Studies (Basingstoke, New York, NY: Palgrave Macmillan, 2007); Daehnhardt, 'Germany', 2011.

[34] Cf. Simon Bulmer and William E. Paterson, 'Germany's Role in the Handling of the European Monetary and Refugee Crisis', in *Jahrbuch der Europäischen Integration 2016*, ed. by Werner Weidenfeld and Wolfgang Wessels, 1st edn (Baden-Baden: Nomos, 2016), pp. 1–10.

[35] Stephen F. Szabo, *Germany, Russia and the Rise of Geo-Economics*, 1st edn (London: Bloomsbury, 2015). Cf. also: John Lough, *Germany's Russia Problem: The Struggle for Balance in Europe* (Manchester: Manchester University Press, 2021). A few earlier studies by Hans-Joachim Spanger and Gunther Hellmann placed the German-Russian relationship in the broader context of Germany's power political socialisation and practices, cf. Spanger, 'Russlandpolitik', 2011; Gunther Hellmann, *Die Deutschen und die Russen: Über Neigungen und machtpolitische Sozialisierungen*, WeltTrends 96 (2014) www.fb03.uni-frankfurt. de/50290123/WeltTrends2014_final.pdf [accessed 2 March 2019].

[36] Cf. Liana Fix, 'The Different 'Shades' of German Power: Germany and EU Foreign Policy during the Ukraine Conflict', in *Germany's Eastern Challenge: A 'Hybrid Ostpolitik' in the Making?*, ed. by Patricia Daehnhardt and Vladimír Handl (= *German Politics*, 27 (2018)), 498–515; Marco Siddi, 'German Foreign Policy towards Russia in the Aftermath of the Ukraine Crisis: A New Ostpolitik ?', *Europe-Asia Studies*, 68.4 (2016), 665–77; Patricia Daehnhardt, 'German Foreign Policy, the Ukraine Crisis and the Euro-Atlantic Order: Assessing the Dynamics of Change', *German Politics*, 26.4 (2018), 1–23; Patricia Daehnhardt and Vladimír Handl, 'Germany's Eastern Challenge and the Russia–Ukraine Crisis: A New Ostpolitik in the Making?', in *Germany's Eastern Challenge: A 'Hybrid Ostpolitik' in the Making?*, ed. by Patricia Daehnhardt and Vladimír Handl (= *German Politics*, 27 (2018)), pp. 445–59; Alyona Getmanchuk and Sergiy Solodkyy, 'German Crisis Management Efforts

Wolfgang Wessels, the Ukraine conflict demonstrated Germany's role as "primus inter pares", whereas Lisbeth Aggestam and Adrian Hyde-Price suggest German leadership was being shaped by the role expectations of its key allies and partners.[37] Only few analyses of Germany's role during the Ukraine conflict took into account a broader view of Germany's role in EU relations with Russia.[38] Marco Siddi's article on German leadership in EU relations with Russia suggested a German hegemonic leadership role.[39] In contrast, Bulmer and Paterson used the Ukraine conflict and the Eurozone crisis as case studies to conclude that Germany's role in these crises does not fit the classical definition of a hegemon and thus German hegemony in the EU. In the Ukraine conflict, Germany has primarily acted as a "supreme facilitator" within the EU.[40]

Taken all together, the literature on Germany's role within the EU and in European Russia policy has generally reflected an awareness of a shift in Germany's European approach. As most analysts agree, Germany's European policy gravitated towards more assertiveness in the sense that "Germany will if necessary, proceed alone (Alleingang) rather than engage in exhaustive consultation"[41] and demonstrated its leadership throughout

---

in the Ukraine–Russia Conflict from Kyiv's Perspective', in *Germany's Eastern Challenge: A 'Hybrid Ostpolitik' in the Making?*, ed. by Patricia Daehnhardt and Vladimír Handl (= *German Politics*, 27 (2018)), pp. 1–18; Nicholas Wright, 'No Longer the Elephant Outside the Room: Why the Ukraine Crisis Reflects a Deeper Shift Towards German Leadership of European Foreign Policy', in *Germany's Eastern Challenge: A 'Hybrid Ostpolitik' in the Making?*, ed. by Patricia Daehnhardt and Vladimír Handl (= *German Politics*, 27 (2018)), pp. 479–97.

[37] Inez von Weitershausen, David Schäfer amd Wolfgang Wessels, 'A 'Primus Inter Pares' in EU Foreign Policy?—German Leadership in the European Council during the Libyan and Ukrainian Crises', *German Politics*, 29.1 (2020), 42–58; Lisbeth Aggestam and Adrian Hyde-Price, 'Learning to Lead? Germany and the Leadership Paradox in EU Foreign Policy', *German Politics*, 29.1 (2020), 8–24.

[38] Cf. Fn. 36.

[39] Marco Siddi, 'A Contested Hegemon?: Germany's Leadership in EU Relations with Russia', *German Politics*, 94 (2018), 1–18.

[40] Simon Bulmer and William E. Paterson (eds), *Germany and the European Union: Europe's Reluctant Hegemon?*, The European Union Series, 1st edn (Oxford: Macmillan Education, 2019).

[41] Bulmer and Paterson, 'Normalized Power', 2010, p. 1052.

diverse crises. Yet, there is no consensus on how to conceptualise this shift. Germany has become more influential within the EU, but the conceptual terminology to explain Germany's influence is still under debate.

Theorising Member States' Influence

How has member states' influence on European foreign policy been explained in different EU research traditions and which approach is most useful for the analysis of Germany's influence on the EU's policy towards Russia?

Liberal intergovernmentalism understands European foreign policy as a domestic preferences-based approach evaluated through the lens of absolute gains: Member states trade foreign policy interests including cross-policy bargains from other fields.[42] It is comparable to an "especially complex poker game" wherein the member states "bring their cards to the table and must then deal amongst themselves to construct the best possible hand".[43] At first glance, liberal intergovernmentalism seems a useful framework for the analysis of member states' influence that could be transferred to an analysis of Germany's influence on the EU's policy towards Russia. However, liberal intergovernmentalism has a narrow, bargaining-focused power conception whereas discussions about European foreign policy do not necessarily take place in a grand bargaining setting, and it leaves out the entire complex of indirect power including discursive and socially constructed meanings of power. As Nicole de Flers and Patrick Müller argue, "member states are encouraged to switch from [a] bargaining negotiation style to arguing and suasion strategies and even to engage in 'problem-solving,' so that common definitions of problems and philosophies for their solution may emerge".[44] Thus, liberal intergovernmentalism is most useful for negotiation contexts in European integration, for example, treaty negotiations, but less so for assessing varieties of power exertion in foreign policy.

---

[42] Ben Tonra and Thomas Christiansen, 'The Study of EU Foreign Policy: Between International Relations and European Studies', in *Rethinking European Union Foreign Policy*, ed. by Tonra and Christiansen, pp. 1–9 (p. 7).

[43] Tonra and Christiansen, *Study of EU Foreign Policy*, 2004, p. 7.

[44] Flers and Müller, 'Dimensions and Mechanisms', 2012, p. 31.

Europeanisation Studies has had a growing academic profile since the 2000s.[45] Initially, Europeanisation Studies focused on the domestic transformation of member states and the impact of EU institutions and policies on domestic political systems (*downloading*).[46] The concept was later converted into a bi-directional model, which incorporates the bottom-up perspective of member states "projecting" or *uploading* policies to imprint their own policy preferences, ideas and interests upon the European agenda.[47] When it comes to Germany's influence on the EU's policy towards Russia, at first glance, *uploading* seems to be a useful concept, but it enters a paradox if a member state predominantly engages in uploading instead of both uploading *and* downloading policies. This begs the question: Can a member state still be described as "Europeanized" if it engages primarily in uploading or is this rather an expression of a member states' dominance in European policy? Germany is a good example as it has been described as much more active in "uploading" than "downloading" and thus as a "different sort of Europeanized state".[48] "Europeanization" becomes devoid of meaning if policy behaviour is treated as "Europeanized" when it is in fact an expression of aggregated national policy.[49] While *uploading* adequately describes the formal mechanism of projecting positions and preferences to the European level, it does not address the process of member state power projection in the EU.

POWER AND THE EUROPEAN UNION

Given the limits of the above-mentioned approaches, why can it be useful to apply a power-theoretical approach from International Relations to the study of member state influence in the EU? The study of power and the European Union have had a difficult relationship. While the external

---

[45] Cf. Ben Tonra, 'Europeanization', in *The SAGE Handbook of European Foreign Policy*, ed. by Jørgensen and others, pp. 182–95.

[46] Cf. Johan P. Olsen, 'The Many Faces of Europeanization', *Journal of Common Market Studies*, 40.5 (2002), 921–52.

[47] Cf. Reuben Y.-P. Wong, 'The Europeanization of Foreign Policy', in *International Relations and the European Union*, ed. by Christopher Hill and Michael Smith, New European Union series, 4th edn (Oxford, New York, NY: Oxford University Press, 2005), pp. 134–53.

[48] Daehnhardt, 'Germany', 2011.

[49] Cf. Roy H. Ginsberg, *Foreign Policy Actions of the European Community: The Politics of Scale*, Adamantine Series Studies in International Relations and World Security, 3 (Boulder: L. Rienner, 1989).

power of the EU, for instance questions regarding the EU's actorness, effectiveness and performance, have been discussed in depth, there are "no agreed definitions of the forms of influence—or power—available within the EU".[50] This, as Vincent Della Sala argues, is because power is predominantly associated with a realist outlook adhering more to International Relations and great power politics and less to the EU as a "sui generis" institution of unprecedented multilateral cooperation between states.

On the one hand, the EU is a "polity that deliberately tries to do away with hierarchical forms of government, whose proponents argue that power is no longer the basis of politics, and that provides even the smallest of its constituent parts a veto over key decisions".[51] The dominance of a member state would contradict the setting of the EU, which has a "political and institutional architecture designed consciously and conspicuously to prevent the concentration of power"[52] and to "ensure that no single institution, member state, or group of member states can concentrate power".[53] At its core, the EU is therefore an "anti-hegemonic project".[54]

On the other hand, scholars have argued that power politics have only been tamed and not transcended in the EU.[55] Power dynamics in the EU have always been present in different constellations: big versus small, poor

---

[50] Helen Wallace, 'Exercising Power and Influence in the European Union', in The Member States of the European Union, ed. by Simon Bulmer and Christian Lequesne (Oxford: Oxford University Press, 2005), pp. 25–44 (p. 36); François Duchêne, 'Europe's Role in World Peace', in Europe Tomorrow: Sixteen Europeans Look Ahead, ed. by Richard Mayne (London: Fontana, 1972), pp. 32–47; Ian Manners, 'Normative Power Europe: A Contradiction in Terms?', Journal of Common Market Studies, 40.2 (2002), 235–58; H. Grabbe, The EU's Transformative Power: Europeanization through Conditionality in Central and Eastern Europe, 1st edn (Basingstoke: Palgrave Macmillan, 2006); Roy H. Ginsberg, The European Union in International Politics: Baptism by Fire, New International Relations of Europe (Lanham, MD: Rowman & Littlefield, 2001).

[51] Vincent Della Sala, 'Leaders and Followers: Leadership amongst Member States in a Differentiated Europe', in The Oxford Handbook of the European Union, ed. by Erik Jones, Anand Menon and Stephen Weatherill, Oxford Handbooks Online (Oxford: Oxford University Press, 2012), pp. 306–16 (p. 306).

[52] Della Sala, Leaders and Followers, 2012, p. 307.

[53] Della Sala, Leaders and Followers, 2012, p. 308.

[54] Simone Bunse and Kalypso Nicolaïdis, 'Large versus Small States: Anti-Hegemony and the Politics of Shared Leadership', in The Oxford Handbook of the European Union, ed. by Jones, Menon and Weatherill, pp. 249–66 (p. 249).

[55] Magnette, Bunse and Nicolaïdis, Big vs Small, 2007, p. 134.

versus rich, northern versus southern members.[56] Member states are guaranteed equality per the Treaty of Lisbon, but inequalities are clearly observable in terms of their respective capabilities. Therefore, according to Della Sala, "the debate about hierarchy in relations between sovereign states is especially relevant for the EU, which has tried to go beyond the calculations of power politics".[57] Also, in thinking about power and the EU, power does not have to be conceived in realist categories, especially not in a "sui generis" entity as the EU.[58] As Stefano Guzzini argued, "taking power analysis seriously leads beyond neorealism".[59]

His line of argumentation departs from the observation that new concepts of power have emerged in recent literature which cannot merely complement the traditional realist notion because of their contrasting ontological foundations.[60] Rather than adhering to paradigmatic lines of realism or constructivism, he proposes a dyadic notion of power, wherein the ontological agency-structure dichotomy provides the crucial divide. He argues that it is impossible to limit power to a single concept at the agent or structure level as "[p]ower lies both in the relational interaction of agents and in the systematic rule that results from the consequences of their actions".[61] Guzzini thus presents *(agent) power* as a concept incorporating direct actions, reflecting Robert Dahl's traditional "A gets actor B to do what A wants" definition, indirect institutional power, reflecting Stephen Krasner's idea of "metapower" as changing the setting in which confrontation occurs,[62] and non-intentional power, including unintended and unconscious power effects.[63] But Guzzini also presents *governance* as a structural power concept which exhibits impersonally crafted effects, where the origin of the produced effect is not located at the level of actors. This includes impersonal empowering, including post-structuralist ideas of linking knowledge and power, and impersonal biases, which

---

[56] Bunse and Nicolaïdis, *Large vs Small States*, 2012.

[57] Della Sala, *Leaders and Followers*, 2012, p. 309.

[58] Cf. Berenskoetter and Williams, 'Editors' Introduction', 2004.

[59] Stefano Guzzini, 'Structural Power: The Limits of Neorealist Power Analysis', *International Organization*, 47.03 (1993), 443–78 (p. 443).

[60] Guzzini, 'Structural Power', 1993.

[61] Guzzini, 'Structural Power', 1993, p. 474.

[62] Guzzini, 'Structural Power', 1993, p. 451.

[63] Guzzini, 'Structural Power', 1993, p. 457.

systematically give an advantage to certain actors due to their specific positions in the international system.[64]

A TAXONOMY OF POWER

Assuming that power is a necessary concept in the study of member states' influence in the EU, the following taxonomy developed by Michael Barnett and Raymond Duvall—encompassing different power conceptualisations from realist, institutionalist, constructivist and structuralist perspectives—will be applied as a theoretical framework for the analysis of Germany's influence in EU Russia policy. The taxonomy will be operationalised to trace which concept of power best accounts for Germany's major or minor influence in the EU policy formation process.[65]

Barnett and Duvall develop their taxonomy from the observation that power cannot be conceived outside of social interactions or in a non-interpretative environment, thereby attaching an "irreducibly social" quality to power.[66] In this line of reasoning, Barnett and Duvall assume an explicit stance towards a social-relational concept of power. In their definition, "[p]ower is the production, in and through social relations, of effects that shape the capacities of actors to determine their circumstances and fate".[67] Barnett and Duvall discern two key ontological dimensions in their taxonomy: The first dimension concerns the specificity of the relationship: Is power produced in a *direct* way, that is through an immediate, direct and specific relationship, or in a *diffuse* way, that is indirect and mediated, operating at a physical, temporal or social distance? The second dimension concerns the type of relationship: Does power function through *interaction*,

---

[64] Guzzini, 'Structural Power', 1993, p. 462.

[65] This framework—the power taxonomy of Barnett and Duvall—has also been applied with a different research design by Tom Casier to the Russia-Ukraine conflict on the level of structural competition between the EU and Russia in the decade preceding the conflict. Casier examined the logic of the EU-Russia relationship through a macro-approach in analysis, taking the EU and Russia as entities. This differs from this study, which focuses on the role of member states and uses the taxonomy of Barnett and Duvall for the analysis of member states' influence within the EU, rather than for the analysis of the EU-Russia relationship on a structural level. Cf. Tom Casier, 'The Different Faces of Power in European Union–Russia Relations', *Cooperation and Conflict*, 53.1 (2017), 101–17 (p. 108).

[66] Barnett and Duvall, 'Power in International Politics', 2005, p. 46.

[67] Barnett and Duvall, 'Power in International Politics', 2005, p. 42.

that is through the behavioural relations and interactions of preconstituted social actors towards one another, or *constitution*, that is through social relations that first constitute the actors as social beings? Along these dimensions, the following four conceptual types of power are arranged:[68]

- *Compulsory Power (direct control over another actor)*

Compulsory power pertains to the direct control over the conditions of existence and/or the actions of another actor, intentionally or unintentionally. Despite the negative connotation of the term "compulsory", it can include positive and symbolic means of power (incentives) and is not exclusively coercive. The concept of compulsory power is related to (neo-) realist theory.

- *Institutional Power (indirectly mediated through formal or informal institutions)*

Institutional power pertains to indirect control over the conditions of existence and/or the actions of a socially distant other. Institutional power is mediated through formal or informal institutions, which can be used to shape agendas, practices and policies to bring about desired effects.[69] The concept of institutional power is related to (rational) institutionalist theory.

- *Structural Power (structural factors that constitute an actor's social capacity)*

Structural power arises from the direct and mutual constitution of the capacities of actors and their interests through structural factors, for example, an employer-employee. In this way, structural power operates even when there are no actions observable to exercise control. The concept of structural power is related to (post-) structuralist theory.

- *Productive power (production of discursive and socially constructed meanings)*

[68] Barnett and Duvall, 'Power in International Politics', 2005, pp. 42–44. Compare also the summary by Forsberg, 'Power in International Relations', 2014, pp. 220–21.
[69] This is not to be confused with the power of institutions in their own right (Barnett and Duvall, 'Power in International Politics', 2005, p. 51).

Table 1.3   Fourfold taxonomy of power

		Relational specificity	
Power works through:		Direct	Diffuse
	Interactions of specific actors	*Compulsory*	*Institutional*
	Social relations of constitution	*Structural*	*Productive*

Source: Table from Barnett and Duvall, 'Power in International Politics', 2005, p. 49.

Productive power arises from discourses, social processes and systems of knowledge which indirectly produce socially constructed meanings. These are not controlled but affected through the meaningful practice of actors. For instance, a particular discourse orients action in one direction and away from others. The productive power concept is related to (social) constructivist theory.

Compulsory and structural power are produced through immediate and *direct* connections between actors, whereas institutional and productive power are socially *diffuse* and work at distance. Compulsory and institutional power exist in the *interaction* between specific actors, whereas structural and productive power *constitute* the actors and their social identities. This generates a fourfold taxonomy (Table 1.3).

The taxonomy also pays attention to the fact that "multiple forms of power are simultaneously present in international politics".[70] The four types of compulsory, institutional, structural and productive power are not mutually exclusive and may reinforce one another, for example, when "productive power makes some instances of compulsory power possible".[71] Despite the criticism towards such an encompassing interdisciplinary taxonomy in one research design, namely that there is no "way of conceptualizing power which enables capturing the totality of social relations",[72] this taxonomy makes it possible to test which power concept has the most explanatory power in a given situation.

Since this study will focus on member states' influence and thus assume a primarily agency-centred perspective of analysis, the taxonomy will be slightly adapted for the empirical analysis: The *structural power* concept, which is the least agency-centred concept in the taxonomy, will be excluded, with compulsory, institutional and productive power remaining.

[70] Barnett and Duvall, 'Power in International Politics', 2005, p. 44.
[71] Ibid.
[72] Berenskoetter, *Thinking about Power*, 2007, p. 2.

This adaption acknowledges that "human agency [is] essential in producing, reproducing and possibly transforming structures".[73] In addition, the analysis benefits from more consistency and parsimony through this adaptation. While *productive power* arguably also highlights the structural effects of creating meanings and systems of knowledge, this analysis will concentrate on the way social meanings and systems of knowledge are effected through the meaningful practice of actors, that is, how actors, for instance Germany, practise discourses or paradigms that orient action in one direction and away from others. The adapted taxonomy allows to explain which concept of power can best account for Germany's major or minor influence in the EU policy formation process towards Russia.

While Barnett and Duvall include two case studies as examples for the empirical analysis, they provide little guidance on how to operationalise the analysis of power concepts. How can one identify a certain power concept when it appears in an empirical analysis, or put differently, how do you know it when you see it?

Power itself is difficult to trace in terms of observables, hence the analysis must look for indirect evidence and observable elements indicating power.[74] The possible indicators are the tools and instruments that are used to exercise the respective form of power. Barnett and Duvall list a range of examples for tools and instruments that can be applied—such as mechanisms of coercion, military means, sanctions, normative pressure, agenda setting, discursive production of subjects and the fixing of meanings[75]—yet, these examples are not systemised in their operationalisation. Therefore, a classification of instruments is necessary which is specific to the particular context of EU policy formation taking place under unanimity. Based on the literature on negotiation and bargaining, agenda setting, deliberation, arguing and discourse framing in the EU, the following instruments were identified as the most relevant for the EU policy formation process and categorised in line with the respective power concepts (Table 1.4).

Instruments of compulsory power are defined as the means to directly influence actor B by winning conflicts in a positive or coercive manner. Therefore, they are typically present in bargaining or negotiation contexts

---

[73] Table from Barnett and Duvall, 'Power in International Politics', 2005, p. 49.

[74] Cf. R. N. Mokken and Frans N. Stokman, 'Power and Influence as Political Phenomena', in *Power and Political Theory: Some European Perspectives*, ed. by Brian Barry (London, New York, NY: Wiley, 1976), pp. 33–54 (p. 40).

[75] Barnett and Duvall, 'Power in International Politics', 2005, pp. 51–53.

Table 1.4   Operationalisation of instruments

	Use of compulsory power	Use of institutional power	Use of productive power
Aim	Direct influence: Winning conflicts	Indirect influence: Shaping the milieu	Indirect influence: Creating socially constructed meanings
Instruments	Veto option Issue linkage Side payments	Agenda setting Mediation and brokering Coalition building Access points	Arguing and suasion Paradigm framing

Source: Author's table, based on literature overview.

Compare for literature on negotiation and bargaining in the EU: Andreas Dür, Gemma Mateo and Daniel C. Thomas, 'Negotiation Theory and the EU: The State of the Art', in *Negotiation Theory and the EU*, ed. by Andreas Dür, Gemma Mateo and Daniel C. Thomas (= *Journal of European Public Policy*, 17 (2010)), pp. 613–18; Ole Elgström and Christer Jönsson, 'Negotiation in the European Union: Bargaining or Problem-Solving?', *Journal of European Public Policy*, 7.5 (2000), 684–704; Stefanie Bailer, 'What Factors Determine Bargaining Power and Success in EU Negotiations?', in *Negotiation Theory and the EU*, ed. by Andreas Dür, Gemma Mateo and Daniel C. Thomas (= *Journal of European Public Policy*, 17 (2010)), pp. 743–57; Jeffrey Lewis, *The Impact of Institutional Environments on Negotiation Styles in EU Decision Making*, Paper prepared for the European Union Studies Association (EUSA) Eleventh Biennial International Conference, Los Angeles, CA, 23–25 April (2009) <http://aei.pitt.edu/33098/1/lewis._jeffrey.pdf> [accessed 2 March 2019]; Jonas Tallberg, 'Explaining the Institutional Foundations of European Union Negotiations', in *Negotiation Theory and the EU*, ed. by Andreas Dür, Gemma Mateo and Daniel C. Thomas (= *Journal of European Public Policy*, 17 (2010)), pp. 633–47; Jonas Tallberg, *Leadership and Negotiation in the European Union* (Cambridge: Cambridge University Press, 2006).

Compare for literature on multilateral negotiation and leadership: I. W. Zartman (ed.), *International Multilateral Negotiation: Approaches to the Management of Complexity*, The Jossey-Bass Conflict Resolution Series, 1st edn (San Francisco: Jossey-Bass, 1994); John S. Odell, 'Three Islands of Knowledge about Negotiation in International Organizations', in *Negotiation Theory and the EU*, ed. by Andreas Dür, Gemma Mateo and Daniel C. Thomas (= *Journal of European Public Policy*, 17 (2010)), pp. 619–32; Jonas Tallberg, 'The Power of the Chair: Formal Leadership in International Cooperation', *International Studies Quarterly*, 54.1 (2010), 241–65, Derek Beach and Colette Mazzucelli (eds), *Leadership in the Big Bangs of European Integration*, Palgrave Studies in European Union Politics (Basingstoke, New York, NY: Palgrave Macmillan, 2007).

Compare for literature on agenda setting: Mark A. Pollack, 'Delegation, Agency, and Agenda Setting in the European Community', *International Organization*, 51.1 (1997), 99–134 <https://www.jstor.org/stable/2703953>; Sebastiaan Princen, 'Agenda-Setting in the European Union: A Theoretical Exploration and Agenda for Research', *Journal of European Public Policy*, 14.1 (2007), 21–38; Sebastiaan Princen, *Agenda-Setting in the European Union*, Palgrave Studies in European Union Politics (Basingstoke, New York, NY: Palgrave Macmillan, 2009); Sebastiaan Princen, 'Agenda-Setting Strategies in EU Policy Processes', *Journal of European Public Policy*, 18.7 (2011), 927–43.

Compare for literature on decision-making and issue linkage: Andreas Warntjen, 'Between Bargaining and Deliberation: Decision-Making in the Council of the European Union', in *Negotiation Theory and the EU*, ed. by Andreas Dür, Gemma Mateo and Daniel C. Thomas (= *Journal of European Public Policy*, 17

(*continued*)

Table 1.4 (continued)

(2010)), pp. 665–79; Thomas Risse and Mareike Kleine, 'Deliberation in Negotiations', in *Negotiation Theory and the EU*, ed. by Andreas Dür, Gemma Mateo and Daniel C. Thomas (= *Journal of European Public Policy*, 17 (2010)), pp. 708–26; Heather E. McKibben, 'Issue Characteristics, Issue Linkage, and States' Choice of Bargaining Strategies in the European Union', in *Negotiation Theory and the EU*, ed. by Andreas Dür, Gemma Mateo and Daniel C. Thomas (= *Journal of European Public Policy*, 17 (2010)), pp. 694–707.

Compare for literature on arguing and socially constructed meanings: Cornelia Ulbert, Thomas Risse and Harald Müller, *Arguing and Bargaining in Multilateral Negotiations*, Paper presented to the Conference on "Empirical Approaches to Deliberative Politics" European University Institute, Swiss Chair (2004) <https://www.polsoz.fu-berlin.de/polwiss/forschung/international/atasp/forschung/projekte_abgeschlossen/argumentieren/ulbert_risse_mueller_2004.pdf> [accessed 2 March 2019]; Harald Müller, 'Arguing, Bargaining and All That: Communicative Action, Rationalist Theory and the Logic of Appropriateness in International Relations', *European Journal of International Relations*, 10.3 (2004), 395–435; Anna Holzscheiter, 'Discourse as Capability: Non-State Actors' Capital in Global Governance', in *Facets of Power in International Relations: Special Issue*, ed. by Felix Berenskoetter and Michael J. Williams (= *Millennium: Journal of International Studies*, 33 (2004)), pp. 723–46; Sebastiaan Princen and Femke van Esch, 'Paradigm Formation and Paradigm Change in the EU's Stability and Growth Pact', *European Political Science Review*, 8.03 (2016), 355–75; Sebastiaan Princen and Paul 't. Hart, 'Putting Policy Paradigms in Their Place', *Journal of European Public Policy*, 21.3 (2014), 470–74; Arne Niemann and Jeannette Mak, '(How) Do Norms Guide Presidency Behaviour in EU Negotiations?', in *Negotiation Theory and the EU*, ed. by Andreas Dür, Gemma Mateo and Daniel C. Thomas (= *Journal of European Public Policy*, 17 (2010)), pp. 727–42.

of policy formation and include in this operationalisation the instruments of a veto option (defined as the evocation of an option to block change on issues that are subject to unanimity), issue linkage (defined as distinct issues discussed simultaneously as an incentive for a joint settlement) and side payments (defined as instrument of compensation in an unequal agreement).[76]

Instruments of institutional power are defined as the means to indirectly influence actor B by shaping the institutional milieu. Therefore, they are evident in problem-solving contexts of policy formation and include in this operationalisation the instruments of agenda setting (defined as having an issue considered by relevant actors), mediation and brokering (defined as resolving conflict by facilitating a compromise on a mutually

[76] Cf. for definitions: Jonathan B. Slapin, *Veto Power: Institutional Design in the European Union*, New Comparative Politics (Ann Arbor, MI: University of Michigan Press, 2015), p. 127; McKibben, 'Issue Characteristics', 2010; Fritz W. Scharpf, *Games Real Actors Play: Actor-Centered Institutionalism in Policy Research*, Theoretical Lenses on Public Policy (Boulder: Westview Press, 1997), pp. 126–27; Helen V. Milner, *Interests, Institutions, and Information: Domestic Politics and International Relations* (Princeton, NJ: Princeton University Press, 1997), p. 112.

agreeable outcome), access points (defined as a privileged relationship to institutionally relevant actors) and coalition building (defined as the ability to initiate, enlarge and empower coalitions).[77]

Instruments of productive power are defined as the means to indirectly influence actor B by affecting socially constructed meanings, perceptions and identities. Therefore, they are most apparent in the discursive contexts of policy formation and include in this operationalisation the instruments of arguing and suasion (defined as the justification and communication of reasons for why an actor should reconceive positions and preferences) and paradigm framing (defined as establishing a set of beliefs, ideas and assumptions determining the very nature of a problem and feasible solutions).[78]

While this classification is certainly not exhaustive, it represents a useful operationalisation of instruments as indirect evidence and indicators of the respective power concepts. It is important to note that an operationalisation of instruments as indicators of power represents but one possible operationalisation of the taxonomy. While this operationalisation is useful for this study, a different operationalisation could include other indicators for the respective power concepts. Also, a particular challenge in Barnett and Duvall's framework is to establish linkages between different power concepts and how these reinforce or weaken each other. According to

[77] Cf. for definitions: Elgström and Jönsson, 'Negotiation in the European Union', 2000; Risse and Kleine, 'Deliberation', 2010; Princen, 'Agenda-Setting', 2007; Princen, *Agenda-Setting in the European Union*, 2009; Princen, 'Agenda-Setting', 2011; Tallberg, *Leadership and Negotiation*, 2006, 14, 69–71; Wallace, *Exercising Power*, 2005, p. 29; Hanns W. Maull, 'Germany and the Art of Coalition Building', *Journal of European Integration*, 30.1 (2008), 131–52; Bailer, 'Factors Determine Bargaining', 2010.

[78] Cf. for definitions: Holzscheiter, 'Discourse as Capability', 2004; Müller, 'Arguing, Bargaining and All That', 2004; Jeffrey T. Checkel, '"Going Native" in Europe?', *Comparative Political Studies*, 36.1–2 (2003), 209–31; Warntjen, 'Bargaining and Deliberation', 2010; Ulbert, Risse and Müller, *Arguing and Bargaining*, 2004; Risse and Kleine, 'Deliberation', 2010; Sebastiaan Princen and Femke van Esch, 'Paradigm Formation and Paradigm Change in the EU's Stability and Growth Pact', *European Political Science Review*, 8.03 (2016), 355–75; Sebastiaan Princen and Paul 't. Hart, 'Putting Policy Paradigms in Their Place', *Journal of European Public Policy*, 21.3 (2014), 470–74. Although Barnett and Duvall argue that entirely voluntary persuasion is not part of any power concept (Barnett and Duvall, 'Power in International Politics', 2005, p. 42), it is unlikely, as they argue, that suasion occurs at all on entirely voluntary terms. Arguing and suasion always evokes power effects to the advantage or disadvantage of one side or the other.

Felix Berenskoetter, Barnett and Duvall "do not touch on the link between these conceptions (…) which allows them to blend out that these connections may be difficult to establish across meta-theoretical divides".[79]

RESEARCH DESIGN AND METHODOLOGY

Departing from this theoretical framework, the research question reads as follows:

- *Which **power concept** can best account for Germany's major or minor influence on the EU's policy towards Russia? Or, put differently: Why was Germany influential in the formation of EU policy towards Russia in some cases and not in others?*

To avoid a selection bias in the selection of case studies, the research question also includes the possibility of a minor German influence and accounts for this variance—why Germany was influential in some cases and not in others. The analytical scheme (Fig. 1.1) illustrates the interplay of variables for the analysis of Germany's influence on the EU's policy formation towards Russia. Germany's positions and preferences represent the starting point and will be understood as those of the respective government, which means that the domestic preference-building process will be excluded from the analysis for the sake of reducing complexity. The main question is therefore not *why* member states wish to be influential in the first place, but *how* member states exert influence and pursue their agenda.

The *dependent variable*, that is, the phenomenon to be explained, is Germany's influence on the EU's policy towards Russia as well as any potential variances thereof. Influence is here understood as the effects of power projection,[80] that is, the extent to which control over the final outcome of the EU's policy towards Russia has been achieved. The more control over the outcome (that is overlap with initial positions and preferences), the more influence an actor can justifiably be assumed to have exerted.

[79] Berenskoetter, *Thinking about Power*, 2007, p. 2.
[80] The effects of power projection include the effects of the projection of compulsory, institutional and productive power.

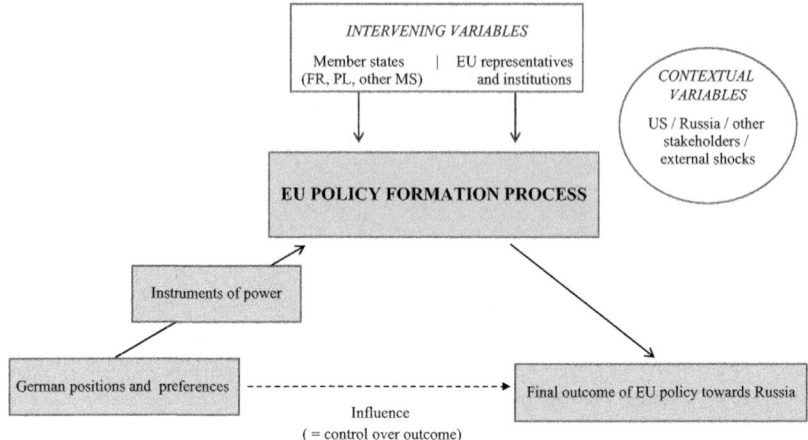

Fig. 1.1 Analytical scheme: German influence on EU policy formation towards Russia. (Source: Author's figure)

As *intervening variables* in this process, the positions and preferences of EU member states (that is their respective governments) and EU institutions and representatives will be analysed. The analysis will focus on the dynamic between Germany, France and Poland, the three key actors in the EU's Russia policy: France as the traditional partner or counterweight to Germany among the "older" member states and Poland as the most outspoken representative of the "newer" EU member states.[81] As *contextual variables* the roles of the US, Russia, further case-related stakeholders as well as external shocks will be taken into account.

Based on the state of research it is assumed that *firstly*, Germany's overall European policy has displayed a tendency towards greater assertiveness since reunification in 1990. *Secondly*, it is assumed that the EU's policy formation towards Russia has become more competitive since the EU's Eastern enlargement in 2004. It thus can be expected that Germany's approach in Russia policy has also become more assertive in this new, more competitive environment of EU policy formation. The main hypothesis of this study therefore suggests that Germany's influence on the

---

[81] Cf. Rachel Le Noan, 'France', in *National Perspectives on Russia*, ed. by David, Gower and Haukkala, pp. 30–47; Cichoki, *Poland*, 2013; Susan Stewart, 'Germany', in *National Perspectives on Russia*, ed. by David, Gower and Haukkala, pp. 13–29.

formation of the EU's Russia policy can be best explained by the use of instruments of compulsory power (such as the veto option or issue linkage).

- *H1: Germany was influential in the formation of the EU's Russia policy after the EU's Eastern enlargement through the use of **instruments of compulsory power**.*
  *Or, put differently: Germany's major or minor influence on the EU's policy towards Russia is best explained by the use or the lack of **instruments of compulsory power**.*

In addition, two sub-hypotheses support the assumption of a greater assertiveness. Firstly, according to the literature, Germany has traditionally been reluctant to engage in security policy issues,[82] especially towards Russia. Yet, in the period after the EU's Eastern enlargement Germany has demonstrated an increased willingness to engage on these issues with Russia. The following sub-hypothesis will therefore be proposed for the analysis:

- *Sub-hypothesis a): Germany displays greater willingness to engage in security policy and crisis situations with Russia in the period after the EU's Eastern enlargement in 2004.*

Secondly, the different contexts of EU policy formation towards Russia—policy initiatives and crisis situations—suggest a different use of instruments of power, such as compulsory instruments in crisis situations or institutional or productive power instruments in policy initiatives. This follows de Flers and Müller's proposition that "it would be conceivable, for instance, that negotiations about less contended foreign policy issues (…) are more likely to encourage a problem-solving or arguing mode of

---

[82] Cf. Miskimmon, *Germany and the Common Foreign and Security Policy of the EU*, 2007; Niklas Helwig, *Europe's New Political Engine: Germany's Role in the EU's Foreign and Security Policy*, Report, Finnish Institute for International Affairs 44 (Helsinki, 2016) https://www.fiia.fi/wp-content/uploads/2017/01/fiiareport44_europes_new_political_engine.pdf [accessed 14 April 2019]; Sebastian Harnisch and Raimund Wolf, *Germany's Changing Security Culture and Governance* (2009) https://www.uni-heidelberg.de/md/politik/harnisch/person/publikationen/harnisch__wolf_2009_germany_____s_changing_security_culture_and_governance.pdf [accessed 2 March 2019].

interest mediation. Highly contested foreign policy issues that are of sub-stantial significance to individual member states, by contrast, can be expected to promote a bargaining style of negotiations".[83]

- *Sub-hypothesis b): A correlation can be observed between the contexts of policy formation, that is crisis situations and policy initiatives, and the use of certain instruments of power.*

These hypotheses will be tested with the method of process-tracing. While it is similar to the method of historical explanations, process-tracing goes one step further and relies on theories and hypotheses to verify causal relationships. According to Andrew Bennet and Jeffrey Checkel, process-tracing comprises the "analysis of evidence on processes, sequences, and conjunctures of events within a case for the purposes of either developing or testing hypotheses about causal mechanisms that might causally explain the case".[84] Causal mechanisms are deemed unobservable per se, yet their footprints can be inferred by concluding causal explanations from empiri-cal observations.[85] Process-tracing is also particularly suited to "assess power explanations by paying careful attention to sequencing and to what information actors had and when they had it".[86] The congruence variant of process-tracing will be used for the analysis.[87] The advantage of congru-ence process-tracing is that it accounts for the causal conditions of a

---

[83] Nicole A. de Flers and Patrick Müller, 'Dimensions and Mechanisms of the Europeanization of Member State Foreign Policy: State of the Art and New Research Avenues', *Journal of European Integration*, 34.1 (2012), 19–35 (p. 27).

[84] Andrew Bennett and Jeffrey T. Checkel, 'Process Tracing: from Philosophical Roots to Best Practices', in *Process Tracing: From Metaphor to Analytic Tool*, ed. by Andrew Bennett and Jeffrey T. Checkel, Strategies for Social Inquiry (Cambridge, New York, NY: Cambridge University Press, 2015), pp. 3–37 (p. 7).

[85] Cf. Alexander L. George and Andrew Bennett, *Case Studies and Theory Development in the Social Sciences*, BCSIA Studies in International Security (Cambridge, MA: MIT Press, 2005), p. 137.

[86] Bennett and Checkel, *Process*, 2015, p. 34.

[87] Cf. for the congruence variant of process-tracing: Joachim Blatter and Till Blume, 'In Search of Co-Variance, Causal Mechanisms or Congruence?: Towards a Plural Understanding of Case Studies', *Swiss Political Science Review*, 14.2 (2008), 315–56; Derek Beach and Rasmus B. Pedersen, *Process-Tracing Methods: Foundations and Guidelines* (Ann Arbor, MI: University of Michigan Press, 2013).

specific outcome without becoming overly mechanistic regarding causal claims.[88] Therefore, rather than focusing on mechanisms, this variant centres on casual configurations generated through "'narratives' with a dense storyline, deep insights into the structures and motivations of (individual, collective or corporate) actors and a fine-grained picture of the critical moments in which various factors came together to produce an important outcome".[89] Careful process-tracing can thus discern what concepts and instruments of power were applied, and at which point in time, to influence a certain phase of the policy formation process.

Since process-tracing requires extensive material, the study will be based on media, literature and document analysis as well as semi-structured elite interviews with different groups of functional elites, including officials and experts, primarily conducted in Berlin and during research stays in Warsaw, Brussels, Paris and Washington.[90] The selection of interviewees reflects the intervening variables in the research design of this study, that is, the focus on France, Poland and EU representatives and institutions. The interviews are anonymised throughout this study and triangulated with media, literature and document analysis to provide a comprehensive picture of Germany's influence in EU policy.

CASE STUDIES

The case studies are selected from a period of EU policy towards Russia spanning from the EU's Eastern enlargement in 2004 to the Ukraine conflict in 2014 and its aftermath. Covering this period of time grants a perspective on the development and possible continuities or changes in Germany's influence. To at least partially control for domestic factors, the selection of cases covers *changing coalitions* in Germany to ensure its influence on EU policy towards Russia is not a single phenomenon under one

[88] Cf. John Gerring, 'Causal Mechanisms: Yes, But...', *Comparative Political Studies*, 43.11 (2010), 1499–526.

[89] Blatter and Blume, 'In Search of Co-Variance', 2008, pp. 323–24.

[90] Cf. David Richards, 'Elite Interviewing: Approaches and Pitfalls', *Politics*, 16.3 (2016), 199–204, Robert Mikecz, 'Interviewing Elites: Addressing Methodological Issues', *Qualitative Inquiry*, 18.6 (2012), 482–93.

Table 1.5   Case studies design

German influence	Policy initiative	Crisis situation
Major influence expected:	*EU-Russia Partnership for Modernisation 2010* (CDU/CSU-FDP coalition)	*Russia-Ukraine Conflict 2014* (Grand Coalition II)
Minor influence expected:	*Meseberg Initiative 2010* (CDU/CSU-FDP coalition)	*Russian-Georgian War 2008* (Grand Coalition I)

Source: Author's table

government. According to these criteria, four cases of EU policy towards Russia are chosen in a most similar/most different design (Table 1.5).[91]

Firstly, cases are chosen which suggest diverging degrees of German influence to avoid a selection bias. Secondly, cases are selected that reflect different contexts of policy making in the EU's Russia policy, namely *policy initiatives* as well as *crisis situations*. According to The Oxford Handbook of Political Leadership, crisis situations are "conditions of serious, urgent and uncertainty-ridden threats to key values and structures of a community or the polity as a whole".[92] They provide "political elites with power chances *and* with acute threats to their legitimacy".[93] In the context of the EU's Common Foreign and Security Policy, crisis situations can be characterised by time constraints and potentially great impact on member states (for instance sanctions or military engagement).[94] Given their salience, they also constitute a more competitive policy formation environment with potentially more resistance by other states to attempts of influencing.[95] The following cases will be tested in the empirical analysis to discern the extent to which a major or minor German influence can be

[91] Cf. Theodore W. Meckstroth, '"Most Different Systems" and "Most Similar Systems": A Study in the Logic of Comparative Inquiry', *Comparative Political Studies*, 8.2 (1975), 132–57.

[92] Chris Ansell, Arjen Boin and Paul 't Hart, 'Political Leadership in Times of Crisis', in *The Oxford Handbook of Political Leadership*, ed. by Rod A. W. Rhodes and Paul 't. Hart (Oxford, New York, NY: Oxford University Press, 2014), pp. 418–29 (p. 418).

[93] Ansell, Boin and Hart, *Political Leadership*, 2014, p. 419.

[94] Wolfgang Wagner, 'Why the EU's Common Foreign and Security Policy Will Remain Intergovernmental: A Rationalist Institutional Choice Analysis of European Crisis Management Policy', *Journal of European Public Policy*, 10.4 (2003), 576–95 [accessed 10 March 2018] (p. 583).

[95] Flers and Müller, 'Dimensions and Mechanisms', 2012, p. 27.

explained by the use of compulsory power instruments, indicating a greater German assertiveness. In addition, the analysis will demonstrate whether a correlation can be observed between crisis situations and policy initiatives and the preferred use of certain instruments.

During the *Russian-Georgian War in 2008* (Grand Coalition I), France assumed a leadership role throughout the crisis under the mandate of its EU Council Presidency and negotiated ceasefire agreements between the conflict parties. While Germany supported France's efforts, it was not in the front row of crisis mediation and opposed further-reaching sanctions. This case therefore suggests minor German influence.

The *EU-Russia Partnership for Modernisation (P4M) from 2010* (CDU/CSU-FDP coalition) followed the model of the German-Russian Modernisation Partnership agreed upon in 2008. In addition to the EU-Russia P4M, twenty-two individual member states in addition to Germany concluded bilateral agreements with Russia. This case would therefore suggest a major German influence on both the European and the member state level.

The *2010 Meseberg Initiative* (CDU/CSU-FDP coalition) was an initiative of the German Federal Chancellery to improve the EU's security cooperation with Russia through the test case of conflict resolution efforts in Transnistria, in return for a EU-Russia Political and Security Committee. The proposal for a joint Committee was not accepted by the EU, nor was sufficient progress achieved in conflict resolution. This case therefore suggests minor German influence.

During the *Russia-Ukraine conflict beginning in 2014* (Grand Coalition II), Germany embraced a leading role in crisis management and spearheaded the EU's sanctions policy towards Russia. This case therefore demonstrates a major German influence and suggests the climax of Germany's influence on the EU's policy towards Russia.

These cases will be tested as to what extent a major or minor German influence can be confirmed and by the use of which instruments of power this influence was achieved. Do they provide evidence for a more assertive approach and greater willingness to engage in crisis situations?

CHAPTER 2

The Russian-Georgian War 2008: Germany as a Junior Partner

The Russian-Georgian War in 2008 was a test case of how the EU could act in a crisis situation in its immediate neighbourhood.[1] It represented a

---

[1] Cf. for general overview: Whitman and Wolff, 'EU as Conflict Manager', 2010; Mouritzen and Wivel, *Explaining Foreign Policy*, 2012; Nicu Popescu, *EU foreign policy and post-Soviet conflicts: Stealth intervention*, Routledge advances in European politics (London: Routledge, 2011); International Crisis Group, *Russia vs Georgia: The Fallout*, Europe Report 195 (Tbilisi, Brussels, 2008) https://www.crisisgroup.org/europe-central-asia/caucasus/georgia/russia-vs-georgia-fallout [accessed 14 April 2019]; Hans-Henning Schröder, *The Caucasus Crisis: International Perceptions and Policy Implications for Germany and Europe*, Research Paper, Stiftung Wissenschaft und Politik (2008) https://www.swp-berlin.org/fileadmin/contents/products/research_papers/2008_RP09_shh_ed_ks.pdf [accessed 30 October 2018]; Michael Brzoska and others, *Der Kaukasuskrieg 2008: Ein regionaler Konflikt mit internationalen Folgen. Eine Stellungnahme aus dem IFSH*, Hamburger Informationen zur Friedensforschung und Sicherheitspolitik 45 (Hamburg, 2008) https://ifsh.de/pdf/publikationen/hifs/HI45.pdf [accessed 13 April 2019]; Elena Kropatcheva, 'Russia's Response to Georgia's Military Operation in South Ossetia', in *OSCE Yearbook 2008: Yearbook on the Organization for Security and Co-Operation in Europe (OSCE)*, ed. by Institute for Peace Research and Security Policy at the University of Hamburg (IFSH), 1st edn (Baden-Baden: Nomos, 2009), pp. 45–61 (pp. 49–50); Lili Di Puppo and others, *Perspectives on the Georgian-Russian War*, Caucasus Analytical Digest 1 (2008) http://www.laender-analysen.de/cad/pdf/CaucasusAnalyticalDigest01.pdf [accessed 24 October 2018]; *Rückblick auf ein Lehrstück: Der Kaukasuskrieg und die Folgen*, ed. by Manfred Sapper (= *Osteuropa*, 11 (2008)); Cornell and Starr (eds), *Guns of August*, 2015; Mike Bowker, 'The War in Georgia and the Western Response', *Central Asian Survey*, 30.2

© The Author(s), under exclusive license to Springer Nature Switzerland AG 2021
L. Fix, *Germany's Role in European Russia Policy*, New Perspectives in German Political Studies,
https://doi.org/10.1007/978-3-030-68226-2_2

new dimension of military conflict involving Russia and was a prime example for "the challenge facing the EU as a security actor".[2] Moreover, the war was a serious challenge to Germany and the EU both in terms of their policy responses and the conflict narrative. How was the conflict to be interpreted for the future of EU-Russia relations? Was it an unexpected, "sui generis"[3] escalation in a long-brewing post-Soviet conflict with both sides to blame, or the manifestation of a new, revisionist Russian foreign policy in its neighbourhood, representing a caesura and requiring a reorientation of the EU's relationship with Russia?

This question was a particular challenge for Germany, which had been at the forefront of shaping EU relations with Russia during the chancellorship of Gerhard Schröder and hereafter.[4] After the accession of Poland and the Baltic states in 2004, the playing field of actors interested in shaping EU Russia policy had altered significantly in the new landscape of an enlarged EU. How much influence could Germany retain on the formation of the EU's policy response to the Russian-Georgian War in comparison to other EU members?[5] Which instruments were applied, especially given the salience of the crisis situation?

(2011), 197–211; Ronald D. Asmus, *A Little War that Shook the World: Georgia, Russia and the future of the West*, 1st edn (New York: Palgrave Macmillan, 2010); Paul Gallis, *The NATO Summit at Bucharest*, Congressional Research Service (Washington, DC, 2008) https://fas. org/sgp/crs/row/RS22847.pdf [accessed 21 October 2018].

[2] Dov Lynch, *Why Georgia Matters*, Chaillot Paper, Institute for Security Studies 86 (Paris, 2006), p. 68 https://infoeuropa.eurocid.pt/files/database/000036001-000037000/000036733.pdf [accessed 14 April 2019].

[3] Cf. Roy Allison, 'Russia Resurgent?: Moscow's Campaign to 'Coerce Georgia to Peace", *International Affairs*, 84.6 (2008), 1145–71.

[4] Cf. Timmins, 'German-Russian Bilateral', 2011.

[5] For an overview of EU member states' positions, compare: Mouritzen and Wivel, *Explaining Foreign Policy*, 2012, p. 114; Henrik B. L. Larsen, 'The Russo-Georgian War and Beyond: Towards a European Great Power Concert', *European Security*, 21.1 (2012), 102–21; Ainius Lašas, 'When History Matters: Baltic and Polish Reactions to the Russo-Georgian War', *Europe-Asia Studies*, 64.6 (2012), 1061–75; Paweł and Świeboda, *The Conflict in Georgia and Its Implications for the Region—the Polish Perspective*, Heinrich Böll Stiftung (2008) https://pl.boell.org/sites/default/files/downloads/Conflict_in_Georgia_by_Pawel_Swieboda.pdf [accessed 24 October 2018]; Laure Delcour and Elsa Tulmets, 'Die deutsch-französischen Beziehungen im russisch-georgischen Konflikt: Parallel laufende diplomatische Initiativen', in *Die Konsenswerkstatt: Deutsch-französische Kommunikations- und Entscheidungsprozesse in der Europapolitik*, ed. by Claire Demesmay, Martin Koopmann and Julien Thorel, Genshagener Schriften—Europa politisch denken, 2 (Baden-Baden: Nomos, 2013), 105-120; International Crisis Group, *Russia vs Georgia*, 2008, pp. 26–30.

The policy formation process within the EU will be traced throughout three conflict phases: From the outbreak of war on 7 August 2008 until the signing of the Six-Point Peace Plan by Russia on 16 August; from 16 August to the signing of the Second Peace Plan on 8 September 2008; and the aftermath of the conflict until the renewal of suspended negotiations on a EU-Russia Partnership and Cooperation Agreement in November 2008. As an additional source, WikiLeaks' documents for this period of time will be taken into account, which were exchanged through US diplomatic channels, mirroring internal US interests as well as discussions with European actors and their respective positions and preferences.[6] Such documents are particularly valuable to identify "the dogs that did not bark" in European policy formation.[7]

German Positions and Preferences

In the prelude to the Russian-Georgian War in August 2008, Germany played a prominent role on two issues: Firstly, the debate about a NATO Membership Action Plan for Georgia, which culminated at the NATO Bucharest Summit on 2–4 April 2008. Then Georgian President Mikheil Saakashvili has declared membership in EU and NATO a top priority for Georgia after the peaceful change of power during the Rose Revolution in 2003 and was supported by US President George W. Bush in his bid. Secondly, Germany assumed a leading role in conflict prevention efforts in Abkhazia as coordinator in the UN Secretary-General's Group of Friends

---

[6] According to Gabriel J. Michael, despite the reluctance among political scientists to engage with leaked documents, ethical objections raised in this context are primarily related to the first-time publication of leaked material, whereas the subsequent scholarly use of already publicly available material is less problematic. Cf. Gabriel J. Michael, 'Who's Afraid of WikiLeaks?: Missed Opportunities in Political Science Research', *Review of Policy Research*, 32.2 (2015), 175–99. In this study, the analysed cables are part of the US diplomatic cables leak from November 2010, including ca. 250,000 cables available on WikiLeaks and partly published by *El País, Der Spiegel, Le Monde, The Guardian* as well as *The New York Times* in redacted form. Many of the WikiLeaks documents that will be used have already been empirically examined in Mouritzen and Wivel's account "International Diplomacy and the Russo-Georgian War", cf. Mouritzen and Wivel, *Explaining Foreign Policy*, 2012. From a methodological perspective, it is important to note that these diplomatic cables provide a US perspective and analysis of the positions and preferences of European partners. As an addition to other sources, they provide a unique insight to otherwise inaccessible assessments of the positions and preferences of key actors.

[7] Michael, 'Who's Afraid of Wikileaks', 2015, p. 194.

on Georgia. Russia supported South Ossetia and Abkhazia throughout the secessionist wars of the early 1990s, including a peacekeeping force of Russian troops alongside an unarmed United Nations Observer Mission in Abkhazia. Berlin approached these two issues with different strategies: While Germany opposed the decision for a NATO membership plan for Georgia in Bucharest, at the same time it assumed an agenda-setting role in conflict prevention efforts in Abkhazia, proposing a "Steinmeier plan" for negotiations.

Opposing NATO Membership Action Plan for Georgia

Germany played a major role in discussions on a NATO Membership Action Plan for Georgia, the precondition for accession to NATO, in the run-up to the Russian-Georgian War in August 2008.[8] While the Bush administration was willing to grant Georgia a membership plan at the NATO Summit on 2–4 April, France, Germany and at least two other governments[9] indicated they hoped the process would proceed more slowly and opposed the US' position. The German government publicly declared its position in advance of the summit. Then German Foreign Minister Frank-Walter Steinmeier warned against unnecessarily provoking Russia[10] and Chancellor Angela Merkel declared NATO accession for Georgia as "too early".[11] Poland in particular tried to pressure Germany, arguing in a letter that Germany had become a NATO member in the past despite its own East-West division.[12] Differences were not reconciled in advance and resurfaced at the summit, where leaders sought a compromise.

In order to reach a consensus in their final communiqué, leaders eventually agreed on the possibility of NATO membership, in line with NATO's open-door policy,[13] yet with unspecific temporal terms. This produced the

---

[8] Cf. Tuomas Forsberg and Graeme Herd, 'Russia and NATO: From Windows of Opportunities to Closed Doors', *Journal of Contemporary European Studies*, 23.1 (2015), 41–57; Emmanuel Karagiannis, 'The 2008 Russian–Georgian War via the Lens of Offensive Realism', *European Security*, 22.1 (2013), 74–93.

[9] Paul Gallis, *The NATO Summit at Bucharest*, Congressional Research Service (Washington, DC, 2008) https://fas.org/sgp/crs/row/RS22847.pdf [accessed 21 October 2018].

[10] 'Steinmeier mahnt zu Rücksicht auf Russland', *Die Welt*, 2 April 2008.

[11] 'Merkel: Nato-Beitritt für Ukraine zu früh', *Bild*, 2 April 2008.

[12] 'Kaczynski rügt deutsche Nato-Politik', *Frankfurter Allgemeine Zeitung*, 2 April 2008.

[13] North Atlantic Treaty Organization (NATO), *NATO Decisions on Open-Door Policy* (2008) https://www.nato.int/docu/update/2008/04-april/e0403h.html [accessed 21 October 2018].

following wording in the final communiqué: "NATO welcomes Ukraine's and Georgia's Euro-Atlantic aspirations for membership in NATO [and] agreed today that these countries will become members of NATO".[14] From a US perspective, this declaration was meant to "signal confidence" in Georgia's and Ukraine's ability to qualify for membership, while "sending a message to Moscow" that countries in its neighbourhood could freely choose their allegiances.[15] According to Ronald Asmus, member of the US administration at that time, Germany played a crucial role on this issue: In his account, countries like France were also sceptical, but would not have stood in the way of a membership plan.[16] While there are different assessments to whether the decision hinged solely on Germany,[17] Berlin contributed to setting the boundaries of European and Transatlantic policy towards Georgia with significant implications for the conflict to come.

Germany's reluctant stance regarding a NATO Membership Action Plan and the wording in the final communiqué would become an issue of heated debate later on: Did the refusal to grant Georgia a membership plan embolden Russia, as argued by Eastern EU member states in a joint declaration following the outbreak of the war,[18] or was it the "emergency brake"[19] preventing further escalation, such as NATO involvement in the Russian-Georgian War?

[14] North Atlantic Treaty Organization (NATO), *Bucharest Summit Declaration: Issued by the Heads of State and Government Participating in the Meeting of the North Atlantic Council, 3 April* (Bucharest, 2008) https://www.nato.int/cps/us/natohq/official_texts_8443.htm [accessed 21 October 2018].

[15] Paul Gallis, *The NATO Summit at Bucharest*, Congressional Research Service (Washington, DC, 2008) https://fas.org/sgp/crs/row/RS22847.pdf [accessed 21 October 2018].

[16] Asmus, *Little War*, 2010, 111ff.

[17] Cf. Ian Traynor, 'Nato Allies Divided over Ukraine and Georgia', *The Guardian*, 2 December 2008; Steven Erlanger and Steven Lee Myers, 'NATO Allies Oppose Bush on Georgia and Ukraine', *The New York Times*, 3 April 2008; 'France and Germany Thwart Bush's Plans', *Spiegel Online*, 3 April 2008; 'Nato: No Map for Georgia or Ukraine, but Alliance Vows Membership', *RadioFreeEurope/RadioLiberty*, 3 April 2008.

[18] Lech Kaczyński and others, *Joint Statement by Presidents of Poland, Estonia, Latvia and Lithuania, 9 August* (2008) https://halldor2.wordpress.com/2008/08/09/joint-statement-by-presidents-of-poland-estonia-latvia-and-lithuania/ [accessed 21 October 2018].

[19] Translation by the author. Wolfgang Ischinger, *Das Russland-Paradox: Vom (richtigen und falschen) Umgang mit Moskau*, Munich Security Conference (MSC) Blog (2016) https://www.securityconference.de/news/article/monthly-mind-juli-2016-das-russland-paradox-vom-richtigen-oder-falschen-umgang-mit-moskau/ [accessed 21 October 2018].

Setting the Agenda in Abkhazia

While Germany was opposing a membership plan for Georgia, it was at the same time leading the agenda on conflict prevention efforts in Abkhazia facilitated by its mandate as the coordinator of the UN Secretary-General's Group of Friends on Georgia.[20] Given increased tensions throughout the spring of 2008, the conflict was most likely expected to erupt in Abkhazia, the region with the fiercest independence aspirations. Then Foreign Minister Steinmeier developed a three-staged plan for conflict mediation,[21] which was coordinated with EU members states, the US and Russia.[22] He travelled to Tbilisi and Sukhumi to garner acceptance for his plan on 17 and 18 July, with the support of the UN Mission.[23] The German ambassador in Tbilisi pursued talk in Sukhumi together with the US Deputy Assistant Secretary of State Mathew Bryza.[24] Yet the efforts were not fruitful and Germany's invitation to the conflict parties to come to Berlin for peace talks in August was met with reluctance.[25]

By the beginning of August, the situation in Abkhazia was overshadowed by the outbreak of war in South Ossetia, where, in contrast to the UN mission in Abkhazia, the Organization for Security and Co-operation in Europe (OSCE) was in the lead in conflict prevention efforts and participated in meetings of the Joint Control Commission, the negotiation mechanism co-chaired by Georgia, South Ossetia, North Ossetia and Russia. The change of the conflict venue to South Ossetia shifted responsibilities for conflict mediation as well as possibilities for Germany to shape the situation through its institutional UN mandate.[26] After the outbreak of war, the institutional legitimacy passed on to France and then President Nicolas Sarkozy as the EU's Council President, who initially also coordinated with the OSCE due to their presence on the ground in South Ossetia. Germany's influence on conflict resolution as coordinator of the

---

[20] 'Germany Takes Lead in Abkhaz Diplomatic Efforts', *Civil.ge*, 16 July 2008.

[21] 'Some Details of German Abkhaz Plan Reported', *Civil.ge*, 23 July 2008.

[22] 'Germany Proposes Peace Plan for Abkhazia', *Spiegel Online*, 7 July 2008.

[23] 'Harte Worte aus Georgien', *ntv*, 17 July 2008.

[24] Interview with German diplomat in Berlin, 09.08.2016.

[25] Delcour and Tulmets, *Die deutsch-französischen Beziehungen*, 2013; Vladimir Socor, *Post-Mortems on the German Plan on Abkhazia*, Eurasia Daily Monitor, The Jamestown Foundation 140 (2008) https://jamestown.org/program/post-mortems-on-the-german-plan-on-abkhazia/ [accessed 21 October 2018]; 'Abkhazia's Separatists Reject German Plan to Prevent Conflict with Georgia', *The New York Times*, 18 July 2008.

[26] Interview with German diplomat in Brussels, 08.03.2016.

UN Secretary-General's Group of Friends on Georgia thus receded after the outbreak of war in South Ossetia, with President Sarkozy grasping the opportunity to leave a mark during his EU Council Presidency.

CRISIS MEDIATION

Conflict Phase I: Supporting France's Conflict Mediation

In the first conflict phase—lasting from the outbreak of war until the Russian signing of the Six-Point Peace Plan agreement on 16 August 2008—President Sarkozy in his function as the EU's Council President asserted the first claim to a conflict mediation role by conducting shuttle diplomacy between Tbilisi and Moscow. The French president used this opportunity to present France as the "political leader of a unified Union capable of delivering foreign policy results",[27] taking advantage of the EU as a multiplier of French influence. Conflict mediation efforts were primarily implemented by France on behalf of the EU, not by EU representatives. The German government followed France's leadership in conflict mediation after the outbreak of hostilities. Poland and the Baltic states, however, put forward their own statement[28] and narrative of the conflict as a clear indication of Russian imperialist ambitions in the region. Two broad positions and narratives thus emerged during the first conflict phase:[29] a Polish position, supported by the Baltic states, and a French position, supported by Germany.

The outbreak of war in South Ossetia on the night of 7 August took the international community by surprise and without warning. Following the Georgian military's artillery assault on the South Ossetian "capital" of Tskhinvali, Russia intervened the next day with a major military incursion.[30] Within a short time, Russian troops drove Georgian forces from South Ossetia and advanced further onto the Georgian capital, Tbilisi.

---

[27] Larsen, 'Russo-Georgian War', 2012, 107f.

[28] Katrin Bennhold, 'Differences emerge in Europe of a response to Georgia conflict', *The New York Times*, 12 August 2008; https://www.nytimes.com/2008/08/12/world/europe/12iht-diplo.4.15218653.html.

[29] Mouritzen and Wivel, *Explaining Foreign Policy*, 2012, pp. 113–38.

[30] Compare for an overview of events the official report and the following conflict timelines: Heidi Tagliavini, *Report of the Independent International Fact-Finding Mission on the Conflict in Georgia: Volume I-III* (2009) http://www.mpil.de//files/pdf4/IIFFMCG_Volume_I2.pdf;   http://www.mpil.de//files/pdf4/IIFFMCG_Volume_II1.pdf;

With international leaders gathered at the Summer Olympics in Beijing, French President Sarkozy used this opportunity to immediately approach Russian then Prime Minister Vladimir Putin, asking for a brief ceasefire to mediate the conflict, which was unheeded.[31] On 12 August, then President Dmitry Medvedev informed High Representative Solana that Russia was concluding its operations in South Ossetia, clearing the way for President Sarkozy to fly to Moscow to negotiate an agreement.[32] In talks with the Russian leaders Medvedev and Putin in Moscow, Sarkozy negotiated a Six-Point Peace Plan which included international talks on the "future status" of South Ossetia and Abkhazia, as well as "security measures" implemented by Russian forces while awaiting international mechanisms.[33] The same day, Sarkozy arrived in Tbilisi to gain approval from the Georgian side for the agreement. Yet, President Saakashvili refused to sign the agreement until the wording was changed from talks on the "future status" of Abkhazia and South Ossetia to talks on "security and stability", thereby not explicitly questioning Abkhazia's and South Ossetia's status and—at least in wording—preserving Georgia's territorial integrity.[34] This adapted agreement was followed by further negotiations in Moscow, with Russia eventually agreeing to this version. EU foreign ministers adopted the plan in an extraordinary meeting on 13 August,[35] calling on the Council Secretariat and the Commission to prepare an EU contribution to monitor the implementation of the plan.[36] Eventually, Moscow signed the agreement on 16 August 2008.

http://www.mpil.de//files/pdf4/IIFFMCG_Volume_III1.pdf [accessed 13 April 2019]; International Crisis Group, *Russia vs Georgia*, 2008; Schröder, *Caucasus Crisis*, 2008.

[31] Asmus, *Little War*, 2010, p. 191.

[32] Ian Traynor and Luke Harding, 'Surrender or Else, Russia Tells Georgia', *The Guardian*, 12 August 2008.

[33] 'Russia "Ends Georgia Operation"', *BBC News*, 12 August 2008.

[34] Jon Swaine, 'Russia and Georgia 'Agree in Principle' to Nicolas Sarkozy-Backed Peace Plan', *The Telegraph*, 13 August 2008.

[35] Compare for English translation of the final version of the Six-Point Peace Plan: Council of the European Union, General Affairs and External Relations, *Press Release, Presse 236, Extraordinary Meeting 13 August* (Brussels, 2008) http://eeas.europa.eu/archives/delegations/georgia/documents/eu_georgia/13august2008_en.pdf [accessed 21 October 2018].

[36] Council of the European Union, General Affairs and External Relations, *Press Release, Presse 236, Extraordinary Meeting 13 August* (Brussels, 2008) http://eeas.europa.eu/archives/delegations/georgia/documents/eu_georgia/13august2008_en.pdf [accessed 21 October 2018].

President Sarkozy's trips to Moscow and Georgia demonstrated that France was willing to take a leadership role in crisis mediation efforts, representing and negotiating on behalf of the EU, with only a limited role for EU or OSCE representatives. EU High Representative Solana did not accompany Sarkozy to Moscow; he was told not to interrupt his August holiday, and thereby effectively sidelined.[37] Solana was only later involved in the negotiation of the second ceasefire agreement from 8 September, and in the preparation of the EU Monitoring Mission. France hence maximised the legitimising effects of the Council Presidency for a leading role, placing an overriding priority in the Six-Point Peace Plan on ceasing hostilities, with little conditionality attached. This pragmatic approach was met with criticism: In a US cable, a Swedish diplomat was quoted complaining about a "Sarkozy Show" and a pro-Russian language in the Peace Plan.[38] According to other US cables, Germany reportedly also voiced criticisms about the unclear terms of the Peace Plan and a lack of French conflict expertise.[39]

Chancellor Merkel and Foreign Minister Steinmeier adopted a position in support of France's efforts, and initially refrained from strongly worded statements towards Russia. According to a US cable, this was a strategic division of labour between Germany and France: "If French efforts failed, Germany should be ready to use direct language toward Russia in public statements (similar to what Germany says they already are using in private discussions with Russia)".[40] In the EU Foreign Affairs Council, Steinmeier explicitly supported France's position: "Do we want strongly-worded statements to air our frustration (…)? Or do we want Europe to remain capable of playing a constructive role (…)"?[41] Another reason for the German government's initially cautious wording towards Russia was also

---

[37] Nicu Popescu, *EU Foreign Policy and Post-Soviet Conflicts: Stealth Intervention*, Routledge Advances in European Politics (London: Routledge, 2011), p. 87.

[38] Andrew Rettman, 'US Cables Shed Light on EU 'Friends of Russia' in Georgia War', *EUobserver*, 1 December 2010.

[39] Cf. WikiLeaks, *Germany Carefully Watching Russian Withdrawal, 22 August* (2008) https://wikileaks.org/plusd/cables/08BERLIN1176_a.html [accessed 24 October 2018]; WikiLeaks, *Merkel "Will Talk Tough" in Sochi: Foreign Office and Bundestag Display Mixture of Resolve and Skepticism, 15 August* (2008) https://wikileaks.org/plusd/cables/08BERLIN1130_a.html [accessed 24 October 2018].

[40] WikiLeaks, *Germany's View of Georgia: Frustration Rising but Awaiting French Results in Moscow, 12 August* (2008) https://wikileaks.org/plusd/cables/08BERLIN1101_a.html [accessed 24 October 2018].

[41] As quoted in Mouritzen and Wivel, *Explaining Foreign Policy*, 2012, p. 188.

the difficult relationship with Georgian President Saakashvili, who was deemed to have an impulsive character after a first meeting in Berlin, especially from the Chancellor's side.[42] His impulsiveness was also considered as having potentially contributed to the outbreak of the war through Georgia's miscalculated military assault on Tskhinvali. In US cables, German diplomats were criticised for adopting a cautious position on the question of who was to blame for the outbreak of the war and refraining from putting the blame squarely on Russia, as argued by Eastern member states. Germany's NATO ambassador was quoted in a US cable that "responsibility for the outbreak of conflict could be shared. (...) There were questions that both Russia and Georgia should be asked".[43] According to Steinmeier, "pointing the finger of blame for the outbreak of the recent escalation won't help anyone".[44]

The question of who was responsible for the war's outbreak became the crucial dividing line in the narrative of the Russian-Georgian War. In the words of Roy Allison, "[t]wo quite contrary narratives are in circulation. Russia claims that its operation and subsequent security measures in Georgia have been sui generis and essentially retaliatory—an ad hoc, exceptional, though large-scale, response to a Georgian attack in South Ossetia. Critics of Moscow's offensive argue, on the contrary, that Russia's ostensible commitment to protect 'Russian citizens', a core justification of the intervention in Georgia, has principally served as a means of coercion and a device to expedite military intervention in that country".[45] According to a Swedish diplomat quoted in a US cable, two "camps" emerged within the EU: "One camp's overriding priority is to stop the suffering and ensure the ceasefire is respected, that it is too early to judge or blame and the EU cannot appear biased. Members include Malta, Cyprus, France, Germany, Ireland and the Netherlands. The other camp says Georgia made mistakes, but the overriding concern is that Russia launched a full-scale invasion of a sovereign nation in violation of international

---

[42] Interview with German official in Berlin, 15.07.2016; Compare also: Henning Krumrey, 'Merkel zwischen Krieg und Frieden', *Focus*, 17 August 2008.

[43] WikiLeaks, *North Atlantic Council Visit to Tbilisi, 30 September* (2008) https://wikileaks.org/plusd/cables/08USNATO352_a.html [accessed 24 October 2018].

[44] As quoted in Mouritzen and Wivel, *Explaining Foreign Policy*, 2012, p. 188.

[45] Allison, 'Russia Resurgent?', 2008, pp. 1145–46.

commitments. (…) Members include England, Belgium, Sweden, Denmark, the Baltic states, Slovenia, Slovakia and Bulgaria".[46]

German diplomats positioned themselves in hindsight inbetween and tended to see the Russian-Georgian War as an unexpected escalation in continuation of twenty years of post-Soviet conflict structures, triggered when a Georgian miscalculation was met with a disproportionate Russian response. At the beginning, however, Germany supported France's neutral mediation role.[47]

In order to contribute to an independent—and commonly accepted— answer to the question of responsibility, Germany was the initiator and strongest advocate for an independent report of the conflict's genesis, the so-called Tagliavini Report, named after the Swiss diplomat Tagliavini who headed the Independent International Fact-Finding Mission.[48] On Foreign Minister Steinmeier's initiative in September 2008, the EU Council of Ministers charged the commission with investigating the causes and the course of the conflict.[49] The report was published a year later and established facts on outbreak and trajectory of the conflict including war crime claims.[50] Yet while the report gathered an immense amount of detail, it concluded there was "no way to assign overall responsibility for the conflict to one side alone".[51] According to a European Council official, at that point in time interest in the report was waning, since all parties had already established their own narratives and used the facts of the report to advance their respective views.[52] The question of whom to blame remained a political question, despite Germany's attempt to establish a common conflict narrative.

A gap in the narrative of the conflict permeated between France and Germany on the one hand, and Poland and the Baltic states on the other hand. Shortly after the outbreak of war, on 9 August, the presidents of

---

[46] Rettman, 'US Cables Shed Light', 2010. Interestingly, Poland was not mentioned, although playing an important role in the second "camp".

[47] Interview with German diplomat in Berlin, 09.08.2016.

[48] Federal Foreign Office, *Steinmeier Commends the Work of the Tagliavini Commission, 30 September* (Berlin, 2009) https://www.auswaertiges-amt.de/en/newsroom/news/090930-tagliavini/233248 [accessed 24 October 2018].

[49] Tagliavini, *Tagliavini report*, 2009, p. 3.

[50] Lili Di Puppo and others, *The EU Investigation Report on the August 2008 War and the Reactions from Georgia and Russia*, Caucasus Analytical Digest 10 (2009) http://www.laender-analysen.de/cad/pdf/CaucasusAnalyticalDigest10.pdf [accessed 24 October 2018].

[51] Tagliavini, *Tagliavini report*, 2009, p. 32.

[52] Interview with European Council official in Brussels, 31.05.2016.

Estonia, Latvia, Lithuania and Poland published a joint declaration open for other signatories, which condemned Russia's "revisionist" actions and implicitly criticised the positions of France and Germany on the question of whom to blame for the war: "aggression against a small country in Europe will not be passed over in silence or with meaningless statements equating the victims with the victimizers".[53] In addition, the letter proposed

> "to refrain from calling Russia a strategic partner, to stop visa facilitation talks and dialogue on a new Partnership and Cooperation Agreement and replace Russian forces in South Ossetia with international forces".

Lastly, the letter criticized those refusing to grant Georgia a MAP at the NATO Summit in Bucharest as giving a green light to Russia—again implicitly reproaching Germany and France for their positions.

Among Eastern European member states, Poland assumed a leadership role, as it perceived the conflict as "one of the most important political incidents of the present decade [which] will shape the strategic reality in Eastern Europe in the upcoming years".[54] On Poland's initiative and to demonstrate solidarity with Georgia, the four presidents together with the Ukrainian president organised their own trip to Tbilisi on 12 August in order to "act as human shields",[55] competing with Sarkozy's trips to Moscow and Tbilisi on the same day. The foreign minister of Lithuania, Petras Vaitiekūnas, had already embarked on a fact-finding mission to Tbilisi on 8 August.[56] While Moscow granted Sarkozy's plane safe passage to Georgia, the Eastern European delegation had to travel in a motor convoy from Azerbaijan.[57] Eastern European member states thereby asserted their own position in the conflict distinctively dissociating them-selves from the positions of France and Germany.

The gulf between these two divergent European positions became sym-bolically most visible when Sarkozy and the Eastern European presidents,

---

[53] Kaczyński and others, *Joint Statement*, 2008; Katrin Bennhold, 'Differences emerge in Europe of a response to Georgia conflict', *The New York Times*, 12 August 2008; https://www.nytimes.com/2008/08/12/world/europe/12iht-diplo.4.15218653.html.

[54] Cf. Paweł and Świeboda, *Conflict in Georgia*, 2008.

[55] Lašas, 'When History Matters', 2012, p. 1065.

[56] Cf. 'Lithuania Sends Foreign Minister to Georgia', *Reuters*, 8 August 2008; Runner, 'EU Diplomats Fly', 2008.

[57] Interview with Polish official in Warsaw, 16.05.2016.

although both in Tbilisi mere meters apart, did not meet except from a handshake, according to US Diplomat Ronald Asmus.[58] The Eastern delegation was addressing a rally outside the Georgian Parliament, while Sarkozy was trying to gain approval for the peace plan negotiated in Moscow, with Saakashvili rushing back and forth between the two delegations.[59] This uncoordinated double EU presence demonstrated the divisions between "old" and "new" member states over the EU's policy towards Russia[60] and the different conflict narratives: One side called for solidarity in the wake of Russia's military intervention, which represented from their point of view a continuation of Russian imperialist behaviour emboldened by EU leaders' reluctance in Bucharest. The other side—Germany and France—framed the conflict during the first conflict phase as an unexpected escalation that required a neutral mediating role from the EU.

Against the backdrop of these diverging positions, the US played an important role as a contextual factor to EU policy formation. While Sarkozy was keen to keep French and European ownership of crisis mediation efforts,[61] ambiguous signals were sent from Washington, welcoming the visit of Eastern European presidents to Tbilisi.[62] Only during a trip to Georgia on 15 August, US Secretary of State Condoleezza Rice clearly placed the US support behind French efforts and tried to secure Saakashvili's signature of the Six-Point Peace Plan.[63] However, the Russia-critical rhetoric from the US—more in line with Eastern European positions than France's and Germany's[64]—further exacerbated the dividing lines in the EU and between France, Germany and the US.[65] According to

---

[58] Asmus, *Little War*, 2010, p. 208.

[59] 'Russia, Georgia Agree to Peace Plan to End Fighting', *RadioFreeEurope/RadioLiberty*, 12 August 2008, Asmus, *Little War*, 2010, p. 205.

[60] Kai-Olaf Lang, 'The Old Fears of the New Europeans', in *The Caucasus Crisis*, ed. by Schröder, pp. 30–33.

[61] Mouritzen and Wivel, *Explaining Foreign Policy*, 2012, p. 141.

[62] Cf. Bowker, 'The War in Georgia', 2011.

[63] Damien McElroy and Jon Swaine, 'Condoleezza Rice in Tbilisi to Secure Georgia Peace Plan', *The Telegraph*, 15 August 2008.

[64] For instance, in remarks on 11 August, then President Bush interpreted the Russian-Georgian War as a Russian effort to depose President Saakashvili: George W. Bush, *Remarks on the Situation in Georgia, 11 August* (2008) https://www.gpo.gov/fdsys/pkg/PPP-2008-book2/pdf/PPP-2008-book2-doc-pg1137.pdf [accessed 30 October 2018].

[65] Stephen Blank, 'America and the Russo-Georgian War', *Small Wars & Insurgencies*, 20.2 (2009), 425–51.

a US cable, the US embassy Berlin even deemed it necessary to underline that "assertions in the German media about a U.S. 'green light' to Saakashvili were entirely baseless",[66] responding to reports that Washington could have emboldened Saakashvili in the period before the outbreak of the war.

Although Eastern European leaders criticised the Six-Point Peace Plan for its failure to affirm Georgia's territorial integrity, they nevertheless supported the Peace Plan in the extraordinary meeting of EU foreign ministers on 13 August. France's activism left little room and options to Eastern member states: Rejecting the Peace Plan would have cast the Eastern European member states as outsiders and reinforced prejudices about Polish and Baltic biased positions towards Russia, which were perceived by Western Europeans as constant "Cassandras calls", according to a former Polish diplomat.[67] Especially in a crisis situation of war and peace, the EU's unity was perceived as a value in and of itself.[68] The Oxford Handbook of Political Leadership stresses the symbolic role of a leader as "iconic for both the response effort and the political community at large".[69] This was particularly visible in Sarkozy's personal engagement and his desire to demonstrate a united European response, with France at the helm.[70] France thus successfully consolidated its leadership role within the EU and was accepted by the conflict parties, bestowed with the legitimising effects of the Council Presidency.

From a German perspective, contesting the French leadership role was neither promising, given that the institutional legitimacy for a conflict mediation role has passed on to France's Council Presidency, nor necessary: The like-minded French positions, prioritising at first a neutral mediation role, reflected Germany's own positions and preferences. Germany could remain under the lee of France's leadership without the need to assume an exposed role itself during the first conflict phase. This has only changed when the situation deteriorated in the second phase. Russia's failure to withdraw Russian troops from Georgia proper further widened the gulf among member states and required Germany to become more

[66] WikiLeaks, *Germany's View of Georgia*, 2008.

[67] Interview with former Polish diplomat in Warsaw, 17.05.2016.

[68] Interview with Estonian diplomat in Berlin, 17.08.2016.

[69] Ansell, Boin and Hart, *Political Leadership*, 2014, p. 421.

[70] Cf. Nicolas Sarkozy, 'L'Union européenne et la Russie dans la gouvernance mondiale', *Politique étrangère*, 4 (2008), 723–32 https://www.cairn.info/revue-politique-etrangere-2008-4-page-723.htm [accessed 21 October 2018].

heavily involved both in crisis mediation efforts with Russia and in reaching consensus among the EU, in particular with Eastern member states.

Conflict Phase II: Keeping the EU Together

In the second conflict phase, the non-withdrawal of Russian forces to the pre-conflict line led to a delay in implementing the Six-Point Peace Plan and to a more explicit and strongly worded German position towards Russia. The recognition of the independence declarations of South Ossetia and Abkhazia by Russia on 26 August[71] resulted in a hardening of the EU's position and required renewed mediation efforts, namely a second, more detailed agreement concluded in Moscow on 8 September 2018. Beforehand, Merkel travelled to Sochi and Tbilisi to support the implementation of the peace plan and visited Eastern European capitals to reconcile divergent positions within the EU while adopting a more outspoken position towards Russia and on the question of Georgia's NATO perspective.

Shortly after the agreement of the Six-Point Peace Plan, Chancellor Merkel travelled to Sochi and Tbilisi on 15 and 17 August to pressure the Russian leadership to withdraw troops to the pre-conflict line.[72] According to a US cable, attempts by the Russian side to add a sightseeing trip to the Olympic Park in Sochi during Merkel's visit were "rebuffed" and the German side adopted a tough stance in talks with President Medvedev.[73] The Chancellor "believed empathetically" that Medvedev was the "appropriate interlocutor" instead of Prime Minister Putin, and contacts with Prime Minister Putin would "needlessly increase" his standing.[74] After the meeting with Medvedev, Merkel criticised Russia's actions in Georgia in a strongly worded statement as "disproportionate" and "unreasonable" and

---

[71] Compare for the recognition of independence the following Russian presidential decrees: Dmitry Medvedev, *Presidential Decree of the Russian Federation "About Recognition of the Republic South Ossetia", No. 1261, 26 August* (2008) http://cis-legislation.com/document.fwx?rgn=24165 [accessed 16 December 2018], Dmitry Medvedev, *Presidential Decree of the Russian Federation "About Recognition of the Republic of Abkhazia", No. 1260, 26 August* (2008) http://cis-legislation.com/document.fwx?rgn=24164 [accessed 16 December 2018].

[72] Federal Chancellor, *Merkel Fordert Schnellen Rückzug Russischer Truppen, 17 August* (Tbilisi, 2008) https://www.bundeskanzlerin.de/bkin-de/merkel-fordert-schnellen-rueckzug-russischer-truppen-609458 [accessed 16 December 2018].

[73] WikiLeaks, *Germany's View of Georgia*, 2008.

[74] WikiLeaks, *Merkel in Sochi*, 2008.

called upon Russia to withdraw its forces.[75] In Tbilisi, Merkel pledged support for Georgia and its NATO perspective, stating that "Georgia will become a member of NATO if it wants to—and it does want to".[76]

This in turn led international media to speculate that Merkel may have reversed her Bucharest stance.[77] In a visit to Vilnius and Tallinn on 26 August, Merkel even went one step further, confirming there was no ambiguity about the question that a NATO Membership Action Plan would follow as a next step.[78] In fact, Merkel did not specify a timeframe and therefore only reaffirmed the unspecified pledge in the Bucharest Communiqué that Georgia would eventually become a NATO member at some point in the future. However, her explicit rhetoric on Georgia's NATO membership perspective can be interpreted twofold: Firstly, a strong message of NATO solidarity with Georgia towards Russia, suggesting that the August war has not diminished Georgia's chances for a NATO membership perspective. Secondly, a message towards Eastern European member states to address the criticism that Germany's and France's "no" to a NATO membership plan for Georgia has emboldened Russia.[79] Germany thereby attempted to bring closer together divergent member states' positions in the EU, especially between France and Germany on the one and Eastern Europeans on the other hand.

According to a US cable, Merkel also stated in a conversation with the Lithuanian president that she was "forward leaning" about a NATO membership plan, but "her coalition situation limited her ability to act" in the face of SPD Foreign Minister Steinmeier's opposition.[80] Merkel was

[75] 'Merkel, Medvedev Clash Over Russia's War in Sochi Talks', *Deutsche Welle*, 15 August 2008.

[76] 'Merkel Signals Support for Georgia's NATO Membership Bid', *Deutsche Welle*, 17 August 2008.

[77] Cf. ibid.; 'Merkel Backs Georgia's Bid to Join NATO in Visit to Tbilisi', *The Jerusalem Post*, 17 August 2008.

[78] Angela Merkel, *Rede von Bundeskanzlerin Dr. Angela Merkel im Rahmen ihres Besuchs in Estland, 26. August* (Tallinn, 2008) https://www.bundesregierung.de/breg-de/service/bulletin/rede-von-bundeskanzlerin-dr-angela-merkel-796320   [accessed   16 December 2018].

[79] Cf. Ralf Beste, Markus Feldenkirchen and Alexander Szandar, 'Germany and the Caucasus Conflict: Merkel's Most Serious Foreign Policy Crisis', *Spiegel Online*, 18 August 2008.

[80] WikiLeaks, *Russia, Georgia, Germany, Lithuania and the EU: Threats and Responses, 27 August* (2008) https://wikileaks.org/plusd/cables/08VILNIUS708_a.html [accessed 16 December 2018].

thereby using the domestic context as a justification of Germany's Bucharest position against the backdrop of continuous criticism from Eastern Europeans. She also referred to Italy and Spain as "weak links" in the EU, according to the US cable, thereby positioning Germany and France as consensual middle ground[81]—which was perceived differently by Eastern Europeans. In her remarks in Tallinn, Merkel again underlined the importance of European unity despite varying historical experiences, mentalities and dependencies.[82] The Chancellery Chief of Staff de Maizière commented according to a US cable on the "difficulties in bringing the EU together on Georgia" and noted "the division of labour taking place between the French and the Germans with the French working on the larger EU members and the Germans on the smaller ones (…) to calm fears and forge consensus".[83] This illustrates that the divergences within the EU were perceived as significant enough for Berlin to assume a mediation role and to engage directly with Vilnius and Tallinn.

The divergent positions within the EU were further exacerbated by Russia's recognition of the independence declarations of South Ossetia and Abkhazia on 26 August,[84] which Merkel strongly condemned and suggested that suspending EU-Russia negotiations on a new Partnership and Cooperation Agreement should be up for discussion at an extraordinary summit of the European Council in September.[85] Despite Merkel's efforts in Sochi to put pressure on the Russian leadership, Russian troops had still not withdrawn from Georgia proper by the end of August. At the extraordinary European Council on 1 September, European leaders thus agreed to suspend negotiations conditioned on Russia's troop withdrawal to positions held prior to 7 August.

The summit also endorsed a visit by President Sarkozy on 8 September to Moscow to implement a more detailed, revised version of the Six-Point

---

[81] WikiLeaks, *Russia, Georgia,* 2008.

[82] Merkel, *Rede in Estland,* 2008.

[83] WikiLeaks, *Lugar Codel: Germans Emphasize Need for Cooperation with Russians on Energy, 10 September* (2008) https://wikileaks.org/plusd/cables/08BERLIN1244_a.html [accessed 16 December 2018].

[84] Compare for the recognition of independence the following Russian presidential decrees: Medvedev, *Presidential Decree South Ossetia,* 2008, Medvedev, *Presidential Decree Abkhazia,* 2008.

[85] Merkel, *Rede in Estland,* 2008.

Peace Plan.[86] Although Moscow reportedly would have preferred Sarkozy to come alone,[87] he was accompanied by then European Commission President José Manuel Barroso and High Representative Solana—the first time EU representatives were involved in crisis mediation efforts. While this added visibility to EU representatives and institutions, the leadership role was still France's: After four hours of talks, Sarkozy announced on 8 September a breakthrough in discussions, with an implementation agreement that Russia would withdraw its forces and checkpoints from Georgia proper, followed by international talks and the deployment of EU observers.[88]

Conflict Phase III: Return to Business-as-Usual

After the conclusion of the implementation agreement on 8 September, European efforts in crisis mediation concentrated on the deployment of an EU observer mission to Georgia. While the idea of EU peacekeepers had already been floated by Estonia before the outbreak of the war in August and was supported by Polish Foreign Minister Radosław Sikorski,[89] it gained real traction when Germany supported the proposal for an unarmed civilian mission tasked to monitor the implementation of the 8 September agreement.[90] On 15 September, the General Affairs and External Relations Council officially approved the EU Monitoring Mission (EUMM) in a CFSP Joint Action.[91] The mission was to deploy approximately 200 monitors on 1 October, to which Germany contributed about one-fifth, including the head of the EUMM, Hansjörg Haber. According to a

[86] Council of the European Union, *12594/2/08: Extraordinary European Council, Presidency Conclusions, 1 September* (Brussels, 2008) http://www.consilium.europa.eu/ueDocs/cms_Data/docs/pressData/en/ec/102545.pdf [accessed 17 March 2019].

[87] Asmus, *Little War*, 2010, p. 212.

[88] Dmitry Medvedev and Nicolas Sarkozy, *Press Conference Following Talks with President of France Nicolas Sarkozy, 8 September* (2008) http://en.kremlin.ru/events/president/transcripts/1330 [accessed 16 December 2018].

[89] WikiLeaks, *GOP Rallies*, 2008.

[90] WikiLeaks, *Germany/Georgia: Status of EU Observer Mission and Other Initiatives, 12 September* (2008) https://wikileaks.org/plusd/cables/08BERLIN1261_a.html [accessed 16 December 2018].

[91] Council of the European Union, *Council Joint Action 2008/736/CFSP on the European Union Monitoring Mission in Georgia, EUMM Georgia, 15 September* (Brussels, 2008) https://publications.europa.eu/en/publication-detail/-/publication/0babfe13-406a-4fa3-b3a9-3b7aa0fe5236/language-en [accessed 17 March 2019].

German diplomat, having a German head of the EUMM represented a major priority for Germany[92] and left a German footprint on at least one part of crisis mediation efforts. In turn and as a concession to France, French Diplomat Pierre Morel was appointed EU special representative for the crisis in Georgia next to the already existing special representative for the South Caucasus and Swedish diplomat, Peter Semneby.[93]

Russia only withdrew its forces from Georgia proper ten days after the mission's deployment on 10 October rather than upon its arrival, as foreseen by the EU, and refused to grant the EUMM access to Abkhazia and South Ossetia.[94] To this very day, the EU mission has only been able to monitor the administrative border line from the Georgian side. Nevertheless, the mission was regarded a success of European foreign policy.[95] In addition, the EU became part of the Geneva talks, the international conflict resolution mechanism envisioned in the agreement. Talks were launched in Geneva on 15 October and co-chaired by the OSCE, the EU and the UN. Participants included representatives of Georgia, Russia, Abkhazia and South Ossetia, as well as the US.

With the withdrawal of Russian forces from Georgia proper, one important condition of the implementation agreement had been fulfilled. Against this backdrop, the question of when and how to normalise relations with Russia was soon raised among Europeans. For Germany and France, this represented an opportunity for at least a partial resumption of EU-Russia cooperation. Already back in Moscow in September, President Sarkozy underlined there was "still a strategic partnership between Russia and Europe"[96] and reacted positively to a scheduling of the next EU-Russia Summit in Nice. According to a US cable, Merkel assumed that the resumption of the Partnership and Cooperation Agreement negotiations "hinges on the fulfilment of point five [Russian withdrawal out of Georgia proper] and not the fulfilment of all six points".[97] Despite disagreements within the EU, Germany pioneered on the bilateral level a resumption of political cooperation with Russia and held—although in a smaller format

[92] Interview with German diplomat in Brussels, 30.05.2016.

[93] Popescu, *EU Foreign Policy*, 2011, pp. 66–94.

[94] Richard Lewington, 'Keeping the Peace in the South Caucasus: The EU Monitoring Mission in Georgia', *Asian Affairs*, 44.1 (2013), 51–69.

[95] Cf. Maria R. Freire and Lícinia Simão, 'The EU's Security Actorness: The Case of EUMM in Georgia', *European Security*, 22.4 (2013), 464–77.

[96] Medvedev and Sarkozy, *Press Conference*, 2008.

[97] WikiLeaks, *Germany/Georgia*, 2008.

and with fewer ministers than usual—bilateral governmental consultations in St Petersburg on 2 October.

The US initially opposed a quick return to business-as-usual relations. The US ambassador to NATO warned that "our current approach on preventing any policy level discussions with Russia at NATO will become unsustainable once the EU holds its Nice Summit".[98] A similar sceptical position towards the resumption of cooperation was shared by Eastern Europeans. The US embassy in Vilnius reported that the Lithuanian Ministry of Foreign Affairs was "very concerned that the EU is going to cave on normalizing relations with Russia in the coming weeks", given pressure from France and Germany to "forgive Russia" and resume Partnership and Cooperation Agreement negotiations.[99] The US embassy in Berlin noted Germany was "concerned about freezing cooperation at a reduced level for an unlimited period of time".[100]

Without having reached an agreement among member states, the French Foreign Minister Bernard Kouchner announced on 28 October in St Petersburg that negotiations on the EU-Russia Partnership and Cooperation Agreement would resume at the EU-Russia Summit on 14 November in Nice.[101] During the summit, the European Commission announced the resumption after a meeting of EU foreign ministers, a decision which could not be blocked by Eastern Europeans as it was in the formal responsibility of the European Commission.[102] EU High Representative Solana was quoted arguing that to "have a relationship with Russia which has a framework is better for the international [community] and the European Union (…) That doesn't mean that we are going to have business as usual".[103] This illustrates Germany's and France's willingness to prevent that the Russian-Georgian War fundamentally affected the future

[98] WikiLeaks, *RFG: NATO-Russia: Maintaining Consensus on "No Business-As-Usual"*, 29 October (2008) https://wikileaks.org/plusd/cables/08USNATO402_a.html [accessed 16 December 2018].

[99] WikiLeaks, *Lithuania, The EU, and Russia: Possible Veto on Business-as-Usual*, 23 October (2008) https://wikileaks.org/plusd/cables/08VILNIUS903_a.html [accessed 16 December 2018].

[100] WikiLeaks, *Germany/Georgia*, 2008.

[101] Vladimir Socor, *EU's French Presidency Rushes Partnership Talks with Moscow*, Eurasia Daily Monitor, The Jamestown Foundation 209 (2008) https://jamestown.org/program/eus-french-presidency-rushes-partnership-talks-with-moscow/ [accessed 14 April 2019].

[102] 'EU Foreign Ministers Consider Restarting Talks with Russia', *alfa.lt*, 11 November 2008.

[103] Ibid.

of EU-Russia relations, despite Merkel's pledge in Tallinn that there would be no more of the same.[104]

Germany continued to advocate for more, not less cooperation with Russia. In a speech in December, Chancellor Merkel argued that the resumption of Partnership and Cooperation Agreement negotiations was sending a positive signal towards Russia ahead of the 60th anniversary of NATO—an act of "political wisdom".[105] Foreign Minister Steinmeier went one step further and called for a re-convention of the suspended NATO-Russia Council in a speech in December and even in a public letter to newly elected President Obama.[106] A general review of EU-Russia relations, published in November 2008, followed Germany's position and called for the EU and Russia to "be able to discuss areas of disagreement in an open and constructive manner (…) We should strive to improve our capacity to manage differences while advancing our common goals".[107] According to a German expert, this reflected "an almost complete consensus on the need to have dialogue with Russia despite—or maybe precisely because of—the crisis caused by the war in Georgia".[108] Within a few months after the end of the war, the EU-Russia relationship returned to business-as-usual after Germany and France advocated for a quick return to normalcy.

[104] Merkel, *Rede in Estland*, 2008.

[105] Angela Merkel, *Regierungserklärung von Bundeskanzlerin Merkel zum Europäischen Rat in Brüssel am 11./12. Dezember 2008 vor dem Deutschen Bundestag, 4. Dezember* (Berlin, 2008) https://www.bundesregierung.de/breg-de/service/bulletin/regierungserklaerung-von-bundeskanzlerin-dr-angela-merkel-zum-europaeischen-rat-in-bruessel-am-11-12-dezember-2008-796120 [accessed 16 December 2018].

[106] Cf. Frank-Walter Steinmeier, *Rede von Außenminister Steinmeier zur gesamteuropäischen Sicherheitspartnerschaft, 11. Dezember* (2008) https://www.auswaertiges-amt.de/de/newsroom/081210-schwarzkopf/219814 [accessed 16 December 2018]; Frank-Walter Steinmeier, "'Im engen Schulterschluss'", *Der Spiegel*, 12 January 2009.

[107] European Union, *MEMO/08/678, Review of EU-Russia Relations, 5 November* (Brussels, 2008) https://www.europa.eu/rapid/press-release_MEMO-08-678_en.pdf [accessed 14 April 2019].

[108] Cf. Sabine Fischer, 'European Policy towards the South Caucasus after the Georgia Crisis', in *Perspectives on the Georgian-Russian War*, ed. by Di Puppo and others, pp. 2–6.

SANCTIONS POLICY

The Russian-Georgian War in August resulted in different levels of sanctions policy within different fora: Within the EU, the debate about sanctions gained traction in particular towards the end of August 2008, fuelled by Russia's unwillingness to withdraw its forces to the pre-conflict line. The role of the US and the debate within NATO, taking place within the same period of time, will be taken into account as contextual factor to the EU policy formation process. In addition, sanctions within the G8—suspending Russia's membership—were proposed by the US, but not implemented.[109]

After the acceptance of the independence declarations of Abkhazia and South Ossetia, the atmosphere had shifted internationally towards increased pressure on Russia: The other G8 leaders condemned the recognition of independence as unacceptable in a joint statement.[110] Within the EU, the question of sanctions—of political and/or economic nature—was for the first time explicitly addressed by French Foreign Minister Kouchner at a press conference in Paris on 28 August, commenting that "sanctions are being considered, and many other means" ahead of the extraordinary European Council meeting on 1 September.[111] Interpreted as a move to "increase diplomatic pressure" on Moscow to withdraw troops from Georgia proper,[112] the French Foreign Minister, however, clarified that France itself was not in favour of sanctions, though the topic should be discussed at the extraordinary Council Meeting on 1 September.[113]

Ahead of the Council Meeting, positions among member states were divided. As reported in a US cable, Lithuania for instance considered a wide menu of sanctions options: "freezing ministerial participation in the G8; suspending the PCA negotiations (…) dropping any mention of 'strategic partnership'; targeting individuals involved in the invasion, including

[109] Henrik B. L. Larsen, 'The Russo-Georgian War and Beyond: Towards a European Great Power Concert', *European Security*, 21.1 (2012), 102–21.

[110] Federal Foreign Office, *Statement on Georgia of Foreign Ministers of Canada, France, Germany, Italy, Japan, the United States and the United Kingdom, 27 August* (2008) https://www.auswaertiges-amt.de/en/newsroom/news/080827-g7-erklaerung-georgien/234804 [accessed 16 December 2018].

[111] 'EU Considers Sanctions on Russia', *BBC News*, 28 August 2008.

[112] Mark Tran, Julian Borger and Ian Traynor, 'EU Threatens Sanctions against Russia', *The Guardian*, 28 August 2008.

[113] 'Crisis in the Caucasus: EU Considers Sanctions as Russia Looks for Friends', *Spiegel Online*, 28 August 2008.

freezing bank accounts and a visa ban list; freezing Russia's CoE membership (…); changing the visa regime for access to the Schengen area; or even more radical ideas like military exercises in Georgia".[114] The Polish government appeared double-headed at the EU summit in a dispute over competencies, with President Kaczyński strongly in favour of sanctions, and Prime Minister Tusk favouring a more moderate stance.[115] In a telephone conversation before the summit, Chancellor Merkel attempted to moderate President Kaczyński, appealing to European unity and support for the efforts of President Sarkozy.[116] Eventually at the summit, Poland advocated for further-reaching political measures, such as postponing the EU-Russia summit in November, but refrained from demanding sanctions of economic nature.[117] The position of Poland was supported by the UK: Prime Minister David Cameron argued in a BBC Radio 4 interview for the necessity to introduce a "carrot and stick" approach towards Russia, calling it a "bully".[118] Nevertheless, this strongly worded statement resulted in the end only in the demand to exclude Russia from the next G8 meeting and to suspend Partnership and Cooperation Agreement negotiations. In other words, the bark was worse than the bite: Both Poland and the UK supported political sanctions yet refrained from economic sanctions.[119]

Berlin argued that the outcome of the Council meeting with regard to sanctions depended decisively on whether Russia was ready to fulfil the Six-Point Peace Plan.[120] Foreign Minister Steinmeier opposed sanctions towards Russia in principle, but left room for manoeuvre for an EU consensus: He suggested in an interview before the summit that Eastern European member states will attempt to cancel the negotiations on a new Partnership and Cooperation Agreement permanently, yet that the likely outcome will be an only temporary suspension of negotiations.[121] He was

[114] WikiLeaks, *Russia, Georgia*, 2008.

[115] Philippa Runner, 'Two-Headed Poland in EU Summit Farce', *EUobserver*, 14 October 2008.

[116] 'Europa sucht eine gemeinsame Haltung zum Georgien-Konflikt', *Deutschlandradio*, 31 August 2008.

[117] Cf. Paweł and Świeboda, *Conflict in Georgia*, 2008.

[118] 'David Cameron Calls for Tough EU Sanctions on Russia', *The Guardian*, 1 September 2008.

[119] Bruno Waterfield, 'Georgia Conflict: Gordon Brown Heads for Clash over Russia at EU Summit', *The Telegraph*, 1 September 2008.

[120] 'EU will keine Sanktionen gegen Russland', *Der Tagesspiegel*, 29 August 2008.

[121] Translations by the author. 'EU-Politik gegenüber Russland: Steinmeier will keine Sanktionen', *Frankfurter Allgemeine Zeitung*, 28 August 2008, cf. also: Frank-Walter

thereby setting the boundaries for how far Germany was prepared to go and implicitly suggested that any further reaching measures would be opposed by Germany: A tougher approach was unreasonable, since "it is in our own interest to return to a normal relationship".[122] Thereby, Steinmeier defined what from a German perspective would be an acceptable—or unacceptable—outcome of EU sanctions policy towards Russia.

In an attempt to contain divisions at the EU summit, France did not circulate pre-prepared position papers among member states ahead of the summit but relied upon talks and discussions on-site.[123] Eventually, leaders agreed at the extraordinary summit to a temporary suspension of Partnership and Cooperation Agreement negotiations, as suggested by Steinmeier, conditioned on Russia's withdrawal to positions held prior to 7 August in Georgia proper.[124] Further discussions on sanctions were postponed to the informal Gymnich meeting of European foreign ministers on 5–6 September.[125] In reality, the debate on sanctions died down after the summit and did not come up again in the following months. According to a scholar, the "discrepancy is remarkable: at the end of the day, Russia has faced only symbolic sanctions after the recognition of Georgia's breakaway republics (…) The 'fervently' hawkish states were unable to mobilize any sanction that would be able to punish Russia as none of the European great powers, even Britain, were willing to run the risk for sacrificing the long-term relations with Russia over Georgia".[126]

The EU policy formation process on sanctions policy was overall marked by ambiguity, especially in the interpretation of the results for domestic audiences. The final outcome was interpreted by British media as a position pushed through by Merkel and Sarkozy, granting a second chance to Russia,[127] although the difference to the UK's position was in fact marginal. Despite strong rhetoric, the sanctions under discussion were

---

Steinmeier and Ansgar Graw, '"Ein sehr fragiler Waffenstillstand"', *Welt am Sonntag*, 17 August 2008.

[122] Ibid.

[123] Severin Weiland, 'Debatte über Russland-Sanktionen: Frankreich bremst Scharfmacher in der EU', *Spiegel Online*, 29 August 2008.

[124] Council of the European Union, *12594/2/08: Extraordinary European Council, Presidency Conclusions, 1 September* (Brussels, 2008) http://www.consilium.europa.eu/ueDocs/cms_Data/docs/pressData/en/ec/102545.pdf [accessed 17 March 2019].

[125] 'EU-Länder fragen nach Ursachen des Kaukasus-Konflikts', *Reuters*, 5 September 2008.

[126] Larsen, 'Russo-Georgian War', 2012, pp. 116–17.

[127] 'Brown Fails to Get EU Sanctions against Russia', *The Daily Telegraph*, 2 September 2008.

primarily of political, not economic nature, revolving around the question whether to temporarily or permanently suspend the talks on a new Partnership and Cooperation Agreement. International media reports were unclear in their interpretation whether or not the temporary suspension of Partnership and Cooperation Agreement negotiations could be termed as sanctions at all in the context of the Russian-Georgian War,[128] illustrating the low threshold of the EU sanctions debate.

How did the US and the debate within NATO on sanctions influence the EU's policy formation? The positions of NATO members were divided from the beginning, with the US adopting an especially critical stance towards Germany. For a preparatory meeting of the NATO Political Committee on 11 August, Germany was described in a US embassy cable as "traditionally cautious" and opposing any consequences for cooperation with Russia in the NATO-Russia Council (NRC), supported by France: "Germany argued that the NRC consultation mechanism was needed now more than ever", "that there is no mechanism for NATO Allies to suspend the NRC ['this is a very useful body']" and "called for more consultations with Russia". In contrast, the "Balts and Poland would like to suspend the NATO-Russia Council".[129]

A cable from the US ambassador to NATO on 12 August was more explicit, assuming that Germany would use its veto option to block consensus on limiting cooperation with Russia in the NRC: "The German-led side (to include Belgium, Spain and Norway) is unlikely to support anything more than a slap on the Russian wrist in the upcoming NATO Ministerial. French views are more nuanced aimed at promoting a French (and EU) leadership role. (…) Germany will surely turn the tables to block consensus on future decisions that require an affirmative NATO action to stop cooperation with Russia".[130] The US favoured a suspension of the NRC, yet feared that "consensus limits us to a calibrated response" and identified Germany "as the standard bearer for the pro-Russia camp". Two days prior to the NATO Ministerial on 19 August, Steinmeier argued in an interview that dialogue within the NATO-Russia Council was "indis-

---

[128] Interview with German diplomat in Brussels, 08.03.2016.

[129] WikiLeaks, *NATO Allies Lack Cohesion during First Meeting on Georgia Crisis, 11 August* (2008) https://wikileaks.org/plusd/cables/08USNATO281_a.html [accessed 16 December 2018].

[130] WikiLeaks, *Debate on Russian Role in OAE Foreshadows Dividing Lines on NATO-Russia Policy, 13 August* (2008) https://wikileaks.org/plusd/cables/08USNATO287_a.html [accessed 16 December 2018].

pensable", and that open channels for communication were needed with both Tbilisi and Moscow,[131] again setting the boundaries for what would be acceptable to Germany as a joint NATO response. He also considered NATO's role in the region as limited,[132] a view shared by the German NATO ambassador who was quoted in a US cable that NATO should have a "supportive role", which was interpreted by the US as "a call for NATO to have the minimum possible role".[133]

Following these internal NATO divisions, in particular between Germany and the US, the final communiqué of the Ministerial only contained a warning that NATO was considering "the implications of Russia's actions for the NATO-Russia relationship (…) We have determined that we cannot continue with business as usual"[134] without outlining concrete measures. Yet, at the following press conference NATO Secretary General Jaap de Hoop Scheffer announced a de facto non-convention of the NATO-Russia Council (NRC): "In other words, if you would ask me what about the NATO-Russia Council, we're not abandoning the NATO-Russia Council, but as long as Russian forces are basically occupying a large part of Georgia, I cannot see a NATO-Russia Council convene at whatever level".[135] The subsequent press release clarified that meetings would be "placed on hold".[136] Although this temporary non-convention represented a step forward from Germany's initial reluctance to any measures, it was still below the measures initially envisaged by the US. International media therefore criticised the decision as weak and Russia's representative to NATO ridiculed the response as "the mountain

[131] Steinmeier and Graw, 'Fragiler Waffenstillstand', 2008.

[132] 'NATO demonstriert Solidarität mit Georgien', *Deutsche Welle*, 19 August 2008.

[133] WikiLeaks, *North Atlantic Council*, 2008.

[134] North Atlantic Treaty Organization (NATO), *Statement: Meeting of the North Atlantic Council at the level of Foreign Ministers held at NATO Headquarters, 19 August* (Brussels, 2008) https://www.nato.int/cps/en/natolive/official_texts_29950.htm [accessed 16 December 2018].

[135] Jaap de Hoop Scheffer, *Press Conference by NATO Secretary General after the Meeting of the North Atlantic Council at the Level of Foreign Ministers, 19 August* (Brussels, 2008) https://www.nato.int/docu/speech/2008/s080819c.html [accessed 16 December 2018].

[136] North Atlantic Treaty Organization (NATO), *NATO's Foreign Ministers Reiterate Their Support to Georgia, 19 August* (2008) https://www.nato.int/docu/update/2008/08-august/e0819a.html [accessed 16 December 2018].

gave birth to a mouse".[137] Meetings of the NATO-Russia Council were eventually resumed in June 2009.

In sum, as contextual factor, the role of the US and the sanctions debate within NATO influenced the EU policy formation process to the extent that according to a British scholar, the "feeble" response of NATO coincidentally strengthened the role of the EU as the main venue for crisis response.[138] Furthermore, the NATO sanctions debate strengthened France's and Germany's positions as seemingly pragmatist middle ground in contrast to supposedly hawkish US and Eastern European positions. This reinforced France's and Germany's role as the most influential actors in the crisis, shaping the narrative of the conflict and making the international response to the Russian-Georgian War an EU-led response as opposed to a US-led one. As noted in a US cable, "Germany (…) did not offer specific German ideas" during the sanctions debate,[139] but instead tried to set the boundaries for what would be a preferable EU and NATO response from Berlin's perspective.

Explaining the Final Outcome

How can the final outcome of EU policy towards the Russian-Georgian War be explained? To what extent did German positions and preferences overlap with the final outcome, compared with alternative influences? Which instruments of power have been applied by Germany, and do they signify a more assertive German approach in shaping EU policy towards Russia? (Table 2.1)

German Influence

Before the outbreak of the war, Germany was influential in crisis mediation through its engagement as the coordinator of the UN Secretary-General's Group of Friends on Georgia in Abkhazia. In this role, Germany

---

[137] Vladimir Socor, *Summit Tests EU's Capacity to Oppose Russia's Reexpansion*, Eurasia Daily Monitor, The Jamestown Foundation 165 (2008) https://jamestown.org/program/summit-tests-eus-capacity-to-oppose-russias-reexpansion/#! [accessed 16 December 2018].

[138] James Sherr, 'The Implications of the Russia-Georgia War for European Security', in *The Guns of August 2008*, ed. by Cornell and Starr, pp. 196–224 (p. 210).

[139] WikiLeaks, *TFGG01: Chancellor Merkel Says Russia Has Not Fulfilled Six-Point Plan*, 25 *August* (2008) https://wikileaks.org/plusd/cables/08BERLIN1181_a.html [accessed 16 December 2018].

Table 2.1 Instruments of power in the Russian-Georgian War

EU policy formation process	Key MS/EU actors	Contextual variables	Instruments of power applied by Germany			Empirical evidence
			Compulsory power	Institutional power	Productive power	
Crisis mediation						
Conflict Phase I: Six-Point Peace Plan	FR, GER, PL, Baltic states	– Bucharest decision – Russian incursion into Georgia	–	–	– Arguing and suasion – Paradigm framing	– Support for France's crisis mediation efforts – Initiation of Tagliavini Report
Conflict Phase II: Second agreement	FR, GER, EU Actors	– Russian acceptance of independence declarations – Lack of withdrawal of troops	–	– Mediation and brokering	– Arguing and suasion	– Visits and speeches in capitals of Eastern member states
Conflict Phase III: Return to cooperation	GER, FR	– Partial withdrawal of Russian troops from Georgia proper	–	–	– Arguing and suasion	– Establishment of EUMM under German leadership – Renewed cooperation with Russia
Sanctions policy						
Temporary suspension of new PCA negotiations	FR, GER, PL, UK	– Suspension NATO-Russia Council – US push for sanctions	– Veto option	–	–	– Opposition to further-reaching sanctions within NATO and EU

Source: Author's table

was able to use the UN institutional mandate to engage in agenda setting on a peace plan. After the outbreak of war in South Ossetia, the institutional legitimacy and agenda-setting role passed on to France, which held the EU Council Presidency. In the ensuing crisis mediation efforts, Germany exerted at first a minor influence, primarily focusing on supporting France's mediation role. Due to the similarity of positions between Germany and France, the leading role of France ensured an outcome that was to a large extent in line with Germany's own positions and preferences. Germany also engaged in arguing and suasion as well as paradigm framing to establish a commonly accepted narrative of the conflict and its causes by initiating the Tagliavini Report.

Only during the second conflict phase has Germany stepped up with visits to Sochi, Tbilisi and Eastern European capitals, using institutional and productive power instruments of arguing and suasion as well as mediation and brokering with Eastern Europeans in light of strong internal divisions. German diplomats remained convinced, however, that the conflict required more, not less cooperation with Russia in the future to prevent a repetition of such a crisis. This narrative facilitated a return to business as usual against the positions of Poland and the Baltic states, who regarded the conflict as evidence for a new imperialist Russian foreign policy in the region and called for reduced cooperation.

In sanctions policy, Germany was influential by opposing further-reaching sanctions in EU and NATO with an implicit veto option and setting the boundaries for a—from a German perspective—"pragmatic" policy response, perceived as "Russia-friendly" by critics.[140] This demonstrates Germany's willingness to use instruments of compulsory power and to adopt a more assertive approach in sanctions policy to achieve an outcome in overlap with German positions and preferences.

Alternative Influences I (EU Actors and Member States)

The most important alternative influence to Germany was France. France was able to activate the "power of the chair" of the Council Presidency[141] and engaged as the main meditator on behalf of the EU, using the presidency's "practical efficiency" to act as a peace broker.[142] French

---

[140] Larsen, 'Russo-Georgian War', 2012, p. 111.
[141] Tallberg, 'Power of the Chair', 2010.
[142] Larsen, 'Russo-Georgian War', 2012, p. 106.

engagement was however less about French interest in Georgia or Eastern Europe in general,[143] but more about demonstrating French leadership in a crisis situation, using the EU as an influence-multiplier. Through instruments of institutional power, France was setting the agenda for the EU in crisis mediation.

Next to France, Poland and the Baltic states played a significant role, advancing an alternative position and narrative towards the conflict. They advocated for a stronger reaction to Russia's intervention in Georgia—although falling short of demanding economic sanctions. Poland and the Baltic states opposed the narrative of more, not less cooperation promoted by Germany and argued that Russia's revisionist foreign policy in the region was the main cause of the conflict, requiring reduced cooperation. However, the position of Eastern European members was perceived as an outlier position in the EU and was sidelined by the French and German wish to preserve EU-Russia relations and to maintain a common European stance, even if it represented only a lowest common denominator position. This placed Eastern European countries under pressure to refrain from using a veto option, especially against powerful big member states[144]—an example for the "distant shadow of the future"[145] in EU negotiations, where using a veto option today could have a negative effect on negotiations in the future.

EU institutions and representatives played a limited role and were only visible during the second conflict phase. Since France used the EU as a platform for its leadership role, EU institutions and representatives were also sidelined, and the EU response remained primarily member-state driven. French conflict mediation was nevertheless regarded a success story for the EU, resulting in the establishment of the EUMM.[146] According to Whitman and Wolff, this demonstrates that the EU's performance as a global security provider under the Lisbon Treaty "leaves much to chance—or, to put it more positively, to the activism, skill, determination and vision of particular individuals, as exemplified in the role played by Sarkozy".[147] In addition, the EU co-chaired together with the United Nations High Commissioner for Refugees (UNHCR) the Geneva talks.[148]

---

[143] Mouritzen and Wivel, *Explaining Foreign Policy*, 2012, p. 140.
[144] Interview with Estonian diplomat in Berlin, 17.08.2016.
[145] Dür, Mateo and Thomas, 'Negotiation Theory', 2010, p. 615.
[146] Whitman and Wolff, 'EU as Conflict Manager', 2010.
[147] Whitman and Wolff, 'EU as Conflict Manager', 2010, p. 101.
[148] Sinkkonen, 'Security Dilemma', 2011, p. 268.

Prior to August 2008, the EU had only enjoyed an observer status within the Joint Control Commission for South Ossetia.

Alternative Influences II (Russia, US, External Shocks)

As contextual factors, Russia, the US and NATO as well as external shocks played a role in the EU's policy formation. Firstly, the outbreak of hostilities in South Ossetia was an external shock that came to the surprise of the international community. Russia's intervention deep into Georgian territory as well as the acceptance of the independence declarations of Abkhazia and South Ossetia contributed to a more outspoken criticism from the European side and to the negotiation of a second implementation agreement. Russia's withdrawal from Georgia proper, that is, the fulfilment of five out of six points in the Peace Plan, then contributed to a quick resumption of EU-Russia cooperation. Russia's (un-) willingness to cooperate in conflict mediation was hence an important factor in the EU policy formation.

The US was a strong supporter of Georgia's NATO membership since Bucharest and pushed for a more outspoken reaction to the Russian-Georgian War, yet accepted European leadership in crisis mediation. Seeking a tougher response at least within NATO, the US advocated for the non-convention of NATO-Russia Council meetings, which was the only measure accepted by other members, in particular by Germany. Despite the support for Polish and Baltic positions within the EU, the US left conflict resolution efforts to France, but was particularly critical of the "dovish" German position. Given the quick return to EU-Russia cooperation, the NATO-Russia Council also resumed meetings in June 2009. As contextual factor, the US thus emboldened divergent views within the EU, but also strengthened the positions of Germany and France by accepting France's leadership role.

CONCLUSION: GERMANY AS A JUNIOR PARTNER

The Russian-Georgian War was the first crisis involving Russia in the immediate neighbourhood of the EU after the accession of Eastern European member states in 2004. In this new landscape, the EU policy formation process during the Russian-Georgian War was marked by divergent views among member states about the policy outcome, resulting under French leadership in a lowest common denominator policy.[149] In a US cable, then German Chancellery Chief of Staff de Maizière was quoted: "When we use strong words, we are not together; when we use weak words, we are together".[150] Germany's influence on the final outlook of EU policy during the conflict was minor compared to France's role as EU Council Presidency. According to Tallberg,[151] the EU Council Presidency is a crucial transmission belt for power within the EU and among member states. In contrast to Germany, France benefitted from the legitimising effects of this mandate to shape the EU's response to the Russian-Georgian War.[152] Germany supported French efforts and attempted to mediate among EU Eastern member states. However, Germany was also setting the boundaries and opposing further reaching sanctions within the EU and NATO. This demonstrates that Germany was willing and able to adopt a more assertive approach to influence the final outcome of EU policy in line with its preferences.

Henrik Larsen goes one step further and argues the fact that "Germany *de facto* [blocked] US insistence on further NATO enlargements and [played] the role as EU-Russia bridge builder witnesses a new self-consciousness characterizing a great power".[153] Despite Germany's limited role in crisis mediation efforts, this demonstrates that influence can be exercised without a formal leadership role: While France was clearly in a leadership position through its EU Council Presidency, Germany was able to exert influence on the outcome of EU policy by setting the boundaries. This shows that an EU policy response can be formed without German leadership, but not without Germany's consent, which can be described as a "negative" leadership role, according to Derek Beach: member states

[149] Cf. Daniel C. Thomas, *The Negotiation of EU Foreign Policy: Normative Institutionalism and Alternative Approaches*, UCD Dublin European Institute Working Paper 08-4 (Dublin, 2008) https://www.ucd.ie/t4cms/WP_08-4_Daniel_Thomas.pdf [accessed 18 March 2018]. Daniel defines the 'lowest common denominator' as the result of competitive bargaining among divergent member states preferences which—due to veto options—can lead to a deadlock or a lowest common denominator policy.

[150] WikiLeaks, *Lugar Codel*, 2008.

[151] Cf. Tallberg, 'Power of the Chair', 2010, Tallberg, *Leadership and Negotiation*, 2006; Beach and Mazzucelli (eds), *Leadership in the Big Bangs*, 2007.

[152] Interview with German diplomat in Berlin, 09.08.2016.

[153] Larsen, 'Russo-Georgian War', 2012, pp. 111–12.

building coalitions in an effort to "fight for the status quo"—such as maintaining the status quo in EU-Russia relations.[154]

Despite statements to the contrary, the Russian-Georgian War did not represent a caesura in relations with Russia, with Germany playing a crucial role in maintaining the status quo of a cooperation paradigm in the EU's relations with Russia for years to come. Germany contributed to a conflict narrative that framed the Georgian-Russian War as an unexpected escalation of a post-Soviet conflict—a Georgian miscalculation met by a disproportionate Russian response—rather than an indication of a new revisionist Russian foreign policy, as argued by Poland and the Baltic states. In consequence, Germany stressed the necessity to return to more, not less cooperation with Russia, which led to a quick resumption of business-as-usual relations with Russia. The positions of member states were thus closely intertwined with their underlying narrative of the conflict: For Eastern European member states, the August war was the precedent that emboldened Russia to take further steps in the neighbourhood, especially in Ukraine in 2014. For German representatives, the August war was proof that NATO's Bucharest decision not to move closer to Georgia represented in hindsight "historical wisdom".[155]

---

[154] Derek Beach and Colette Mazzucelli, 'Introduction', in *Leadership in the Big Bangs of European Integration*, ed. by Beach and Mazzucelli, pp. 1–21 (p. 6).

[155] Former Chancellery Chief of Staff Ronald Pofalla at a public discussion in Berlin, 10.05.2016.

CHAPTER 3

The EU-Russia Partnership for Modernisation 2010: Germany as Agenda-Setter

The EU-Russia Partnership for Modernisation was proposed at the Stockholm Summit in November 2009, only a year after the Russian-Georgian War. It was eventually concluded at the EU-Russia Summit in Rostov-on-Don on 1 June 2010. As outlined in the EU-Russia Joint Statement on the Partnership for Modernisation, the idea behind the initiative was to breathe new life into the EU-Russia relationship,[1] as negotiations over a new Partnership and Cooperation Agreement were stalled for years. It was based on the assumption that Russia was both willing and able to modernise its economy and society, and that the EU was able to benefit from and contribute to this process.[2] In the words of then European Commission President Manuel Barroso, the initiative represented "the most efficient way to improve EU-Russia relations" by "combining a strategic view of our future with a pragmatic and transformational agenda".[3] This initiative did not appear out of thin air: a precedent was set by the bilateral German-Russian Modernisation Partnership, introduced by

---

[1] Council of the European Union, *Joint Statement*, 2010.

[2] Council of the European Union, *Joint Statement on the Partnership for Modernisation EU-Russia Summit 31 May–1 June* (Rostov-on-Don, 2010) http://europa.eu/rapid/press-release_PRES-10-154_en.htm [accessed 17 March 2019].

[3] Jose M. Barroso, 'Bringing EU-Russian Relations to a New Level', in *Selected Articles on Modernisation and Innovation in Russia*, ed. by Hanna Mäkinen, Electronic Publications of Pan-European Institute (Turku, 2012).

© The Author(s), under exclusive license to Springer Nature Switzerland AG 2021
L. Fix, *Germany's Role in European Russia Policy*, New Perspectives in German Political Studies,
https://doi.org/10.1007/978-3-030-68226-2_3

German Foreign Minister Steinmeier in May 2008 in a speech in Yekaterinburg.[4] Subsequent to the German-Russian Modernisation Partnership, twenty-two other EU member states concluded their own Modernisation Partnership agreements with Russia.[5]

The fact that the German idea of a Modernisation Partnership was adopted both at the EU and at the member state level suggests a strong German agenda-setting role. From the outset, the German-Russian Modernisation Partnership aspired to a "European dimension", as outlined by Foreign Minister Steinmeier in his speech in Yekaterinburg.[6] According to a German diplomat, this ambition to extend the German-Russian Modernisation Partnership to the European level resulted from the perception that there was "not enough Russia policy" taking place at the European level.[7] Instead, there was a strong focus on the Eastern neighbours in light of the Eastern Partnership initiation in May 2008.[8]

Although Eastern Europeans were sceptical of the new modernisation paradigm,[9] Poland was among the first to conclude a Modernisation Partnership with Russia. How can the success of the modernisation partnerships be explained, and does it provide evidence for a major German

---

[4] Frank-Walter Steinmeier, *"Time for a German-Russian Modernization Partnership"*: *Frank-Walter Steinmeier, Federal Minister for Foreign Affairs, at the Department of International Relations of the Urals State University in Yekaterinburg*, 13 May (2008) https://www.auswaertiges-amt.de/en/newsroom/news/080513-bm-russland/232842 [accessed 13 April 2019]. Cf. Also Petersburger Dialog, *Gemeinsame Erklärung des Deutschen und des Russischen Lenkungsausschusses des Petersburger Dialoges zur Gestaltung der Modernisierungspartnerschaft*, 2. *Oktober* (St. Petersburg, 2008) http://www.petersburger-dialog.de/files/Unterzeichnung%20Modernisierungspartnerschaft%20dt.pdf [accessed 8 March 2018].

[5] Cf. Tatiana Romanova and Elena Pavlova, 'What Modernisation?: The Case of Russian Partnerships for Modernisation with the European Union and Its Member States', *Journal of Contemporary European Studies*, 22.4 (2014), 499–517.

[6] Steinmeier, *Yekaterinburg*, 2008.

[7] Interview with German diplomat in Warsaw, 20.05.2016.

[8] Interview with German diplomat in Warsaw, 20.05.2016.

[9] Cf. Stefan Meister, *Reframing Germany's Russia Policy—An Opportunity for the EU*, Policy Brief, European Council on Foreign Relations (2014), p. 7 https://www.ecfr.eu/page/-/ECFR100_GERMANY_RUSSIA_BRIEF_AW.pdf [accessed 14 April 2019]; Hans-Joachim Spanger, 'Modernisierungspartnerschaft zwischen EU und Russland', *Strategie und Sicherheit*, 2012.1 (2012), 395–407 https://www.degruyter.com/view/j/sus.2012.2012.issue-1/sus.2012.2012.1.395/sus.2012.2012.1.395.xml (p. 398).

influence on the EU's policy formation? The policy formation within the EU will be analysed focusing on the policy initiation on the EU level as well as on the level of member states' Modernisation Partnerships with Russia.

German Positions and Preferences

Berlin's idea for a new initiative towards Russia took shape in the context of Germany's EU Council Presidency in 2007. In the run-up, German diplomats in the policy planning division started working on a comprehensive, three-pronged concept for the region of Eastern Europe, Russia and Central Asia:[10] For Eastern Europe, the concept of an Eastern Neighbourhood Policy Plus (ENP+) was developed, which later formed the basis of the Eastern Partnership.[11] For Central Asia, the EU-Central Asia Strategy was designed and adopted during Germany's Council Presidency in 2007.[12] For Russia, Foreign Minister Steinmeier introduced the concept of "Annäherung durch Verflechtung" (rapprochement through interlocking),[13] a variation of the traditional German "Ostpolitik" (Eastern Policy) paradigm of "change through rapprochement". The Modernisation Partnership was built on this "Ostpolitik" paradigm,[14] seizing upon the modernisation discourse in Russia that emerged in the wake of the election of Dmitry Medvedev as president in March 2008.

[10] Cf. Kai-Olaf Lang, 'Polen, Deutschland und die EU-Ostpolitik: Spannungsfelder und Kooperationspotentiale', in *Deutschland und Polen: Die europäische und internationale Politik*, ed. by Thomas Jäger and Daria W. Dylla (Wiesbaden: VS Verlag für Sozialwissenschaften, 2008), pp. 123–36 (pp. 132–33).

[11] Liana Fix and Anna-Lena Kirch, *Germany and the Eastern Partnership after the Ukraine Crisis*, Note du Cerfa, French Institute of International Relations (Paris, Brussels, 2016) https://www.ifri.org/sites/default/files/atoms/files/ndc_128_kirch_fix_en.pdf [accessed 9 March 2018].

[12] Cf. Referat Mittel- und Osteuropa der Friedrich-Ebert-Stiftung, *Partnership with Russia in Europe: Economic and Regional Topics for a Strategic Partnership*, Gesprächskreis Partnerschaft mit Russland in Europa (2007) http://library.fes.de/pdf-files/id/04688.pdf [accessed 14 April 2019].

[13] 'Berlin schlägt in der EU-Russlandpolitik eine "Annäherung durch Verflechtung" vor', *Frankfurter Allgemeine Zeitung*, 4 September 2006.

[14] Manfred Huterer, 'Strategie ist möglich: Diplomat Huterer über Deutschlands Ostpolitik', in *Zeit im Spiegel: Das Jahrhundert der Osteuropaforschung*, ed. by Manfred Sapper and Volker Weichsel (= *Osteuropa*, 2–3 (2013)), pp. 269–76 (p. 270).

By December 2007, policy planning staff at the foreign ministry and experts at the German Institute of International and Security Affairs, a German think tank advising the government on foreign policy, had developed an unpublished scenario paper on Russia's future in response to the new modernisation discourse in Russia. This paper outlined three possible scenarios and potential Western responses:[15] It envisaged a "Russian Davos" as a best-case scenario of an "efficient modernisation of the country". This would include "Russia's integration in the global economy and gradual adoption of European standards such as the rule of law", possibly resulting in a "strategic union" with Russia.[16] However, as quoted in *Der Spiegel*, the paper noted that Western Europe should "avoid putting too much pressure on a Russian reform government, for instance by putting Georgia on track for NATO membership".[17] The second scenario was based on "selective partnership", describing the "decline of cooperation into a kind of 'confrontational cherry picking' where the two sides cooperate only if and when they feel they stand to gain from it".[18] The third scenario described the emergence of an "authoritarian and imperialist Russia" and a "cold peace", where "the West would have to counteract 'Russian foreign policy audacity' by strengthening the EU and NATO".[19]

The election of President Medvedev four months later in March 2008 seemed to indicate that the first "Russian Davos" scenario could very well be possible, and consequently, that Medvedev's reform-oriented agenda should be supported. This optimistic overall assessment of Medvedev's presidency presented a window of opportunity from a German policy-making perspective. Germany's early conceptual preparation and scenario analysis meant it had the conceptual groundwork prepared to move forward with a policy initiative.

An important contextual factor was the new modernisation discourse in Russian government and expert circles accompanying the election of then

---

[15] Ralf Beste, Uwe Klußmann and Gabor Steingart, 'The Cold Peace', *Spiegel Online*, 1 September 2008 (p. 3); Interviews with current and former experts from the German Institute for International and Security Affairs (SWP) in Berlin, May–July 2016. A German expert suggested that the paper was leaked on purpose to *Der Spiegel* after the Russian-Georgian War to prepare the ground for future policy making: Adomeit, *Russlands "Modernisierungspartnerschaften"*, 2011, p. 47.

[16] Beste, Klußmann and Steingart, 'Cold Peace', 2008, p. 3.

[17] Ibid.

[18] Ibid.

[19] Ibid.

President Dmitry Medvedev.[20] At the time, Russia was hard-hit by the global economic and financial crisis. According to a British expert, the downturn put "the domestic social contract under increasing strain" and a rapprochement with the West was seen as "a potential bolster for the regime rather than a threat".[21] In a widely discussed article "Russia, Vpered!" (Go, Russia!)[22] from September 2009, President Medvedev laid out the modernisation agenda for Russia during his presidential term. The Institute of Contemporary Development (INSOR), a Russian think tank headed by Igor Yurgens and closely associated with Medvedev, contributed a blueprint for Russia's development in the twenty-first century, with a comprehensive economic reform and modernisation plan.[23] Modernisation, primarily understood as technological modernisation of the economy with only a limited component of societal modernisation or even democratisation, became the new *leitmotif* in Russian politics in the following years.[24]

From a German perspective, Russia's modernisation discourse was perceived as credible and sincere as well as worthy of support.[25] It provided Germany with the chance to position itself as the ideal partner for a modernisation agenda with Russia—given ample historical precedents, dating as far back as Peter the Great[26]—and as the leading proponent of a modernisation policy in the EU. According to a German expert, "the quest for modernisation was seen as a genuine opportunity for cooperation and the

---

[20] Cf. Paul Flenley, 'The Partnership for Modernisation: Contradictions of the Russian Modernisation Agenda', *European Politics and Society*, 16.1 (2014), 11–26.

[21] Andrew Wilson, *The Rostov Summit*, ECFR Commentary (2010) http://www.ecfr.eu/article/commentary_the_rostov_summit [accessed 8 March 2018].

[22] Dmitry Medvedev, *Россия, вперёд! 10 September* (Moscow, 2009) http://www.kremlin.ru/news/5413 [accessed 13 April 2019]; English version: Dmitry Medvedev, *Go Russia! 10 September* (Moscow, 2009) http://en.kremlin.ru/events/president/news/5413 [accessed 13 April 2019].

[23] Alexander Goltz and others, *Russia in the 21st Century: Vision for the Future*, Institute of Contemporary Development (INSOR) (Moscow, 2010) http://www.riocenter.ru/files/INSOR%20Russia%20in%20the%2021st%20century_ENG.pdf [accessed 14 April 2019].

[24] Cf. Vladimir Gel'man (ed.), *Authoritarian Modernization in Russia: Ideas, Institutions, and Policies*, Studies in Contemporary Russia (London, New York, NY: Routledge, 2017).

[25] Interview with German diplomat in Warsaw, 20.05.2016.

[26] Cf. Flenley, 'Partnership of Modernisation', 2014.

transformation of Russia into a more democratic, prosperous and reliable partner".[27]

In May 2008, Foreign Minister Steinmeier presented an outline of the German-Russian Modernisation Partnership in a speech at the University of Yekaterinburg.[28] This speech constitutes an important document to understand the thinking behind Germany's idea of a Modernisation Partnership. The location and audience—a University in Yekaterinburg rather than an official format in Moscow—indicate the initiative sought to reach not only government officials and experts, but the broader Russian society as well. Steinmeier titled his speech "Time for a German-Russian Modernisation Partnership" and started out with a reference to the Second World War and the Cold War, arguing the era of confrontation had become obsolete: "We can only solve our key problems by working together".[29] From his point of view, Russia was an indispensable partner in guaranteeing security and stability in Europe, and this could not be achieved "without—much less against—Russia". Subsequently, Steinmeier explained how the world has changed through a globalised economy and with new emerging power centres. He used this introduction to define what makes a country successful in the "first truly global" century: not sheer landmass or tanks and missiles, but new formulas for success such as "knowledge, innovation and flexibility".[30] The Foreign Minister added: "The future is there for countries and societies that vigorously modernise, are innovative and courageously tackle structural change".[31]

According to Steinmeier, modernisation is hence a precondition for a country's positive standing in the twenty-first century and an open society is best suited to achieve such modernisation. This cannot be "shouldered by the state alone", but requires a lively civil society, entrepreneurial culture, the rule of law and a public debate where competition between divergent opinions is promoted.[32] Steinmeier thus conceived   of   modernisation   as   something   not   purely

---

[27] Sabine Fischer, 'EU-Russia Relations: A Partnership for Modernisation?', in *From Cooperation to Partnership: Moving Beyond the Russia-EU Deadlock*, ed. by Bertelsmann-Stiftung, Europe in Dialogue, 2013, 1 (Gütersloh: Bertelsmann Stiftung, 2013), 26–34 (27f).

[28] Steinmeier, *Yekaterinburg*, 2008.

[29] Ibid.

[30] Ibid.

[31] Ibid.

[32] Ibid.

economic-technocratic. Instead, he advocated for a broader societal and democratic modernisation, linking economic modernisation to the political and societal sphere, thereby positioning himself against a model of "authoritarian modernisation".[33]

On the basis of this modernisation concept, Steinmeier identified new potential avenues for cooperation between Germany and Russia as well as the EU and Russia, demonstrating that his initiative had the ambition to have an impact beyond the bilateral German-Russian level. According to Steinmeier, the Modernisation Partnership should include a "European dimension": Germany and the EU are "natural partners" for Russia's modernisation agenda and should contribute to make this "historically unique process" a success.[34] Steinmeier introduced a discourse of complementarity, high potential and mutual benefit: The EU and Russia were ideally suited to cooperate within an EU-Russia strategic partnership for a potential future free-trade area. Without yet explicitly mentioning the possibility of an EU-Russia initiative, Steinmeier adopted an agenda-setting role on behalf of the EU early on in the policy formation. This implicit assumption that the EU should follow Germany's initiative flowed naturally from Germany's understanding of its leading role in European Russia policy and the perception that there was "not enough Russia policy" taking place at the European level.[35]

In the second half of his speech, Steinmeier identified a common agenda for the German-Russian Modernisation Partnership encompassing climate, energy, health, demography, education and science. The Modernisation Partnership should address these concrete policy fields (including the promotion of Russia's accession to the WTO) and be based on the rule of law. The concrete sector-specific areas of cooperation were later specified in a "Declaration on Key Directions of Economic

---

[33] Cf. Bobo Lo and Lilia Shevtsova, *21st Century Myth: Authoritarian Modernization in Russia and China*, Carnegie Moscow Center (Moscow, 2012) https://carnegieendowment.org/files/BoboLo_Shevtsova_web.pdf [accessed 16 December 2018]; Walter Laqueur, 'Moscow's Modernization Dilemma: Is Russia Charting a New Foreign Policy?', *Foreign Affairs*, 89.6 (2010), 153–60 https://www.jstor.org/stable/20788726 [accessed 16 December 2018]; Sirke Mäkinen, Hanna Smith and Tuomas Forsberg, "With a Little Help from my Friends': Russia's Modernisation and the Visa Regime with the European Union', *Europe-Asia Studies*, 68.1 (2016), 164–81 https://www.tandfonline.com/doi/pdf/10.1080/09668136.2015.1123223.

[34] Steinmeier, *Yekaterinburg*, 2008.

[35] Interview with German diplomat in Warsaw, 20.05.2016.

Cooperation in the Framework of the Partnership for Modernisation" between the Russian Minister of Economic Development and the Federal Ministry of Economy and Technologies in November 2010.[36] The title of the declaration illustrates the discrepancy in expectations: From the Russian side, the focus was to be placed primarily on economic cooperation, whereas at least initially, the German side hoped for a broader societal modernisation in Russia.

At a meeting of the bilateral steering committee of the Petersburg Dialogue in July, a government-supported forum to foster cooperation between Russia and Germany, Steinmeier stated he was "optimistic" that the time was ripe to "deepen" the German-Russian and European-Russian relationship. He also emphasised that it was a "great opportunity" and "vital that we don't squander it", reflecting a sense of urgency in his argumentation.[37] Although the Russian-Georgian War in August 2008 put these plans on hold and suggested that the scenario of "cold peace" could be more likely than a "Russian Davos", the war did not change the principled willingness of German policy makers to move ahead with the bilateral Modernisation Partnership and to invest in more, not less cooperation with Russia.[38] In October 2008, the German and Russian sides signed a joint statement for a German-Russian Modernisation Partnership at the St Petersburg Dialogue.[39]

In sum, according to Steinmeier's first presentation of the Modernisation Partnership in Yekaterinburg, a triad of economic, security and transformational interests were behind the launch of the initiative. Russia not only represented an important partner for energy resources, but also an enticing potential market for German and

---

[36] Bundesministerium für Wirtschaft und Technologie, *Erklärung über Schwerpunkte der deutsch-russischen wirtschaftlichen Zusammenarbeit im Rahmen ihrer Modernisierungspartnerschaft, 26. November* (Berlin, 2010) https://russische-botschaft.ru/wp-content/uploads/2014/11/Erkl%C3%A4rung-%C3%BCber-Moderniserungspartnerschaft.pdf [accessed 14 April 2019].

[37] Frank-Walter Steinmeier, *"Tackling global challenges together—prospects for the German-Russian modernization partnership": Speech by Federal Minister Steinmeier at the meeting of the bilateral steering committee of the Petersburg Dialogue, 3 July* (2008) https://www.auswaertiges-amt.de/en/newsroom/news/080703-petersburger-rede-bm/232866 [accessed 13 April 2019].

[38] Cf. Matthias Dembinski and others (eds), *Nach dem Kaukasus-Krieg: Einbindung statt Eindämmung Russlands,* HSFK-Report, 2008, 6 (Frankfurt a. M.: Hessische Stiftung Friedens- und Konfliktforschung, 2008).

[39] Petersburger Dialog, *Gemeinsame Erklärung,* 2008.

European goods, in exchange for German and European technological know-how and knowledge transfer.[40] From a German perspective, it was assumed that by economically interlocking Russia in a web of cooperation, the cost for Russia of withdrawing from this web and putting the relationship at risk by misbehaviour—such as in Georgia—would be too high.[41] In addition, a successful economic modernisation could lead to the strengthening of the rule of law and good governance, which would in turn facilitate a transformation towards a more open and democratic society.[42] A German diplomat summarised the rationale as follows:[43] "The strategic approach of this concept is to offer Russia support and cooperation for its modernisation. (...) The basic philosophy is to involve the country in a web of cooperation to put our relationship on an even broader fundament, which can withstand differences and difficulties. It of course also serves our foreign economic interests".[44] Although a comparison with Germany's traditional "Ostpolitik" (Eastern policy) approach was rejected as an "abridged" interpretation of the Modernisation Partnership, the similarities are difficult to overlook: The Modernisation Partnership stipulates that economic and societal transformation could be achieved through economic cooperation, resembling indeed the "Ostpolitik" approach of "Wandel durch Annäherung" (change through rapprochement), which was already recycled in Steinmeier's 2006 concept of "Annäherung durch Verflechtung" (rapprochement through interlocking).[45]

Given these similarities, the policy design of the German-Russian Modernisation Partnership was criticised as new wine in old wine skins and representing an "umbrella" for existing projects, which made the initiative difficult to monitor and implement.[46] However, the initiative was more than just an "empty signifier":[47] It fulfilled an important discursive function for the relationship with Russia, as it represented a "powerful

---

[40] Interview with British expert in Brussels, 08.03.2016.
[41] Interview with German diplomat in Berlin, 15.07.2016.
[42] Interview with German diplomat in Brussels, 30.05.2016.
[43] Translations by the author. Huterer, 'Strategie ist möglich', 2013, p. 270.
[44] Ibid.
[45] Stewart, 'Germany', 2013, p. 23.
[46] Ibid.
[47] Romanova and Pavlova, 'What Modernisation?', 2014, p. 511.

tool for [the] discursive 'normalization' of Russia"[48] as just another country facing the modernisation challenges of the twenty-first century. Furthermore, the concept of a Modernisation Partnership proved successful as a projection surface for the transformational ambitions of the German side and the narrow, technical interpretation of modernisation put forward by the Russian side. The broad policy design bridged the contradiction between a value- versus interest-based policy towards Russia.[49] This in turn facilitated the later adoption of the initiative by the EU and member states, as it offered points of reference for a broad range of aspirations and activities.

Policy Initiation (EU Level)

Steinmeier's idea for a "European dimension" of the German-Russian Modernisation Partnership fell on fertile soil in Brussels and with European institutions: The EU-Russia relationship has stalled long before the fallout of the Russian-Georgian War and the subsequent suspension of negotiations on a new Partnership and Cooperation Agreement: With ongoing trade disputes,[50] the bi-annual EU-Russia summits and meetings of the EU-Russia Permanent Partnership Cooperation Council—installed to foster a continuous dialogue between European and Russian representatives—have turned into rituals devoid of meaning and concrete results.[51]

A new initiative in EU-Russia relations seemed therefore urgently needed and long overdue, especially in light of the overall favourable political environment after the US-Russian reset in March 2009.[52] Against this backdrop, the German-Russian bilateral agenda setting provided a welcome opportunity for EU institutions, particularly the Commission, to use the German idea as an example for a new EU-wide initiative. According to a European Commission official, the idea for an EU-Russia Partnership for Modernisation indeed stemmed from the German example, yet it was developed not "at the behest" of Germany, but rather inspired by the

---

[48] Makarychev and Meister, 'Modernisation Debate', 2014, pp. 80–81.

[49] Spanger, 'Modernisierungspartnerschaft', 2012, p. 399.

[50] Cf. Heinz Timmermann, 'EU-Russland: Hintergründe und Perspektiven einer schwierigen Beziehung', *integration* (2008), 159–78.

[51] Cf. Stewart, 'Germany', 2013.

[52] Cf. Angela Stent, 'US–Russia Relations in the Second Obama Administration', *Survival*, 54.6 (2012), 123–38.

"courage and comprehensiveness" of "Steinmeier's people".[53] This demonstrates that the EU was intent on keeping the ownership of the EU-Russia Partnership for Modernisation, and credited Germany only with an inspirational leadership role, despite the obvious similarity of the modernisation initiatives.

At the EU-Russia Stockholm Summit in November 2009, over a year after the outbreak of the Russian-Georgian War, European Commission President Manuel Barroso and President Medvedev "spontaneously"[54] agreed to initiate an EU-Russia Partnership for Modernisation. In February 2010, the Commission delivered a written proposal to Russian authorities for the shape of a future EU-Russia Partnership for Modernisation. According to a German expert, the European Commission's initial proposal was much more value based and political than the final outcome:[55] The first draft from February 2010 prioritised values such as democracy and the rule of law over economic and technological cooperation but was met with scepticism by the Russian side, which in turn charged the Russian Ministry of Economic Development with the elaboration of the final agreement, demonstrating Russia's priority for an economic-technological focus.[56] According to Romanova and Pavlova, the final agreement thus adopted only a "mildly political" approach for the EU-Russia Modernisation Partnership.[57] Compared with the EU's previous approach towards Russia, the Partnership for Modernisation indicated a "shift away from the discourse of democratization (...) that used to underlie the relationship to a more pragmatic economic vision, although a political dimension remains".[58]

The joint EU-Russia statement released at the adoption of the EU-Russia Partnership for Modernisation defined it as a "flexible framework for promoting reform" and identified "priority areas of the Partnership".[59] Here, the more political and transformational issues such as judicial reform, the fight against corruption, people-to-people links and dialogue with civil society were lower priorities compared to the economic

---

[53] Interview with European Commission official in Brussels, 30.05.2016.

[54] Cf. Knut Fleckenstein, 'The EU-Russia Modernisation Partnership—What's in It?', in *Selected Articles on Modernisation and Innovation in Russia*, ed. by Mäkinen, p. 3.

[55] Adomeit, *Russlands "Modernisierungspartnerschaften"*, 2011, p. 47.

[56] Adomeit, *Russlands "Modernisierungspartnerschaften"*, 2011, p. 48.

[57] Romanova and Pavlova, 'What Modernisation?', 2014, p. 511.

[58] David and Romanova, 'Modernisation in EU–Russian Relations', 2015, p. 4.

[59] Council of the European Union, *Joint Statement*, 2010.

elements,[60] and the same prioritisation was also reflected in the working plan for the Partnership for Modernisation, agreed upon in December 2010 to be regularly monitored via progress reports.[61] At the summit, EU Council President Van Rompuy described the rationale behind the initiative: "We want to be Russia's partner in modernisation (…) With you we have a most intensive and dynamic dialogue. With Russia we do not need a 'reset'. We want a 'fast forward'".[62] This ambition was mirrored by the Russian side: the Russian Ambassador to the EU Vladimir Chizov called the Partnership for Modernisation a "gas pedal" for their relationship.[63] Both statements conceive the new initiative as a mutually beneficial window of opportunity for deeper cooperation, reflecting the overall atmosphere of a thaw in relations with Russia.

In an article from 2011, Commission President Barroso underlined that the EU-Russia Partnership for Modernisation pursues a transformational ambition from the EU's perspective:[64] He argued that the relationship was strategic since it is in the long-term interest of both sides; pragmatic since it was based on already existing networks and contacts; and transformative since the strengthening of trade and technological

---

[60] Romanova and Pavlova, 'What Modernisation?', 2014, p. 506.

[61] Hugues Mingarelli and Andrei Slepnev, *Progress Report Agreed by the Coordinators of the EU-Russia Partnership for Modernisation for Information to the EU-Russia Summit of 7 December 2010* (2010) http://eeas.europa.eu/archives/docs/russia/docs/eu_russia_progress_report_2010_en.pdf [accessed 13 April 2019]; Gunnar Wiegand and Andrei Slepnev, *Progress Report Agreed by the Coordinators of the EU-Russia Partnership for Modernisation for Information to the EU-Russia Summit of 9–10 June 2011* (2011) http://www.eeas.europa.eu/archives/delegations/russia/documents/news/20110610_01_en.pdf [accessed 19 April 2019]; Gunnar Wiegand and Alexey Likhachev, *Progress Report Agreed by the Coordinators of the EU-Russia Partnership for Modernisation for Information to the EU-Russia Summit of 21 December 2012* (2012) http://www.eeas.europa.eu/archives/docs/russia/docs/2012_p4m_progress_report_signed_en.pdf [accessed 14 April 2019]; Gunnar Wiegand and Alexey Likhachev, *Progress Report Approved by the Coordinators of the EU-Russia Partnership for Modernization for information to the EU-Russia Summit on 28 January 2014* (2014) https://web.archive.org/web/20140705232631/https://eeas.europa.eu/russia/docs/eu_russia_progress_report_2014_en.pdf [accessed 19 April 2019].

[62] European Council, *EUCO 158/14: Statement by the President of the European Council Herman Van Rompuy and the President of the European Commission in the name of the European Union on the agreed additional restrictive measures against Russia, 29 July* (Brussels, 2014) http://www.consilium.europa.eu/media/22015/144158.pdf [accessed 17 March 2018].

[63] 'Russia-EU Relations Need a Gas Pedal Rather Than Reset Button', *Amber Bridge*, 13 December 2011.

[64] Barroso, *EU-Russian Relations*, 2012.

cooperation through the Partnership for Modernisation would improve the rule of law in Russia and facilitate contact between civil society on both sides. These facets strongly resemble the "Ostpolitik" (Eastern policy) paradigm of Steinmeier's modernisation concept, namely that economic cooperation contributes in the long term to political transformation and that modernisation could spur an interlinking of economic and societal transformation. This demonstrates the similarities in the underlying modernisation paradigm of the EU-Russia Partnership for Modernisation and the German-Russian Modernisation Partnership. The Russian paradigm of modernisation, in contrast, included a much narrower definition as an economic and technological endeavour.[65] For Russia, modernisation was "primarily understood as *innovation* [which] entails that the EU serves as a reform supporter and a technology provider".[66] For the EU, modernisation was "closely connected to *liberalization* (…) necessarily wide-ranging and entails deep reforms to promote a market-based economy, the rule of law and democratization". [67] To some observers, due to these differences in the conception of modernisation on the European and Russian sides, the EU was set up for failure from the start.[68]

Shortly before the adoption of the Partnership for Modernisation, the new German Foreign Minister Westerwelle and his Russian counterpart Lavrov published an article for the German newspaper *FAZ* and explicitly claimed ownership of the idea, stating that the EU-Russia Partnership for Modernisation followed the "German-Russian example" and that the "bilateral experiences" would be "beneficial" for the EU-Russian project.[69] Noticeably, Germany not only claimed ownership of the idea for the EU-Russia Partnership for Modernisation, but also kept track of its implementation: According to a Polish diplomat, Germany was the most vocal attendant in the Committee of Permanent Representatives and frequently

---

[65] Romanova and Pavlova, 'What Modernisation?', 2014, p. 505.

[66] Laure Delcour, *The EU and Russia's Modernisation: One Partnership, Two Views*, International Affairs at LSE Blog (2011) http://blogs.lse.ac.uk/ideas/2011/04/the-eu-and-russia%e2%80%99s-modernisation-one-partnership-two-views/   [accessed   8 March 2018].

[67] Delcour, *EU and Russia's Modernisation*, 2011.

[68] Cf. Katinka Barysch, 'The EU-Russia Partnership for Modernisation', in *The EU-Russia Modernisation Partnership,* The EU-Russia Centre Review (2010), pp. 28–32; Marina Larionova, 'Can the Partnership for Modernisation Help Promote the EU–Russia Strategic Partnership?', *European Politics and Society*, 16.1 (2014), 62–79.

[69] Translations by the author. 'Die deutsch-russische Modernisierungspartnerschaft', *Frankfurter Allgemeine Zeitung*, 30 May 2010.

asked for results of the EU-Russia Partnership for Modernisation.[70] This underlines that Germany's Modernisation Partnership was not only an example and inspiration for the EU, but that Germany actively followed-up on the implementation through institutional access points.

In sum, during the policy initiation at the EU-level, Germany exerted influence by projecting the German idea and concept of a modernisation partnership with Russia on the European level: Through agenda setting and institutional access points with the European Commission, but also by framing a modernisation paradigm based on Russia's ability and willingness to modernise and the opportunity to link economic cooperation with political and societal transformation. This approach allowed Germany to claim ownership for the *idea*, but leaving the ownership for the *implementation* of the EU-Russia Partnership for Modernisation to the Commission. Thus, the EU-Russia Partnership for Modernisation was understood as Commission policy, relieving Germany from responsibility for success or failure of the initiative. While the Commission underlined its institutional ownership—not acting "on the behest"[71] of Germany—Germany's ideational leadership role in the initiation, as well as the similarities in the underlying modernisation paradigm of the initiatives, demonstrates a major German influence.

Policy Initiation (Member State Level)

To what extent have other member states with their own Modernisation Partnerships followed Germany's agenda setting, and which overlap or divergences with the German-Russian Modernisation Partnership and the EU-Russia Partnership for Modernisation can be observed? A comprehensive comparison of Modernisation Partnerships between Russia and EU member states has been conducted by Romanova and Pavlova.[72] According to Tatiana Romanova, member state Modernisation Partnerships represented a significant "thickening" of the EU-Russia Partnership for Modernisation: "For the first time in the history of EU-Russian relations the same agenda was promoted at the EU and national levels".[73] In addition, the

[70] Interview with Polish diplomat in Brussels, 23.03.2016.

[71] Interview with European Commission official in Brussels, 30.05.2016.

[72] Romanova and Pavlova, 'What Modernisation?', 2014.

[73] Tatiana Romanova, 'The Partnership for Modernisation Through the Three Level-of-Analysis Perspectives', *European Politics and Society*, 16.1 (2014), 45–61 (p. 54).

member state Modernisation Partnerships were "carefully promoted at the EU-Russia level"[74] with EU reports tracking the status of negotiations.[75] This demonstrates that these Modernisation Partnerships were understood as part of a broader European policy approach towards Russia.[76]

After the German-Russian Modernisation Partnership in 2008, a further twenty-two Modernisation Partnerships were concluded from 2010 to 2013 between EU member states and Russia.[77] The frontrunners were Denmark, Cyprus and Slovenia, followed by Spain, Italy, Poland, Belgium and France in 2010.[78] Russia played an important role by approaching member states with initial offers of bilateral Modernisation Partnerships and providing the first agreement draft, coordinated by the Russian Ministry of Economic Development, which was responsible for the internal and external processes of modernisation.[79] These agreement drafts provided the basis for negotiations with member states, but were significantly revised in bilateral talks to account for the specific priorities of each individual EU member state. In these draft agreements, member states injected their own interpretation of the modernisation paradigm.[80] Views on the modernisation paradigm ranged from a "narrow" understanding of the concept as mere innovation and technology to a "wide-ranging and systemic reform process dealing also with good governance and the rule of law".[81]

According to Romanova, some member states' modernisation partnerships barely mentioned "political aspects", while others argued "extensively and ardently for the need to promote democracy and human rights in Russia", revealing the "differences in the extent to which various

---

[74] Romanova, 'Partnership for Modernisation', 2014, p. 54.

[75] Ibid.

[76] Ibid.

[77] Romanova and Pavlova, 'What Modernisation?', 2014, p. 501. They mention 24 MPs including Germany, but only because they count Germany twice with the October 2008 declaration and the agreement of Economic Ministers in 2010.

[78] Ibid.

[79] Romanova and Pavlova, 'What Modernisation?', 2014, p. 506.

[80] Cf. Barysch, 'EU-Russia Partnership', 2010.

[81] Delcour, *EU and Russia's Modernisation*, 2011.

member states were prepared to politicize their Ps4M with Russia".[82] Not all member states followed the EU concept of a "mildly political" approach.[83] Instead, according to Romanova and Pavlova, member states' Modernisation Partnerships were an arena for "conceptual battles" about modernisation.[84] The fact that despite these differences in the interpretation of modernisation, the majority of member states nevertheless concluded Modernisation Partnerships can be partially explained by contextual factors: Firstly, the EU and German agenda setting provided an incentive to follow suit and not to miss out on a lucrative economic opportunity.[85] Secondly, the overall state of relations between Russia and EU member states was conducive to new initiatives:[86] At that period of time, EU member states were "closer together on Russia than they [had] been for a long time", not least because of the US-Russian reset, leaving "nearly all the main member states in favour of a 'reset' of relations".[87]

Surprisingly, Poland was among the frontrunners to conclude a bilateral Modernisation Partnership with Russia. Given the country's generally critical stance towards Russia, one would expect greater scepticism towards the modernisation paradigm. According to a Polish diplomat, the Modernisation Partnership was indeed perceived as driven largely by Germany and German economic interests.[88] Similarly, a Polish think tank criticised the Partnership for Modernisation as a "façade, legitimizing in the process the vested interests of some EU member states".[89] However, Poland supported the EU-Russia Partnership for Modernisation and signed one of the least political and most economic-technical agreements. Furthermore, a joint Polish-German letter authored by Foreign Minister Westerwelle and Polish Foreign Minister Radosław Sikorski to High Representative Ashton in November 2011 called for a joint approach and

---

[82] Romanova, 'Partnership for Modernisation', 2014, p. 54. For an overview of positions of member states, cf. Romanova and Pavlova, 'What Modernisation?', 2014, p. 509.

[83] Romanova and Pavlova, 'What Modernisation?', 2014, p. 511.

[84] Romanova and Pavlova, 'What Modernisation?', 2014, p. 500.

[85] Interview with German diplomat in Brussels, 09.03.2016.

[86] Iris Kempe, 'Die EU und Russland', in *Jahrbuch der Europäischen Integration 2011*, ed. by Werner Weidenfeld and Wolfgang Wessels, 1st edn (Baden-Baden: Nomos, 2012), pp. 317–22.

[87] Wilson, *Rostov Summit*, 2010.

[88] Interview with Polish diplomat in Brussels, 23.03.2016.

[89] Ćwiek-Karpowicz and Formuszewicz, *Partnership*, 2010, p. 230.

continuation of the modernisation agenda with Russia.[90] Two interlinked developments provide some context and explanation: A Polish-Russian rapprochement process, which started under new Polish Prime Minister Donald Tusk in 2008, unfolded alongside a German-Polish coordination policy towards Russia and German-Polish-Russian cooperation in a trilateral format.[91] Trilateral meetings between Poland, Germany and Russia on the level of foreign ministers and state secretaries took place from 2009 until 2013.[92] In addition, a regular exchange between Polish and German policy planning staff and think tank experts regarding Russia policy was established in Warsaw and Berlin.[93] According to a German diplomat, as a result of this rapprochement and Germany's mediation, German and Polish positions grew closer and Russia policy became less of a "divisive issue" for Poland.[94] The trilateral cooperation contributed to facilitating a common European understanding on Russia, benefitting the Partnership for Modernisation and Polish-Russian relations overall.

In contrast to Poland, the traditionally Russia-sceptic Lithuania and Sweden concluded much more politicised modernisation agreements that focused on human rights. Estonia even "failed to find a consensus on the definition of modernisation" with Russia[95] and therefore refrained from signing a Modernisation Partnership. On the other hand, France and southern member states concluded overall very "pragmatic" Modernisation Partnerships, which, according to Romanova and Pavlova, "leave the impression that their parties are for pragmatic cooperation and (...) rather

[90] Guido Westerwelle and Radosław Sikorski, '"Europa endet nicht an der Ostgrenze Polens"', *Tagesspiegel*, 5 November 2010.

[91] Cf. for overview on these efforts: Andrzej Turkowski, *The Polish-German Tandem*, Carnegie Endowment for International Peace (Washington, DC, 2011) http://carnegieendowment.org/2011/11/17/polish-german-tandem/7wgo [accessed 14 April 2019]; Jarosław Ćwiek-Karpowicz, *Polish Foreign Policy Toward its Eastern Neighbors: Is a Close Cooperation with Germany Possible?*, DGAPanalyse kompakt 6 (Berlin, 2011) https://dgap.org/en/think-tank/publications/dgapanalyse-compact/polish-foreign-policy-toward-its-eastern-neighbors [accessed 18 December 2018]; Stefan Meister, *German Eastern Policy: Is a Partnership with Poland Possible?*, DGAPanalyse kompakt 7 (2011) https://dgap.org/en/think-tank/publications/dgapanalyse-compact/german-eastern-policy [accessed 18 December 2018].

[92] Federal Foreign Office, *German, Polish and Russian Foreign Ministers Meet in Berlin, 20 March* (Berlin, 2012) https://www.auswaertiges-amt.de/en/newsroom/news/120320-trialog/249316 [accessed 16 December 2018].

[93] Interview with Polish diplomat in Warsaw, 17.05.2016.

[94] Huterer, 'Strategie ist möglich', 2013, p. 271.

[95] Romanova, 'Partnership for Modernisation', 2014, p. 54.

leave to the EU the thankless task of promoting human rights, democracy and the rule of law.[96] According to a French official, France did not object to the Modernisation Partnership or the idea that "Russia could be sweetened" as it saw an opportunity for French companies to invest in Russia and hoped for better legal security for its economic commitments.[97] France's economic-technocratic approach is also visible in its Modernisation Partnership, which focused almost exclusively on economic aspects.[98] This reflected France's overall position towards Russia, marked primarily by pragmatism.[99]

In sum, whereas certain member states, such as Lithuania and Sweden, concluded more politicised bilateral Modernisation Partnership with Russia, the key member states France and Poland concluded primarily economic-technocratic agreements, not too far away from Germany's own approach. Apart from Estonia, which did not conclude a modernisation agreement, most member states subscribed to the modernisation paradigm put forward by Germany and the EU—that Russia was able and willing to modernise—out of concern to miss out on a lucrative economic opportunity.[100] Germany's modernisation initiative was hence setting the agenda not only for the EU's, but also for member states' policy towards Russia. However, the content and the orientation of the Modernisation Partnerships, ranging from more political to more economic approaches, were negotiated individually between member states and Moscow, giving Russia significant leeway in bilateral relationships.

---

[96] Romanova and Pavlova, 'What Modernisation?', 2014, p. 511.

[97] Interview with French official in Paris, 23.11.2016.

[98] Romanova and Pavlova, 'What Modernisation?', 2014, p. 510.

[99] Cf. for overview of France's position towards Russia at that time: Le Noan, *France*, 2013; Marie Mendras, *Russia–France: A Strained Political Relationship*, Russian Analytical Digest 130 (2013) http://www.css.ethz.ch/content/dam/ethz/special-interest/gess/cis/center-for-securities-studies/pdfs/RAD-130-2-8.pdf [accessed 18 December 2018]; Thomas Gomart, 'France's Russia Policy: Balancing Interests and Values', *The Washington Quarterly*, 30.2 (2007), 147–55; Isabelle Facon, 'La relation France-Russie à l'épreuve', *Annuaire français de relation internationales*, 16 (2015), 117–31 https://www.frstrategie.org/web/documents/publications/autres/2015/2015-facon-afri-relation-france-russie.pdf; Sénat, *Les relations avec la Russie. Comment sortir de l'impasse?: Part A: L'histoire récente et ses occasions manquées* (Paris, 2015) http://www.senat.fr/rap/r15-021/r15-0214.html [accessed 18 December 2018].

[100] Romanova and Pavlova, 'What Modernisation?', 2014, p. 509.

Explaining the Final Outcome

How can the final outcome of EU policy towards Russia—the conclusion of the EU-Russia Partnership for Modernisation and twenty-two member states modernisation agreements—be explained? To what extent did German positions and preferences overlap with the final outcome, compared to alternative influences? Which instruments of power have been applied by Germany, and do they signify a greater German assertiveness? (Table 3.1)

German Influence

Germany's idea to support Russia's domestic modernisation agenda and to rejuvenate the EU-Russia relationship with a "European dimension" of the Modernisation Partnership had a major influence on the final outcome of EU policy. Germany was the frontrunner and agenda setter both for the EU as well as for member states and made use of the window of opportunity in Russia's domestic modernisation agenda early in Medvedev's presidency. Germany used institutional access points with the Commission, followed up on the implementation of the initiative and advanced a narrative of Russia being able and willing to modernise not only economically, but also with regard to a broader societal and democratic transformation—an effort worthy of support by the EU and to the mutual benefit of all sides. The German modernisation paradigm reflected traditional assumptions of German "Ostpolitik", but left in its broad conception enough room for the European Commission and member states to situate their own concepts of modernisation as either a comprehensive political and societal transformation (liberalisation) or as an economic-technocratic reform agenda (innovation)[101] in their modernisation agreements with Russia.

The EU-Russia Partnership for Modernisation reflected a "mildly political" approach similar to the German-Russian Modernisation Partnership, although the EU aimed initially for a stronger human rights focus, which was rejected by Russia. Other member states diverged in their outlook, with the key member states in Russia policy—France and Poland—adopting an even more "pragmatic" and economic-oriented approach than Germany did in their individual agreements with Russia. The fact that

---

[101] Delcour, *EU and Russia's Modernisation*, 2011.

Table 3.1 Instruments of power in the EU-Russia partnership for modernisation

EU policy formation process	Key MS/ EU actors	Contextual variables	Instruments of power applied by Germany			Empirical evidence
			Compulsory power	Institutional power	Productive power	
EU policy initiation						
EU-Russia P4M	GER, EU Actors	– Russian domestic modernisation agenda – US-Russian reset	–	– Agenda setting – Institutional access points	– Paradigm framing	– Steinmeier speech about modernisation – Exchange with Commission – German agreement as example
MS policy initiation						
Member states' agreements with Russia	GER, FR, PL	– Russia offering draft agreements – Polish-Russian rapprochement	–	– Agenda setting	– Paradigm framing	– "Ostpolitik"-inspired modernisation paradigm – Trilateral Dialogue with Poland on Russia

Source: Author's table

twenty-two agreements between EU member states and Russia were concluded until 2013 demonstrates an unprecedented "thickening"[102] of EU policy on the member state level, inspired by Germany's ideational leadership and early bilateral agenda-setting role. The German-Russian Modernisation Partnership from 2008 gained thus a significant follower-ship among member states by instruments of agenda setting, institutional access points and paradigm framing, without the need for more assertive instruments.

Alternative Influences I (EU Actors and Member States)

The modernisation policy was not contested by most other member states and represented "consensus stuff"[103] among EU institutions and member states. Despite criticism for instance from Estonia, no member state fundamentally opposed the EU-Russia Partnership for Modernisation. To the contrary, even Poland adopted an economic-technocratic approach in its modernisation agreement, which can be explained by the positive environment of a Polish-Russian rapprochement taking place at the time, supported by Germany in the form of intensified exchanges with Poland in bi- and trilateral formats.

EU institutions and representatives, in particular the European Commission, played an important role and developed and implemented the EU-Russia Partnership for Modernisation on an institutional level. Acknowledging Germany's role as idea provider and agenda setter, the European Commission assumed ownership of the implementation of the EU-Russia Partnership for Modernisation and monitored at the bilateral level the conclusion of member states' agreements.

Alternative Influences II (Russia, US, External Shocks)

As an alternative influence, domestic developments within Russia—in particular the emergence of President Medvedev's reform-oriented government with an explicit modernisation agenda—contributed as contextual factor to the EU policy formation process and provided the window of opportunity that was needed for a new institutional initiative. The Russian

---

[102] Romanova, 'Partnership for Modernisation', 2014, p. 54.
[103] Interview with British expert in Brussels, 08.03.2016.

side engaged beyond the EU-Russia Partnership for Modernisation in advancing modernisation agreements with member states, providing the first drafts by the Ministry of Economic Development which were adapted by member states according to their own priorities. Moscow's proactive approach to negotiations with member states thereby contributed significantly to the widespread adoption of modernisation agreements. Finally, the US-Russian reset from the beginning of 2009 provided another contextual factor and contributed to a favourable international environment, adding further legitimacy for an outreach initiative towards Russia.[104] Against this backdrop, the external shock of the Georgian-Russian War—which took place less than a year before the first proposal of an EU-Russia Partnership for Modernisation—did not play a major role. From Germany's view, the conflict rather reinforced the necessity to invest in relations with Russia.

Conclusion: Germany as Agenda-Setter

With its idea of a Modernisation Partnership, Germany was setting the agenda for institutional EU-Russia relations and bilateral member states' relations with Russia. This resulted from the perception that "not enough Russia policy" was taking place at the European level due to a strong focus on the Eastern neighbourhood[105] at that time. The window of opportunity of Medvedev's presidency and a US-Russian reset allowed Germany to step in early with its conceptual ideas and to lay the ground for an "Ostpolitik"-inspired modernisation paradigm. The assumption that Germany's modernisation policy needs a "European dimension" flowed naturally from Germany's understanding of its leading role in European Russia policy. While Germany claimed ownership for the idea, it left the implementation of the EU-Russia Partnership for Modernisation to the Commission which prevented a perception of a too dominant German role.[106] Germany thus relied on an ideational leadership role to advance

---

[104] Cf. European Council, The President, *PCE 110/10: Remarks by Herman Van Rompuy, President of the European Council, at the EU-Russia Summit, 1 June* (Rostov-on-Don, 2010) https://www.consilium.europa.eu/media/27756/114736.pdf   [accessed   9   March 2018] (p. 2).

[105] Interview with German diplomat in Warsaw, 20.05.2016.

[106] Interview with British expert in Brussels, 08.03.2016.

the initiative through agenda setting and paradigm framing, with the German-Russian Modernisation Partnership as example for others to follow.

Germany's influence in the case of the EU-Russia Partnership for Modernisation was lauded as an example of "constructive bilateralism" in European policy making.[107] A German diplomat described the Partnership for Modernisation as a successful case of "Europeanisation".[108] Russia's interest in a modernisation policy with the EU and its willingness to negotiate and advance a range of modernisation agreements with member states played a significant role for the widespread adoption of the Modernisation Partnership in the EU. However, Russia's primary focus remained an economic agenda, in contrast to the ambitious transformational hopes of Germany and the EU.

In the end, the modernisation policy did not succeed in their overall aim, despite the initial optimism:[109] At the time when the EU-Russia agreement was concluded, Medvedev's presidency had entered its second year and serious doubts about the credibility of his modernisation agenda were raised.[110] The European Commission seemed almost too late joining the modernisation policy by 2010 as the "gap between the EU's concept of modernisation and the Russian official discourse" has widened even further.[111] Furthermore, the Modernisation Partnership adopted and modified traditional "Ostpolitik" (Eastern Policy) assumptions of "change

[107] Forsberg and Haukkala, *European Union and Russia*, 2016, 91.

[108] Huterer, 'Strategie ist möglich', 2013, p. 270.

[109] Cf. Justyna Gotkowska, *The German-Russian Modernisation Partnership—Failing to Meet Great Expectations*, OSW Analyses (Warsaw, 2010) https://www.osw.waw.pl/en/publikacje/analyses/2010-07-21/german-russian-modernisation-partnership-failing-to-meet-great [accessed 9 March 2018]; Hannes Adomeit, 'Russlands "Modernisierungspartnerschaften": Ursprünge, Inhalte und Erfolgsaussichten', in Russland modernisiert sich—oder doch nicht?, ed. by Hannes Adomeit, Sozialwissenschaftliche Schriftenreihe, 36/37 (Vienna: Internationales Institut für Liberale Politik Wien, 2011), pp. 25–72.

[110] Cf. Susan Stewart, *Die deutsch-russische Modernisierungspartnerschaft: Skepsis angebracht*, Kurz gesagt, Stiftung Wissenschaft und Politik (Berlin, 2011) https://www.swp-berlin.org/kurz-gesagt/die-deutsch-russische-modernisierungspartnerschaft-skepsis-angebracht/ [accessed 14 April 2019]; Alena V. Ledeneva, *Can Russia Modernise?: Sistema, Power Networks and Informal Governance* (Cambridge: Cambridge University Press, 2013).

[111] Fischer, 'EU-Russia Relations', 2013, 29.

through rapprochement", which were not necessarily transferable to twenty-first-century German-Russian and EU-Russian relations. In hindsight, according to a German diplomat, the modernisation policy seemed a misunderstanding of Russian interests. At that time, it was perceived as an objective analysis of complementary interests. In 2010, the question which course Russia would take was still open-ended from a German perspective.[112]

This demonstrates a "naiveté" of German policy makers that Germany and Europe could contribute to democratising Russia in the long run.[113] Shortly after the Russian-Georgian War, policy initiatives developed *before* the conflict—such as the modernisation policy—were resumed by Germany without questioning their assumptions, based on the conviction that more, not less outreach with Russia was necessary. The EU-Russia Partnership for Modernisation thus contributed to a "discursive normalization"[114] of Russia shortly after the August war, yet without delivering in return the desired results: A broad economic and societal modernisation of Russia remained an unfulfilled promise. Both Germany and the EU have overestimated their leverage on Russia, and underestimated the pitfalls of a modernisation policy, which followed Russia's narrow economic interests and benefitted the ruling elite and their hold on power rather than Russian society. The partnership morphed into "trade without change" and instead of modernisation, neopatrimonialism became the defining feature of the relationship.[115] Eventually, all hopes were dashed after the Duma election protests in 2011 and Vladimir Putin's return to the Presidency. For the EU's Russia policy, the Modernisation Partnerships were "the final attempt at creating a semblance of cooperative and even expanding partnership"[116] before the relationship with Russia turned sour.

---

[112] Interview with German diplomat in Berlin, 09.08.2016.

[113] Meister, 'Entfremdete Partner', 2012, p. 481.

[114] Makarychev and Meister, 'Modernisation Debate', 2014, pp. 80–81.

[115] Fabian Burkhardt, 'Neopatrimonialisierung statt Modernisierung: Deutsche Russlandpolitik plus russischer otkat', *Osteuropa*, 63.8 (2013), 95–106.

[116] Forsberg and Haukkala, *European Union and Russia*, 2016, p. 33.

CHAPTER 4

The Meseberg Initiative 2010: Germany as a Deal-Maker

The Meseberg initiative represents a German attempt under the direction of the Federal Chancellery to capitalise on the overall détente with Russia with an initiative in the area of security policy. Existing mechanisms and fora, such as the NATO-Russia Council, have proven ineffective during the Russian-Georgian War.[1] It proposed—in exchange for Russian cooperation in the solution of the Transnistrian conflict—the establishment of an EU-Russia Political and Security Committee between EU High Representative Ashton and Russian Foreign Minister Lavrov.[2] The initiative was designed as a response to President Medvedev's call for a new European Security Treaty in November 2009,[3] which was perceived by Germany as having not received an adequate response from Europeans.[4]

---

[1] Cf. Erich Reiter (ed.), *Problemlage und Lösungsansätze im Transnistrienkonflikt*, Schriftenreihe zur internationalen Politik, 5 (Vienna, Cologne, Weimar: Böhlau, 2012).

[2] Here and in the following, the Romanian spelling is used, as in the Meseberg agreement itself.

[3] Dmitry Medvedev, *The Draft of the European Security Treaty, 29 November* (2009) http://en.kremlin.ru/events/president/news/6152 [accessed 12 March 2019].

[4] Interview with German official in Berlin, 01.08.2016. Cf. also Manfred Huterer, *The Russia Factor in Transatlantic Relations and New Opportunities for U.S.-EU-Russia Cooperation*, Working Paper, The Brookings Institution 4 (Washington, DC, 2010) https://www.brookings.edu/wp-content/uploads/2016/06/06_us_eu_russia_huterer.pdf [accessed 14 April 2019].

© The Author(s), under exclusive license to Springer Nature Switzerland AG 2021
L. Fix, *Germany's Role in European Russia Policy*, New Perspectives in German Political Studies,
https://doi.org/10.1007/978-3-030-68226-2_4

The Meseberg initiative is an interesting test case to trace German influence on European policy towards Russia, as it seems to indicate a more assertive German approach: The launch of the initiative on a bilateral German-Russian level, without prior formal endorsement by the EU, suggests that Germany was likely self-confident about its ability to gain acceptance for the initiative as well as its room for manoeuvre within the EU to assume a leading role in European security policy.

Germany and Russia concluded a bilateral agreement without involvement of the EU on the main outline of the initiative in Meseberg in June 2010, at the same time as the EU-Russia Partnership for Modernisation was concluded.[5] The agreement linked two distinctive policy areas: conflict resolution in Transnistria with a new mechanism for EU-Russia security cooperation. The conflict in Transnistria was considered a "test case": If cooperation with Russia proves successful in this area, it would demonstrate that Russia can be in the future a constructive actor in European security instead of an unconstructive actor as in the Russian-Georgian War.[6] This would open the way for the resolution of protracted conflicts in the region and more cooperative interaction on other security issues.

Germany's approach in the Meseberg initiative stands out for three reasons: Firstly, the initiative was designed in the area of security policy, in which Germany is usually considered to be a rather reluctant actor,[7] and it

---

[5] Angela Merkel and Dmitry Medvedev, *Memorandum (Meeting of Chancellor Angela Merkel and President Medvedev, 4–5 June 2010)* (Meseberg, 2010) https://archiv.bundesregierung.de/resource/blob/656928/389532/da09e7a21880fb55dfd2d868996295ce/2010-06-05-meseberg-memorandum-data.pdf [accessed 27 September 2017];

For German version, see: Angela Merkel and Dmitry Medvedev, *Memorandum (Treffen zwischen Bundeskanzlerin Angela Merkel und Präsident Dmitri Medwedew, 4. und 5. Juni)* (Meseberg, 2010) https://archiv.bundesregierung.de/resource/blob/656928/452948/9e765ba1c0f63f45787cd6eb06a28968/2010-06-07-meseberg-memorandum-deutsch-data.pdf [accessed 12 March 2019];

For Russian version, see: Angela Merkel and Dmitry Medvedev, *Меморандум по итогам встречи Президента России Д.Медведева и Федерального канцлера Германии А.Меркель, 4–5 июня* (Meseberg, 2010) http://www.kremlin.ru/supplement/575 [accessed 13 April 2019].

[6] Manfred Grund, Hans M. Sieg and Kristin Wesemann, 'Transnistria and the Future Security Architecture in Europe: KAS International Reports (2011)' pp. 60–90 (p. 60).

[7] Cf. Miskimmon, *Germany and the Common Foreign and Security Policy of the EU*, 2007; Harnisch and Wolf, *Germany's Changing*, 2009.

excluded traditional European security actors, such as the US and NATO.[8] Secondly, the transactional approach of the Meseberg initiative, linking two separate policy issues, was considered a rather atypical and "geopolitical"[9] style of policy making, especially for Germany: According to a German diplomat, linking two separate issues resembled a "Realpolitik" policy making, which is more common for US than German foreign policy.[10]

Lastly, according to the former head of the OSCE mission in Moldova, such initiatives are "usually staffed out vertically and horizontally, producing detailed proposals and position papers coordinated among appropriate entities and agencies".[11] In this case, however, Germany concluded the Meseberg memorandum without prior formal endorsement by the EU and official discussion with member states, which resulted in criticism from those the negotiations bypassed. Especially Eastern Europeans perceived the Meseberg initiative as Germany making arrangements with Russia on behalf of the EU in a "secretive way",[12] and EU representatives were thus reluctant to take ownership of the initiative. According to a European Commission official, the initiative was considered by some in Brussels the biggest mistake of German policy in the Eastern neighbourhood.[13]

The policy formation in the EU will be traced focusing on the policy initiation on the bilateral German-Russian level and on the EU level. Furthermore, since the EU policy formation process continued with conflict mediation efforts in Transnistria, the phase of policy implementation will also be taken into account.

---

[8] Vladimir Socor, *Meseberg Process: Germany Testing EU-Russia Security Cooperation Potential*, Eurasia Daily Monitor, The Jamestown Foundation 191 (2010) https://jamestown.org/program/meseberg-process-germany-testing-eu-russia-security-cooperation-potential/ [accessed 27 September 2017].

[9] Interview with former Moldovan official and expert, 06.12.2016.

[10] Interview with German diplomat in Warsaw, 20.05.2016.

[11] Philip Remler, *Negotiation Gone Bad: Russia, Germany, and Crossed Communications*, Carnegie Europe (2013) http://carnegieeurope.eu/2013/08/21/negotiation-gone-bad-russia-germany-and-crossed-communications-pub-52712 [accessed 27 September 2017].

[12] Interview with Moldovan expert in Berlin, 26.05.2016.

[13] Interview with European Commission official in Brussels, 30.05.2016.

German Positions and Preferences

The starting point for Germany's thinking about the Meseberg initiative dates back to the Russian-Georgian War in 2008.[14] Although French President Sarkozy's efforts to broker a ceasefire were successful, there has been no further progress in conflict resolution, and Abkhazia and South Ossetia have since turned into protracted conflicts in the neighbourhood between Russia and the EU. This raised the question how to manage an unstable crisis situation in the European landscape in the future. Six months after the August War, on the occasion of the Munich Security Conference in February 2009, French President Sarkozy and Chancellor Merkel outlined their perspective on stability and security in Europe in a common article.[15] The article, addressing NATO's 60th anniversary in April and Germany's and France's co-hosting role, constitutes an in-depth analysis of the challenges European security was facing and also offers an insight in German-French thinking about relations with Russia: Although the Russian-Georgian War was criticised as a caesura and the first war on European soil in the twenty-first century,[16] the article's focus is on the necessity to re-establish partnership and return to an improved status quo ante with Russia. The article outlines concrete measures and gives some first indications of Germany's thinking about a new initiative in security policy towards Russia.

Responding to Medvedev's Proposals

Medvedev presented his idea on a new European Security Treaty[17] in a speech in Berlin on 5 June 2008.[18] Primarily, his proposals included put-

---

[14] Meister, *New Start*, 2011, p. 12.

[15] Translations by the author. Angela Merkel and Nicolas Sarkozy, *"Wir Europäer müssen mit einer Stimme sprechen"*: *Süddeutsche Zeitung*, 4. Februar (2009) http://www.sueddeutsche.de/politik/sicherheitskonferenz-merkel-und-sarkozy-wir-europaeer-muessen-mit-einer-stimme-sprechen-1.473581 [accessed 28 September 2017].

[16] Merkel and Sarkozy, *Wir Europäer*, 2009.

[17] Medvedev, *Draft Treaty*, 2009; Cf. also Bobo Lo, *Medvedev and the New European Security Architecture*, Policy Brief, Centre for European Reform (2009) https://www.cer.eu/sites/default/files/publications/attachments/pdf/2011/pbrief_medvedev_july09-741.pdf [accessed 12 March 2019]; Layton, 'Reframing European Security', 2013; Marcel de Haas, 'Medvedev's Alternative European Security Architecture', *Security and Human Rights*, 21.1 (2010), 45–48.

[18] Medvedev, *Speech at Meeting*, 2008.

ting into law OSCE security principles, such as indivisible and equal security, and general clauses for crisis management. Although the proposals were criticised as undermining transatlantic security, Berlin considered it useful to find an adequate response to bolster Medvedev's position at home and to demonstrate the willingness for cooperation in security policy with Russia.[19] In June 2009, the Corfu-Process was established within the OSCE to work on Medvedev's proposals, but it was perceived by some observers as sidelining the proposals.[20] In their joint article, Merkel and Sarkozy express willingness to respond to Medvedev's proposal, but emphasise the principle of transatlantic cooperation, the necessity to include the US in discussions, and to remain on the basis of existing treaties and agreements within the context of the EU, NATO, OSCE and arms control and disarmament regimes. Much less ambitious, but in line with Medvedev's idea for security cooperation between the EU and Russia, Merkel and Sarkozy call for an intensification of existing cooperation mechanisms between the EU/NATO and Russia, for instance within the NATO-Russia Council and in form of a better EU-Russia dialogue on security policy.[21]

The article offers concrete examples of how Russian can be better included in European security and mentions in the context of the outstanding ratification of the Adapted Treaty on Conventional Armed Forces in Europe for the first time the Transnistria conflict as a potential area of cooperation: "With good will, through a fast resolution of the Transnistria problem an improvement of the negotiation atmosphere could be achieved". On this issue, the Western side's ratification of the Adapted Treaty hinged upon the withdrawal of Russian troops from Moldova and Georgia, according to the Istanbul commitments.[22] It is notable that the

[19] Interview with German official, 01.08.2016.

[20] Cf. Organisation for Security and Co-operation in Europe (OSCE), *Restoring Trust: The Corfu Process, 1 December* (2010) http://www.osce.org/mc/87193 [accessed 13 April 2019]; Werner Hoyer, 'A German View on the OSCE Corfu Process: An Opportunity to Strengthen Cooperative Security in Europe', *Security and Human Rights*, 21.2 (2010), 114–18.

[21] Merkel and Sarkozy, *Wir Europäer*, 2009.

[22] Cf. Wolfgang Zellner (ed.), *Die Zukunft konventioneller Rüstungskontrolle in Europa = The Future of Conventional Arms Control in Europe*, Demokratie, Sicherheit, Frieden, 194, 1st edn (Baden-Baden: Nomos, 2009); Wolfgang Richter, *Return to Security Cooperation in Europe: The Stabilizing Role of Conventional Arms Control*, Deep Cuts Working Paper 11 (Hamburg, 2017) http://deepcuts.org/images/PDF/DeepCuts_WP11_Richter.pdf [accessed 14 April 2019].

Transnistria conflict is only mentioned in the context of arms control agreements, whereas the overall topic of conflicts in the Eastern neighbourhood and their role for European security is not further elaborated upon. This demonstrates that the Transnistria conflict was regarded as test case for improving security relations with Russia. Was the focus on Transnistria in the Meseberg initiative a Franco-German brainchild, given that the issue was first mentioned in a common article by Merkel and Sarkozy? According to a French diplomat, the Quai d'Orsay was surprised at the mentioning of the Transnistria conflict in the article as there was little interest in Paris in Transnistria.[23] This passage in the article was thus likely coming from Germany. If the French interest in Transnistria was limited, how then did the topic enter the German political agenda?

Moldova as a Test Case

Moldova and the conflict in Transnistria were met with "benign neglect"[24] by member states (apart from Romania[25]), but attracted a constantly growing interest from EU representatives, especially High Representative Solana, since 2002. EU representatives have been able to carve out a role for the EU in conflict resolution efforts, for instance, as observer to the 5 + 2 talks[26] (together with the US) and through de-politicised, technical policy issues, such as the EU Border Assistance Mission to Moldova and Ukraine.[27] A role for the EU in security policy, for instance through an

[23] Interview with French diplomat in Paris, 25.11.2016.

[24] Anneli U. Gabanyi, 'Der Konflikt in Transnistrien im Kontext der europäischen Sicherheitspolitik', *Strategie und Sicherheit*, 2012.1 (2012), 357–68 https://www.degruyter.com/downloadpdf/j/sus.2012.2012.issue-1/sus.2012.2012.1.357/sus.2012.2012.1.357.pdf (p. 358).

[25] Romania has been a strong supporter of Moldova's European integration and has founded the group of friends of Moldova within the EU in 2010. Cf. Octavian Milevschi, 'Romania: From Brotherly Affection with Moldova to Disillusionment and Pragmatism', in *Moldova: Arena of International Influences*, ed. by Marcin Kosienkowski and William Schreiber (Lanham, MD: Lexington Books, 2012), 159–182.

[26] The format includes representatives of the conflict parties, mediators and observers: Moldova, Transnistria, the OSCE, Russia, Ukraine, the EU and the US.

[27] For an overview of the EU's engagement in conflict resolution efforts in Transnistria, cf.: Popescu, *EU Foreign Policy*, 2011, pp. 38–65; Florian Küchler, *The Role of the European Union in Moldova's Transnistria Conflict*, Soviet and post-Soviet politics and society, 78 (Stuttgart: Ibidem, 2008). For an overview of the conflict's origins and the role of the OSCE, cf.: Institut für Friedensforschung und Sicherheitspolitik an der Universität Hamburg, *Protracted Conflicts in the OSCE Area: Innovative Approaches for Co-Operation in the Conflict*

EU-led peacekeeping mission,[28] was met with continuous resistance by member states. Security issues related to Transnistria remained a prerogative of member states. Since 2009, the Eastern Partnership added visibility to Moldova and the Transnistria conflict on the European agenda.[29]

Germany's interest in Moldova and the conflict in Transnistria had two reasons:[30] Firstly, the conflict in Transnistria is commonly referred to as one of the post-Soviet conflicts easiest to solve because of a lack of contact violence and limited ethnic cleavages.[31] According to the former head of the OSCE mission in Moldova, Transnistria was considered "the 'low-hanging fruit' that might provide a mediator with a quick and easy accomplishment".[32] The German Foreign Office also considered Transnistria the conflict where Moscow had the fewest stakes.[33] Merkel's foreign and security policy advisor Christoph Heusgen was involved in negotiations conducted by EU High Representative Javier Solana on this issue in 2003 and was therefore personally interested in the case.[34] In a US

Zones, OSCE Network of Think Tanks and Academic Institutions (Hamburg, 2016) http://osce-network.net/file-OSCE-Network/documents/Protracted_Conflicts_OSCE_WEB.pdf [accessed 14 April 2019]; Andrew Williams, 'Conflict Resolution after the Cold War: The Case of Moldova', *Review of International Studies*, 25.1 (1999), 71–86 https://www.cambridge.org/core/journals/review-of-international-studies/article/conflict-resolution-after-the-cold-war-the-case-of-moldova/58308F770325D67DFBF05AA2A1FD90BE#fndtn-information; Claus Neukirch, 'From Confidence Building to Conflict Settlement in Moldova?', in *OSCE Yearbook 2011: Yearbook on the Organization for Security and Co-operation in Europe (OSCE)*, ed. by Institute for Peace Research and Security Policy at the University of Hamburg (IFSH), 1st edn (Baden-Baden: Nomos, 2012), pp. 137–50 (p. 144); William H. Hill, 'The OSCE and the Moldova-Transdniestria Conflict: Lessons in Mediation and Conflict Management', *Security and Human Rights*, 24.3–4 (2014), 287–97; Stefan Wolff, *The OSCE in Moldova: from confidence building to conflict settlement?* (2018) https://events.uta.fi/experiencesandopportunities2018/wp-content/uploads/sites/51/2018/11/Wolff_The-OSCE-in-Moldova-From-confidence-building-to-conflict-settlement.pdf [accessed 14 April 2019].

[28] Cf. Popescu, *EU Foreign Policy*, 2011, pp. 66–94.

[29] Gabanyi, 'Konflikt in Transnistrien', 2012, 359f.

[30] Cf. Dareg A. Zabarah, 'Germany: Increased Attention towards Moldova?', in *Moldova*, ed. by Kosienkowski and Schreiber, pp. 87–104.

[31] Cf. Stefan Wolff, 'A Resolvable Frozen Conflict?: Designing a Settlement for Transnistria', *Nationalities Papers*, 39.6 (2011), 863–70.

[32] Remler, *Negotiation Gone Bad*, 2013.

[33] Interview with German diplomat in Berlin, 09.08.2016.

[34] Remler, *Negotiation Gone Bad*, 2013.

cable, Heusgen was quoted stating that "Moscow could accomplish 'in about a month'"[35] to solve the conflict. Secondly, contextual factors in Moldova contributed to the perception of a window of opportunity. From a German perspective, the Alliance for European Integration's success in Moldova's parliamentary elections in July 2009 provided an opportunity to cooperate and work together with a pro-European government on the unresolved issue of Transnistria.[36]

The new Moldovan government circulated an aide memoire that it was willing to engage on conflict resolution efforts, to which EU High Representative Catherine Ashton responded in a statement welcoming these positive signals.[37] At the same time, a joint declaration by the Russian and Ukrainian presidents Medvedev and Yanukovych on Transnistria in May 2009 provided fertile soil for a new dynamic in conflict resolution.[38] These favourable circumstances, and a good working relationship between Moldovan Foreign Minister Leancă and Merkel's foreign policy advisor Heusgen, proved conducive for the genesis of the Meseberg initiative.[39]

Newly elected Moldovan Prime Minister Vladimir Filat's first visit to Germany in May 2009 was taken as an opportunity to discuss German ideas on conflict resolution in Transnistria with their respective Moldovan counterparts. In a two-hour conversation, Chancellor Merkel revealed her intention to make the Transnistria issue a priority and to push Russia for progress.[40] She also inquired about constitutional arrangements with Transnistria, relations with Romania, the presence of Russian troops and

---

[35] Remler, *Negotiation Gone Bad*, 2013 takes this quote from the following Wikileaks source: WikiLeaks, *National Security Advisor Heusgen on Afghanistan, Middle East, Iran, Detainees, Russia, Nukes and Balkans, 12 November* (2012) https://wikileaks.org/plusd/cables/09BERLIN1433_a.html [accessed 13 March 2019].

[36] Interview with German official in Berlin, 15.07.2016.

[37] Catherine Ashton, *A 77/10: Statement by High Representative Catherine Ashton on Moldova/Transnistria, 17 May* (Brussels, 2010) https://euronest.blogspot.de/2010/05/statement-by-high-representative_18.html [accessed 28 September 2017].

[38] Cf. Centre for Eastern Studies (OSW), *Ukraine Supports the Russian Position on Transnistria*, Analyses (2010) https://www.osw.waw.pl/en/publikacje/analyses/2010-05-19/ukraine-supports-russian-position-transnistria [accessed 28 September 2017].

[39] Interview with former European diplomat, 28.12.2016.

[40] Interview with former Moldovan official and expert, 06.12.2016.

economic dependence on Russia.[41] In a press conference after the meeting, Merkel referred to the conflict as a relic of old times, called for a political solution and announced that Germany would engage in further talks with Russia: with a bit of political goodwill, this conflict was "solvable".[42] Through this early meeting with Filat, Moldova was included at an early stage of policy design to disperse perceptions that Germany and Russia would negotiate the fate of Moldova above its head. In an interview with German media, Prime Minister Filat stressed that he felt an "honest interest" on behalf of Germany, underlining the importance of Germany's role in helping solve Moldova's "problems" and bringing the country closer to the EU.[43]

The pro-European government in Moldova offered from a German perspective the opportunity to take the seemingly resolvable conflict in Transnistria as a "test case"[44] to demonstrate that an inclusion of Russia in European security issue is not per se futile or counterproductive.[45] According to a German diplomat, in Georgia, Russia has demonstrated how it can create conflicts and conduct war: now Russia should demonstrate how it can solve conflicts.[46] In return for Russian concessions in the conflict, Russia would receive the offer of closer cooperation on European security.[47] For Moldova, progress in conflict resolution could in turn result in progress for Moldova's path towards Europe.

[41] Ibid.

[42] Translations by the author. Angela Merkel and Vladimir Filat, *Pressestatement Bundeskanzlerin Merkel und der Ministerpräsident der Republik Moldau, Vladimir Filat, 12. Mai* (Berlin, 2010) https://www.bundesregierung.de/ContentArchiv/DE/Archiv17/Mitschrift/Pressekonferenzen/2010/05/2010-05-12-filat-merkel.html [accessed 28 September 2017].

[43] Translations by the author. Vlad Filat and Lavinia Pitu, '"Deutschland gehört zu unseren Freunden": Interview mit Vlad Filat', *Deutsche Welle*, 14 May 2010.

[44] Grund, Sieg and Wesemann, 'Transnistria', p. 60.

[45] Interview with German diplomat in Berlin, 15.07.2016.

[46] Interview with German diplomat in Berlin, 09.08.2016.

[47] The initial Russian proposal for conflict resolution, the Kozak memorandum, has been rejected in 2003 after intervention of the EU and the US, and led to a worsening of the relationship between the EU and Russia in this policy area. Cf. William H. Hill, *Russia, the Near Abroad, and the West: Lessons from the Moldova-Transdniestria Conflict* (Washington, DC, Baltimore, MD: Woodrow Wilson Center Press and Johns Hopkins University Press, 2012).

POLICY INITIATION (BILATERAL LEVEL)

The initiation of the Meseberg initiative on the bilateral German-Russian level took place over a two-day closed meeting between President Medvedev, Chancellor Merkel and a limited number of advisors at Schloss Meseberg outside Berlin on 4–5 June 2010.[48] The length and remote location of the meeting was intended to give Merkel and Medvedev time to discuss and build trust among each other.[49] The policy initiation occurred without the involvement of EU, Moldovan or Transnistrian representatives.

The final result of the meeting was the conclusion of a memorandum between Chancellor Merkel and President Medvedev. In this memorandum, the idea to link conflict resolution in Transnistria to security cooperation with Russia was poured into a more concrete outlook: The memorandum proposed "to explore the establishment of an EU-Russia Political and Security Committee between High Representative Ashton and Foreign Minister Lavrov"[50] and elaborated in five points what the committee could be charged with:

> (1) Serve as forum for the exchange of views on current topics of the international political and security agenda, (2) Establish ground rules for joint EU-Russia civil/military crisis management operations, (3) Exchange views and draft recommendations on specific issues of cooperation, including various conflicts and crisis situations which the EU and Russia jointly contribute to resolve within the framework of appropriate multilateral formats, (4) (…) the EU and Russia will cooperate in particular towards a resolution of the Transnistria conflict with a view to achieve tangible progress within the established 5 + 2 format (Russia, Ukraine, Moldova, Transnistria, OSCE, EU, US). This cooperation could include a joint EU-Russia engagement, which would guarantee a smooth transition of the present situation to a final stage, (5) The next EU-Russia summit will review progress made within the new Committee.[51]

Although conflict resolution in Transnistria is mentioned as late as the fourth point, its importance in the memorandum becomes apparent since

---

[48] Cf. Andrew Rettman, 'Germany and Russia Call for New EU Security Committee', *EUobserver*, 7 June 2010.

[49] Cf. Stefan Kornelius, 'Der Russland-Test', *Süddeutsche Zeitung*, 16 July 2010.

[50] Merkel and Medvedev, *Memorandum eng.*, 2010.

[51] Ibid.

it is the longest and most concrete paragraph of the five. Yet the language regarding conflict resolution efforts is kept vague and leaves ample room for interpretation and negotiation on what "tangible progress" and "transition" to a "final stage" mean, and whether a "joint EU-Russia engagement" also implies a withdrawal of Russian troops from Transnistria, for instance to be replaced by EU observers.

Furthermore, the linkage (and chronological sequence) between point four, progress in conflict resolution in Transnistria, and the establishment of the security committee is left unclear in the memorandum. Would the establishment of the new committee precede or be made conditional on progress in conflict resolution? And if the latter, what would be the concrete benchmark for "progress"? This unclear interpretation of the sequencing later resulted in a difficult conundrum about which steps of the agreement should follow at which point of time. According to a German official, Berlin expected Russia to front-load its commitments by delivering results in conflict resolution first after which the establishment of the EU-Russia Political and Security Committee would follow.[52] For the Russian side, the vagueness of the sequencing was an invitation to bargain, according to the former head of the OSCE mission in Moldova: "how much of a settlement" in Transnistria should Russia deliver for "how much" of a say in EU security affairs in return?[53]

The wording on the establishment of the committee is equally vague and non-committal ("proposed to explore the establishment", "committee could be charged") as the language on conflict resolution. Most importantly, the question whether the committee would work under unanimity—that is, including a Russian veto right in the committee—was left unaddressed. Germany lacked the authority to establish such a potentially far-reaching new institutional mechanism to the EU-Russia relationship[54] on a bilateral basis with Russia and to define its tasks on behalf of the EU. Therefore, the memorandum framed the committee as a proposition and the cautious wording also reflects the fact that Brussels and member states had not yet approved of the memorandum's content. Nevertheless, Germany was confident that it would be able to convince Brussels and

---

[52] Interview with German official in Berlin, 15.07.2016. Cf. Andrey Devyatkov, 'Russian Policy toward Transnistria: Between Multilateralism and Marginalization', *Problems of Post-Communism*, 59.3 (2012), 53–62 [accessed 29 October 2017] (p. 57).

[53] Remler, *Negotiation Gone Bad*, 2013.

[54] Cf. Socor, *Meseberg Process*, 2010.

member states to agree to this proposal: The last point of the memorandum assumes that by the next EU-Russia summit, scheduled for December 2010, the committee's progress could already be reviewed.

In sum, while the Meseberg agreement established a link between conflict resolution in Transnistria and the establishment of the Political and Security Committee, the vagueness in details reflects the necessity to make the agreement acceptable to all those who were not present at the bilateral negotiation of the agreement, such as EU and Moldovan representatives. Merkel and Medvedev defended the bilateral form of policy initiation of the Meseberg agreement in a subsequent press conference.[55] When asked whether he was bypassing the EU with this agreement, Medvedev replied by stressing the need for good ideas to be developed at the personal, bilateral level which could then be taken further:

> Every decision has its initiators, its supporters and lobbyists, and in this respect, I think it can be useful to discuss good ideas at the bilateral level first, and then make the relevant proposals to the EU, European Commission and other organisations that make decisions at the overall European level. (…) These steps in no way mean that we want to end our cooperation with Brussels or replace it with cooperation with other countries, even with partners as close and important to us as Germany. But, as I just said, good ideas need to crystallise at the personal level first, and then we can take them further.[56]

Merkel described the Meseberg agreement as "not a bilateral agreement", but "serving the explicit purpose" of European-Russian security cooperation, arguing there are "always situations where a member state

---

[55] For German transcript, see Angela Merkel and Dmitry Medvedev, *Pressestatements von Bundeskanzlerin Angela Merkel und dem Präsidenten der Russischen Föderation, Dmitri Medwedew, 5. Juni* (Meseberg, 2010) https://archiv.bundesregierung.de/archiv-de/dokumente/pressestatements-von-bundeskanzlerin-angela-merkel-und-dem-praesidenten-der-russischen-foederation-dmitri-medwedew-am-5-juni-2010-in-meseberg-846802 [accessed 13 April 2019]; For Russian transcript, see: Angela Merkel and Dmitry Medvedev, *Совместная пресс-конференция с Федеральным канцлером Германии Ангелой Меркель по итогам российско-германских переговоров, 5 июня* (Meseberg, 2010) http://kremlin.ru/events/president/transcripts/7973 [accessed 13 April 2019]; For English translation of the Russian transcript, see: Angela Merkel and Dmitry Medvedev, *Joint News Conference with German Federal Chancellor Angela Merkel following Russian-German Talks, 5 June* (Meseberg, 2010) http://en.kremlin.ru/events/president/transcripts/7973 [accessed 28 September 2017].

[56] English translation of the Russian transcript. Merkel and Medvedev, *Joint News Conference*, 2010.

advances a certain topic a bit".[57] She also expressed hope for a positive EU reaction and referenced implicitly the Russian-Georgian War and the expectation that better security cooperation could prevent a repetition: The initiative could help "bringing cooperation between the EU and Russia to a new level, which will better withstand in a difficult situation than it has been the case in the past". She also made a reference to President Medvedev's proposals for a European Security Treaty, thereby framing the Meseberg agreement as a response to these proposals and argued that the proposed committee would enhance cooperation to a qualitatively new level. The situation in Transnistria is from her point of view a "particularly favourable" example to demonstrate the usefulness of such mechanisms for crisis mediation.[58]

Merkel announced that Germany would introduce the initiative at the next meeting of the EU's Political and Security Committee. She also mentioned in the press conference that "many European partners" were "consulted" regarding the initiative.[59] There are different accounts about which EU institutions, representatives and member states were notified by Germany informally about the initiative ahead of the Meseberg meeting, but it is clear that the proposal had not been formally discussed[60] because of the assumed resistance of some member states.[61] According to a German diplomat, alternative options to the bilateral approach—for instance to pre-negotiate a consensual agreement in Brussels and to launch it at the EU-Russia Summit in Rostov-on-Don, taking place just a few days before Medvedev's and Merkel's meeting in Meseberg—were considered unrealistic and not leading to consensus, since everyone would start co-drafting.[62] The "disconnect" between the Meseberg meeting and the summit in Rostov-on-Don underlines, according to a German expert, the "lack of coordination between the Commission in Brussels and the initiatives of EU member states".[63]

---

[57] Translations by the author from the German transcript. Merkel and Medvedev, *Pressestatements*, 2010.

[58] Ibid.

[59] Ibid.

[60] Rettman, 'Germany and Russia Call', 2010.

[61] Interview with Moldovan expert in Berlin, 26.05.2016.

[62] Interview with German diplomat in Brussels, 30.05.2016.

[63] Meister, *New Start*, 2011, pp. 8–9.

Through this bilateral policy initiation, Germany was setting the agenda on behalf of the EU, instead of within the EU. Germany entered a dual bargaining process with Russia on the one and EU institutions, representatives and member states on the other hand: Towards Russia, Germany assumed responsibility for the establishment of the security committee, while not (yet) enjoying the EU's support for it. Towards the EU, Germany assumed responsibility for progress in conflict resolution in Transnistria, without (yet) being able to demonstrate a constructive Russian role. By linking these issues in one policy design, Germany presented two separate issues for simultaneous discussion as incentive for joint settlement towards both Russia and the EU: If the EU agrees to the establishment of an EU-Russia Political and Security Committee, it would gain the solution of a conflict in its neighbourhood and better cooperation with Russia in return. If Russia agrees to work towards progress in Transnistria, it would gain an elevated role in European security. Both sides were interlinked in unclear sequencing with Germany as broker in-between. To make the policy design even more complicated, Germany assumed with the agreement responsibility as a mediator in conflict resolution in Transnistria, without major prior experience or institutional involvement, in contrast to the EU or the OSCE.[64]

Policy Initiation (EU Level)

The first formal presentation of the Meseberg initiative at the EU-level took place at the meeting of the EU Political and Security Committee on 8 June 2010, a few days after the meeting in Meseberg. The initial echo was interested, including critical questions, but no outright rejection, according to a German diplomat.[65] Yet the fact that member states were not involved in talks before was a cause for irritation.[66] From a German perspective, it was argued that a sense of proportion should be maintained: the establishment of the committee would be a mid-term perspective, with results in conflict resolution to be delivered first before an informal, non-committal meeting including Russia could take place, thereby depicting the committee as more of a consultative instead of decision-making body.[67]

---

[64] Cf. Wolff, 'Resolvable Frozen Conflict', 2011.
[65] Interview with German diplomat in Berlin, 09.08.2016.
[66] Ibid.
[67] Ibid.

The initial response of EU institutions and representatives was also reluctant. According to a European Commission official, the Chancellery had no right to make concessions on behalf of the EU as one out of twenty-seven.[68] Ashton's cabinet was also reluctant to push for the agreement given that it was not even the High Representative's own initiative.[69] Only the European Parliament adopted a resolution in October 2010 approving the Meseberg initiative and the establishment of the security committee to discuss regional issues such as a settlement of the Transnistria conflict.[70] Apart from this resolution, no other formal declaration by EU institutions or representatives has been issued endorsing the initiative.[71]

When it comes to member states, France and Poland, the key actors in the EU's Russia policy, in principle accepted the Meseberg initiative, yet with only superficial support. It was discussed during a meeting of the so-called Weimar Triangle, a discussion format between France, Poland and Germany, in Paris on 23 June, to which Russian Foreign Minister Lavrov was also invited. In his remarks to the press after the meeting, he expressed his expectation for "approval for this initiative by the European Union" as "participants of today's meeting actively called for the EU to do so".[72] Poland's acceptance of the Meseberg initiative is at first glance surprising, given its traditionally sceptical stance towards closer cooperation with Russia, in particular in the sphere of security. Yet, it can be explained against the backdrop of a rapprochement between Poland and Russia after Polish Prime Minister Tusk took office in 2007 as well as the close cooperation between Germany and Poland in Russia policy, particularly by their foreign ministers.[73] In a joint interview by the German and Polish

---

[68] Interview with European Commission official in Brussels, 30.05.2016.

[69] Interview with European Council official in Brussels, 31.05.2016.

[70] European Parliament, *New Momentum in EU-Moldova Relations, 21 October* (Brussels, 2010) http://www.europarl.europa.eu/news/en/press-room/20101020IPR89508/new-momentum-in-eu-moldova-relations [accessed 28 September 2017].

[71] Cf. Vladimir Socor, *Moscow Signals Interest in Berlin Initiative on Transnistria*, Eurasia Daily Monitor, The Jamestown Foundation 63 (2011) https://jamestown.org/program/moscow-signals-interest-in-berlin-initiative-on-transnistria/ [accessed 28 September 2017].

[72] The Ministry of Foreign Affairs of the Russian Federation, *Transcript of Remarks and Response to Media Questions by Russian Foreign Minister Sergey Lavrov at Joint Press Conference after Meeting of Weimar Triangle Foreign Ministers, June 23* (Paris, 2010) http://www.mid.ru/en/web/guest/posledniye_dobavlnenniye/-/asset_publisher/MCZ7HQuMdqBY/content/id/244486 [accessed 13 March 2019].

[73] Cf. for an overview of Polish-Moldovan relations: Marcin Kosienkowski, 'Poland: Rediscovering Moldova', in *Moldova*, ed. by Kosienkowski and Schreiber, pp. 143–58.

foreign ministers in October 2010, Foreign Minister Westerwelle praised the joint coordination, for instance in regional conflict resolution such as in Moldova.[74] By working closer with Germany, Poland demonstrated its aspiration for "a central role in the formulation of policy towards Russia and the other eastern neighbors".[75]

France was interested in general in security cooperation with Russia, but was neither particularly interested in Transnistria,[76] nor had it been a major political partner for Moldova.[77] According to a French diplomat, France was tolerant towards the proposals of the memorandum and glad that Germany took on security issues in the neighbourhood, yet without big expectations.[78] A high-level summit between the French, German and Russian leaders in Deauville on 18–19 October 2010—the first such meeting since 2006, dubbed the "European equivalent" of the US reset on Russia[79]—was a particularly good opportunity to discuss the issue of security cooperation with Russia. However, this happened with different outlooks from the French and German side. Chancellor Merkel used the opportunity to advance the Meseberg initiative, linking once again EU-Russia security cooperation to the Transnistria conflict—which was even mentioned in the final declaration.[80] The French side floated an alternative proposal for security cooperation with the idea "to have a single zone of security and economic cooperation (...) that will pull Russia closer

[74] Cf. 'Poland joins Western World's Policy of Détente towards Russia', *Newsweek Polska*, 24 May 2010.

[75] Meister, *New Start*, 2011, p. 10.

[76] Interview with French diplomat in Paris, 25.11.2016.

[77] Cf. Florent Parmentier, 'France: Unfulfilled Potential as Major Partner', in *Moldova*, ed. by Kosienkowski and Schreiber, pp. 77–86 (p. 85); David Rinnert and Florent Parmentier, *Finding Common Denominators in the Eastern Partnership Region: Towards a Strategic French-German Cooperation in the Transnistrian Conflict*, Policy Brief, The Institute for Development and Social Initiatives "Viitorul" and Friedrich Ebert Stiftung (Chisinau, Paris, Berlin, 2013), p. 9 http://www.fes-moldova.org/media/pdf/Policy_Policy_Brief_2013_1.pdf [accessed 28 September 2017].

[78] Interview with French official in Paris, 23.11.2016.

[79] Robert Marquand, 'Facing a Rising China, Russia Looks to Boost Europe Ties', *The Christian Science Monitor*, 18 October 2010.

[80] Angela Merkel, Nicolas Sarkozy and Dmitry Medvedev, *Déclaration finale: Rencontre Allemagne-France-Russie, 19 Octobre* (Deauville, 2010) https://uk.ambafrance.org/Rencontre-Allemagne-France-Russie [accessed 13 April 2019]; Angela Merkel, Nicolas Sarkozy and Dmitry Medvedev, *Pressekonferenz Merkel, Sarkozy und Medwedew, 19. Oktober* (Deauville, 2010) https://www.bundeskanzlerin.de/ContentArchiv/DE/Archiv17/Mitschrift/Pressekonferenzen/2010/10/2010-10-19-pk-deauville.html [accessed 28 September 2017].

to Europe".[81] This should, according to the German newspaper *Der Spiegel*, represent "a 'technical, human and security partnership' with Russia—led by the French, of course, not by the Germans".[82] Despite France's acceptance of the Meseberg initiative, Sarkozy's proposal underscored the French ambition to remain the key player in European security and to build a counterweight to Germany's security policy entrepreneurship towards Russia in Meseberg.[83] More plainly, France saw the necessity to reassert its traditional status as a leader in European security towards Russia at the Deauville summit with its own, albeit vague, proposal.

Key member states in policy towards Russia—France and Poland—accepted and superficially supported the initiative in Deauville and during the Weimar Triangle meeting. EU institutions and representatives, however, did not officially endorse the Meseberg memorandum and were reluctant to voice support. This demonstrates a lack of support and institutional access points garnered by Germany from within the EU—in particular from the EU High Representative, who was to play a prominent role in the planned EU-Russia Political and Security Committee. Instead, the agenda was set on a bilateral level with Russia first, on behalf of the EU.

Apart from involving Poland and France, Germany also reached out to Romania, back then a new EU member state, to remove a stumbling block in implementing the Meseberg initiative: The lack of a border treaty between Romania and Moldova, one of the reasons that complicated conflict resolution since Transnistrian elites feared they would become a "disadvantaged peripheral province" in a hypothetical unification.[84] Chancellor Merkel paid a state visit in October 2010 to Bucharest and appealed for further progress in negotiations about a Romanian-Moldovan border treaty.[85] The visit was preceded by a trip of German Foreign Minister Westerwelle both to Bucharest and to Chișinău in June together with the British foreign minister. As a result of these efforts, on 8 November 2010

---

[81] Steven Erlanger and Katrin Bennhold, 'Sarkozy to Propose New Bond With Russia', *The New York Times*, 1 October 2010.

[82] 'French-German-Russian Summit: Sarkozy Dreams of a European Security Council', *Spiegel Online*, 18 October 2010.

[83] Meister, *New Start*, 2011, p. 9.

[84] Grund, Sieg and Wesemann, 'Transnistria', 60, 65.

[85] Angela Merkel and Emil Boc, *Pressestatements von Bundeskanzlerin Angela Merkel und dem Premierminister von Rumänien, Emil Boc, 12. Oktober* (Bucharest, 2010) https://www.bundeskanzlerin.de/ContentArchiv/DE/Archiv17/Mitschrift/Pressekonferenzen/2010/10/2010-10-12-pk-bk-bukarest.html [accessed 28 September 2017].

the Treaty on the State Border Regime between Romania and Moldova was signed.[86]

Shortly after the conclusion of the Meseberg agreement, Russia entered the bargaining process on the interpretation of the content and the sequencing of the agreement. On 21 July 2010, in a letter addressed directly to High Representative Ashton, Foreign Minister Lavrov presented the Russian interpretation of the agreement and Russia's priorities: Lavrov proposed a "commission" of twenty-seven EU member states and Russia, operating by consensus, which means including a Russian right to veto.[87] Ashton responded by prioritising conflict resolution in Transnistria over the establishment of the Political and Security Committee, as documented by a request of the European Parliament, arguing that "the influence of this [progress on Transnistria] on the internal discussion in the EU [on the security committee] cannot be overestimated".[88] This demonstrates the reluctance within the EU towards the establishment of the committee and that the question of sequencing—whether the committee should predate or follow progress in conflict resolution—was interpreted differently: The Russian side expected a near-term establishment of the committee to discuss progress on Transnistria,[89] contrary to Ashton's position that first Russian goodwill in Transnistria would be necessary to convince the EU and member states of the idea.

Foreign Minister Lavrov's letter further complicated Germany's position as the initiator and broker of the Meseberg agreement: By directly addressing Ashton, Russia was bypassing Germany and trying to put the EU under pressure, all the more troublesome in a case where the EU did not have a sense of ownership over the initiative. Russia's maximum bargaining position—a Russian veto right in decision making—was clearly not acceptable and dividing member states on this issue, providing further

---

[86] Ministry of Foreign Affairs of Romania, *Romania and Republic of Moldova sign Treaty on State Border Regime, Cooperation and Mutual Assistance in Border Matters, 8 November* (2010) https://mae.ro/en/node/5904 [accessed 13 March 2019].

[87] Remler, *Negotiation Gone Bad*, 2013; Interview with former European diplomat, 28.12.2016.

[88] European Parliament, *Parliamentary Questions, Reply, 25 January* (Brussels, 2011) http://www.europarl.europa.eu/sides/getAllAnswers.do?reference=E-2010-8055&language=MT [accessed 28 September 2017].

[89] Manfred Grund, Hans M. Sieg and Kristin Wesemann, *Transnistrien und die künftige Sicherheitsarchitektur in Europa*, KAS Auslandsinformationen 9/10 (2011), p. 64 http://www.kas.de/wf/doc/kas_28726-544-1-30.pdf?110908153915 [accessed 27 September 2017].

ammunition for critics in Brussels and capitals. It also conflicted with Germany's explanation of the committee as initially consultative body.[90] Furthermore, Russia denied the issue linkage to conflict resolution in Transnistria at first: In a meeting with the Moldovan Foreign Minister Leancă in March 2011, Lavrov underlined that from a Russian perspective, setting up the committee was not dependent on progress in Transnistria, and expressed frustration at the lack of EU reaction to a proposal initiated "by the leader of the biggest EU country and the president of Russia, strategic partner to the EU".[91]

This also demonstrates a Russian understanding of EU policy formation as a process mainly decided by big member states with others expected to follow suit. Nevertheless, in the same meeting with the Moldovan foreign minister, Lavrov also acknowledged that a solution to the Transnistria conflict should be found within a unified Moldovan state, and stated the official 5 + 2 talks should be resumed (broken off in 2006).[92] He thereby implicitly accepted the issue linkage in the Meseberg memorandum and indicated how far Russia was prepared to go in conflict resolution: Russia considered the resumption of negotiations in the 5 + 2 format a sufficient contribution to conflict resolution, at least for the establishment of the committee[93]—whereas the Meseberg memorandum spoke of "tangible progress" and "transition" to a "final stage" through a joint EU-Russia engagement, implying the withdrawal of Russian troops from Transnistria.[94]

Policy Implementation

A formal agreement to resume the 5 + 2 negotiations was only reached in September 2011, since the official Russian position was to wait until after elections in Moldova and so-called elections in Transnistria in November/December 2010 when negotiation parties were established.[95] Yet through-

---

[90] Interview with German diplomat in Berlin, 09.08.2016.

[91] As quoted from Russian news agency Interfax by Socor, *Moscow Signals Interest*, 2011.

[92] 'Лавров: РФ выступает за особый статус Приднестровья в единой Молдавии', *Ria Novosti*, 29 March 2011.

[93] Cf. Centre for Eastern Studies (OSW), *Russia's Superficial Concession on Transnistria*, Analyses (2011) https://www.osw.waw.pl/en/publikacje/analyses/2011-04-06/russias-superficial-concession-transnistria [accessed 13 March 2019].

[94] Cf. Hans M. Sieg, *Der Transnistrien-Konflikt: Voraussetzungen für eine Konfliktlösung*, Südosteuropa Mitteilungen 51 3 (2011).

[95] Devyatkov, 'Russian Policy toward Transnistria', 2012, p. 57.

out 2010, Moscow already exerted pressure on the Transnistrian leadership, including supporting another candidate than the incumbent for the so-called elections in December.[96] While five informal meetings of the 5 + 2 took place in 2010 and Moldovan Prime Minister Filat and Transnistrian leader Igor Smirnov met twice in 2010 on the sidelines at Europa League football matches in a show of "football diplomacy",[97] the first serious attempt to initiate official talks was made on 21 June 2011 in Moscow.[98] In the run-up, Russia tried to broker an agreement without the involvement of other mediators in the 5 + 2 format, which led to a "multiplication of competing drafts, each acceptable to one side or the other, but not to both".[99] This approach alienated the other involved parties and the meeting was suspended under a "stopping the clock"[100] procedure to be continued in Moscow on 22 September. In Moscow, an agreement was eventually found for the resumption of official 5 + 2 talks.[101]

The OSCE played a significant role as mediator for the resumption of talks, yet the "key enabling factor" for the resumption of talks was attributed to Germany's role and the impetus from the Meseberg memorandum.[102] Germany's agenda setting resulted in pressure to make progress for Chişinău and Tiraspol from Moscow, Berlin and Brussels. Financed by the German Foreign Office, the OSCE organised two conferences on Confidence-Building Measures (CBM) in November 2010 and September 2011 in Germany with chief negotiators and co-chairs in attendance.[103] The September meeting in Bad Reichenhall, where Moldovan and Transnistrian leaders met on the sidelines and agreed on a basic document detailing the statute of the Joint Expert Working Groups on CBMs, was especially decisive for the resumption of negotiations. A November

[96] Socor, *Moscow Signals Interest*, 2011, Devyatkov, 'Russian Policy toward Transnistria', 2012, pp. 58–59.

[97] Andrey Devyatkov, 'Russia: Relations with Moldova under a Paradigm of Ambiguity', in *Moldova*, ed. by Kosienkowski and Schreiber, pp. 183–204 (p. 196).

[98] 'Идея независимости Приднестровья не поддерживается какой-либо международной структурой', *Interfax*, 5 June 2011.

[99] Neukirch, *Confidence Building*, 2012, p. 144.

[100] Ibid.

[101] Cf. Andrei Zagorski, 'Russland und der Transnistrienkonflikt', in *Problemlage und Lösungsansätze im Transnistrienkonflikt*, ed. by Reiter, pp. 77–102.

[102] Neukirch, *Confidence Building*, 2012, pp. 146–47.

[103] Neukirch, *Confidence Building*, 2012, p. 142.

meeting between Smirnov and Filat made the first official 5 + 2 meeting in Vilnius on 30 November and 1 December 2011 possible.[104]

Although not officially part of it, Germany further supported the 5 + 2 negotiations, and circulated a non-paper, outlining ideas for a conflict resolution agreement.[105] In April 2012, an agreement on the basic principles of future negotiations was reached,[106] and in August 2012, Merkel visited Moldova calling for further progress in negotiations.[107] However, the appointment of hardliner Dmitri Rogozin as Russian Special Representative for Transnistria[108] under President Putin who returned to the presidency in 2012 led to a "hardening" of Russian and Transnistrian positions[109] and caused conflict resolution efforts to lose momentum.[110] While the resumed talks were a success for Germany, there was still "no agreement within the EU on whether, and if so when to establish the proposed EU-Russia Political and Security Committee".[111] According to a former European diplomat, Russia's conflict resolution efforts were seen as lukewarm and insufficient for some member states to agree to a EU-Russia Political and Security Committee, since they expected "tangible progress"—including the question of Russian troops in Transnistria—and not merely a resumption of official 5 + 2 negotiations.[112] In a minor

---

[104] Neukirch, *Confidence Building*, 2012, p. 139.

[105] Socor, *German Diplomacy Tilts*, 2011.

[106] Hans M. Sieg, *The EU's Role or Absence in "Frozen Conflicts" in Transnistria and Caucasus* (Berlin), p. 3 http://nbn-resolving.de/urn:nbn:de:0168-ssoar-394784 [accessed 29 September 2017].

[107] Federal Chancellor, *Erste Schritte in Richtung EU: Staatsbesuch in der Republik Moldau,* 22. August (Chisinau, 2012) https://www.bundeskanzlerin.de/ContentArchiv/DE/Archiv17/Reiseberichte/moldau-2012-08-22-merkel.html [accessed 29 September 2017].

[108] Andrey Makarychev and Sergunin Alexander, 'The EU, Russia and Models of International Society in a Wider Europe', *Journal of Contemporary European Research*, 9.2 (2013), 313–29 https://www.jcer.net/index.php/jcer/article/view/506/408 (p. 324).

[109] German Bundestag, *Drucksache 18/1745: Antwort der Bundesregierung auf die Kleine Anfrage der Abgeordneten Sevim Dağdelen, Dr. Alexander S. Neu, Heike Hänsel, weiterer Abgeordneter und der Fraktion DIE LINKE, 12. Juni* (Berlin, 2014) https://www.bundesanzeiger-verlag.de/fileadmin/Betrifft-Recht/Dokumente/edrucksachen/pdf/1801745.pdf [accessed 13 April 2019] (p. 10).

[110] Devyatkov, 'Russian Policy toward Transnistria', 2012; Andrey Makarychev, *A Farewell to Meseberg?*, PONARS Eurasia (2012) http://www.ponarseurasia.org/article/farewell-meseberg [accessed 29 September 2017].

[111] Neukirch, *Confidence Building*, 2012, p. 146.

[112] Interview with former European diplomat, 28.12.2016; Grund, Sieg and Wesemann, *Transnistrien*, 2011, p. 62.

interpellation from November 2011, the Alliance 90/The Greens party inquired as to why the proposed committee had not been established in the EU. In its reply,[113] the German Government described the resumption of talks as a first sign of progress and that it was committed to engage for the implementation of the committee with the EU and Russia.[114]

In sum, Germany emerged as an important new conflict mediator in cooperation with the OSCE and the EU, although it was earlier not institutionally involved in conflict resolution in Moldova. While the German government stressed that its role was only "indirect",[115] in reality, Germany assumed ownership for the Transnistria case both politically and diplomatically, including the funding of Confidence-Building Measures. Since ownership from EU institutions for the initiative remained limited, Germany took on a bilateral agenda-setting role. According to a critic, thereby Germany substituted the EU's policy in the 5 + 2 talks for its own.[116] Although Confidence-Building Measures financed by Germany continued to take place, Berlin acknowledged that getting to the "substance" of conflict resolution remained difficult.[117]

When tensions escalated over the Eastern Partnership Association Agreement with Ukraine in 2013, neither the EU-Russia Political and Security Committee nor a conflict resolution agreement in Transnistria had been established. By then, the modus operandi between the EU and Russia had shifted from cooperation to contestation in the Eastern neighbourhood,[118] with no chances for the Meseberg initiative to succeed. Russia blamed the EU for the failure to establish the committee, not Germany: According to Russian Foreign Minister Lavrov, "neither Russia

---

[113] German Bundestag, *Drucksache 17/8239*, 2011.

[114] German Bundestag, *Drucksache 17/8239*, 2011, p. 2.

[115] German Bundestag, *Drucksache 17/8239: Antwort der Bundesregierung auf die Kleine Anfrage der Abgeordneten Viola von Cramon-Taubadel, Volker Beck (Köln), Marieluise Beck (Bremen), weiterer Abgeordneter und der Fraktion BÜNDNIS 90/DIE GRÜNEN, Stand des Meseburg-Memorandums, 21. Dezember* (2011) http://dipbt.bundestag.de/dip21/btd/17/082/1708239.pdf [accessed 27 September 2017].

[116] Vladimir Socor, *German Diplomacy Tilts toward Russia on Transnistria Negotiations*, Eurasia Daily Monitor, The Jamestown Foundation 108 (2011) https://jamestown.org/program/german-diplomacy-tilts-toward-russia-on-transnistria-negotiations/ [accessed 28 September 2017].

[117] German Bundestag, *Drucksache 18/1745*, 2014, p. 11.

[118] Cf. Hiski Haukkala, 'From Cooperative to Contested Europe?: The Conflict in Ukraine as a Culmination of a Long-Term Crisis in EU–Russia Relations', *Journal of Contemporary European Studies*, 23.1 (2015), 25–40.

nor Germany is to blame for the fact that the Meseberg initiative failed to make it through the 'sieve' of internal EU clearances".[119] Furthermore, Moldova assumed that the outcome would reflect primarily Moldovan preferences and lacked the political will for far-reaching concessions and compromise.[120] Despite significant efforts from Germany, the Meseberg initiative and the proposal of a EU-Russia Political and Security Committee was ultimately not implemented, nor has a withdrawal of Russian troops from Transnistria been achieved.[121] Although the EU did not disavow or resist the initiative in principle, it also did not take ownership or endorse it formally as EU policy.

Explaining the Final Outcome

Despite all German efforts, the Meseberg initiative remained a bilateral, rather than a European policy outcome. How can this final outcome be explained? Which alternative factors have contributed to it? Can the initial assumption, namely that the Meseberg initiative demonstrates a more assertive German approach, be confirmed? (Table 4.1)

German Influence

The Meseberg initiative was neither adopted nor fully supported by the EU. Germany thus exerted only a minor influence on official EU policy. Without sufficient progress coming from the Russian side—which contributed to a resumption of 5 + 2 talks but did not go beyond towards a Russian troops withdrawal—EU institutions and representatives remained cautious and sceptical towards the initiative. Russia's lack of response to the initiative complicated Germany's bargaining position in the EU, which was difficult from the beginning due to the bilateral policy initiation and design of the initiative.

---

[119] The Ministry of Foreign Affairs of the Russian Federation, *Foreign Minister Sergey Lavrov Makes a Speech and Answers Questions Following His Talks with German Foreign Minister Frank-Walter Steinmeier, 18 November* (Moscow, 2014) http://www.mid.ru/en/press_service/minister_speeches/-/asset_publisher/7OvQR5KJWVmR/content/id/790869 [accessed 28 September 2017].

[120] Remler, *Negotiation Gone Bad*, 2013; Neukirch, *Confidence Building*, 2012, p. 146.

[121] Katinka Barysch, *The EU and Russia: All Smiles and No Action?*, Policy Brief, Centre for European Reform (2011), p. 6 https://www.cer.eu/sites/default/files/publications/attachments/pdf/2011/pb_russia_april11-157.pdf [accessed 14 April 2019].

Table 4.1 Instruments of power in the Meseberg initiative

EU policy formation process	Key MS/EU actors	Contextual variables	Instruments of power applied by Germany			Empirical evidence
			Compulsory power	Institutional power	Productive power	
Bilateral Policy Initiation						
German-Russian Meseberg agreement	GER	– Medvedev's proposals on European security – Moldovan pro-European government	– Issue linkage	–	–	– Meeting in Meseberg and bilateral conclusion of Meseberg agreement
EU-level Policy Initiation						
Introduction of the agreement to EU representatives and member states	GER, FR, PL, Romania, EU Actors	– Russian letter to HR Ashton – Conclusion of Moldovan-Romanian border treaty	–	– Coalition building	– Arguing and suasion	– Presentation of initiative for EU and member states – Inclusion of France/Poland at Deauville/Weimar Triangle
Policy Implementation						
Conflict resolution in Transnistria	GER	– Russian contribution to 5 + 2 talks resumption – OSCE mediation and brokering	–	– Agenda setting	–	– Confidence-Building Measures leading to resumption of 5 + 2 talks

Source: Author's table

Germany initiated the policy first on a bilateral level, without sufficient ownership by the EU. This demonstrates a lack of institutional and productive power instruments applied by Germany such as arguing and suasion or institutional access points. EU High Representative Ashton only referenced the Meseberg initiative as a bilateral German proposal[122]—despite being expected to play a prominent role in the envisioned committee. Concluding the memorandum on behalf of the EU thus led to scepticism and reluctance on the European side and with member states. Some perceived the Meseberg initiative as Germany making arrangements with Russia on behalf of the EU in a "secretive way" and "outrunning EU-Russia relations".[123] In addition, the policy design of the initiative—linking two separate issues that have no direct relation to each other—reflects a geopolitical style of policy making, which is not considered a typical part of the toolbox of German foreign policy. Applying this instrument and implementing a new initiative in the area of security policy demonstrates thus a greater assertiveness in policy making from Germany's side.

Germany involved France and Poland at summits and foreign ministers' meetings to advance the idea in an attempt of coalition-building, but received only lukewarm support. In the phase of policy implementation, Germany played a key enabling role in support of renewed talks and OSCE Confidence-Building Measures within the 5 + 2 format, which led to the resumption of official negotiations. Germany engaged successfully also with Romania for the resolution of the border issue with Moldova. However, this success in conflict resolution had only limited influence on the EU's policy towards Russia, as it was not followed by further steps, such as a withdrawal of Russian troops from Transnistria. Member states were not convinced of "Germany's capacity to insist that Russia deliver actual results, rather than process".[124]

---

[122] European Parliament, *Parliamentary Questions*, 2011.

[123] Interview with Moldovan expert in Berlin, 26.05.2016; Vladimir Socor, *Meseberg Process: Germany Testing EU-Russia Security Cooperation Potential*, Eurasia Daily Monitor, The Jamestown Foundation 191 (2010) https://jamestown.org/program/meseberg-process-germany-testing-eu-russia-security-cooperation-potential/   [accessed   27 September 2017].

[124] Socor, *Moscow Signals Interest*, 2011.

Alternative Influences I (EU Actors and Member States)

EU institutions and representatives have influenced the EU policy formation process to the extent that they were hesitant to endorse the Meseberg
initiative as EU policy. Neither has the Council adopted a formal conclusion on the initiative nor have subordinated committees done so. Only the
EU Parliament explicitly supported the proposal. While member states, in
particular the key actors France and Poland, accepted the initiative in
meetings at Deauville or at the Weimar Triangle, they remained reluctant
and adopted a "wait and see approach",[125] continuing to pursue their own
policies towards Russia. The lack of ownership in particular of EU representatives and institutions, who were excluded from the policy initiation,
contributed to the fact that the Meseberg initiative did not become part of
the EU's official policy towards Russia.

Alternative Influences II (Russia, Moldova, US, External Shocks)

Russia, as signatory to the memorandum, was the most significant contextual factor and alternative influence on the EU policy formation process.
Russia's maximum bargaining position towards the security committee,
including Russian veto rights, as well as the slow and limited progress in
conflict resolution, contributed to the EU's reluctance to endorse the initiative and made Germany's efforts to convince the EU all the more challenging. Russia expected the German-Russian Meseberg memorandum to
have a much greater influence on EU policy, assuming a policy initiated by
Germany would unquestionably be adopted by others, and put pressure
on the EU to follow up on Germany's commitment. Furthermore, both
Transnistrian leaders had been foot-dragging to achieve a compromise and
deliver results.[126] A lack of will for compromise on the Moldovan side
complicated the resumption of talks and further progress,[127] although representatives were involved in the initiative from the beginning. The US
played a limited role as a contextual factor to the extent that the US-Russian
reset provided the overall atmosphere of détente for a security initiative
with Russia.

---

[125] Socor, *German Diplomacy Tilts*, 2011.
[126] Wolff, 'Resolvable Frozen Conflict', 2011.
[127] Neukirch, *Confidence Building*, 2012, p. 146.

Conclusion: Germany as a Deal-Maker

Does the Meseberg initiative indicate the limits of German power in EU foreign policy? Despite Germany's readiness to engage for the first time in a security policy initiative with Russia, Germany exerted only a minor influence on the final outcome of the EU's policy towards Russia. Germany's assertive approach towards the EU in the Meseberg initiative proved not successful. Combined with Russia's limited willingness to contribute to further-reaching steps in conflict resolution, it resulted in the initiative's failure to be implemented and adopted as official EU policy. The Meseberg initiative remained a bilateral German-Russian agreement rather than a European initiative.

In as much as the Meseberg initiative was a test case for EU-Russia security cooperation, it was also a test case for German power within the EU: Berlin has overestimated its capacity to negotiate an issue with two sides, Brussels and Moscow, at the same time, with only lukewarm support by member states and institutions in an unfamiliar terrain (security policy and protracted conflicts). In addition, the Russian side was complicating efforts by putting forward a maximum bargaining position. By using a bilateral approach to policy initiation, Germany failed to tie the initiative to an institutional EU context and engaged in "freewheeling personal diplomacy at the highest level",[128] put differently: in bilateral deal-making with Russia.

This was in turn met with scepticism by Brussels and capitals. The initiative might also have failed with a stronger EU involvement, given Russia's reluctance to engage in substantial conflict resolution efforts. But the fact that the initiative remained a bilateral German-Russian initiative made it a distinctly German failure. This was different in the case of the EU-Russia Partnership for Modernisation. Both initiatives—the Meseberg initiative and the EU-Russia Partnership for Modernisation—tried to exploit the window of opportunity of the Medvedev presidency in relations with Russia: However, the EU-Russia Partnership for Modernisation demonstrated an explicit EU ownership, in contrast to Meseberg. The proximity in the timing of these two initiatives—the Partnership for Modernisation was concluded by EU representatives just days before Merkel and Medvedev met in Meseberg—makes the differences in approaches particularly apparent.[129] Instead of "constructive

[128] Remler, *Negotiation Gone Bad*, 2013.
[129] Meister, 'Entfremdete Partner', 2012.

bilateralism",[130] the Meseberg initiative failed to advance the EU-Russia security relationship and instead added frustration and misunderstanding. Germany's design of the initiative as a "test case",[131] which should not lead to strategic losses for Germany or the EU,[132] turned out to be an illusion and damaged Germany's credibility in the EU.[133]

A certain naiveté towards the conflict in Transnistria as the "easiest to solve" should also be noted, underestimating the complexities of protracted conflict resolution. The assumption of converging interests in Transnistria on both the European and Russian side[134] was based on a too optimistic reading of the goals of Medvedev's security proposals. Russia's willingness to cooperate on security issues and the resolution of protracted conflicts in the neighbourhood was overestimated, as well as Medvedev's position and room for manoeuvre within the Russian power elite. From a Russian perspective, the conflict represented a useful lever in Russia's claim for a sphere of influence. To give it up would have required significant concessions, such as a veto option for Russia in European security affairs, an inherently inacceptable demand for Europeans. With the return of Vladimir Putin to the Russian presidency in 2012, the initiative entirely lost its momentum.[135] In the end, Germany's bold attempt to improve relations with Russia through cooperation in the neighbourhood was not successfull. Only to a limited extent was the Meseberg initiative a new German "Ostpolitik" (Eastern policy), which was "more skeptical about Russia and more focused on its neighbors", as claimed by *The Economist*[136]—dubbing Chancellor Merkel "Frau fix-it": a deal-maker in the East.

---

[130] Forsberg and Haukkala, *European Union and Russia*, 2016, p. 91.

[131] Grund, Sieg and Wesemann, 'Transnistria', p. 60.

[132] Interview with German expert in Berlin, 16.08.2016.

[133] Cf. Judy Dempsey, 'Challenging Russia to Fix a Frozen Feud', *The New York Times*, 27 October 2010.

[134] Meister, *New Start*, 2011, p. 17.

[135] Richard Sakwa, *Russia against the Rest: The Cold Peace and the Breakdown of the European Security Order* (Cambridge, New York, NY: Cambridge University Press, 2017), p. 273.

[136] 'Frau Fix-It: A New Role for Germany in the East: Make Friends, Fix Problems', *The Economist*, 18 November 2010.

CHAPTER 5

The Russia-Ukraine Conflict 2014: Germany as a Leading Power

The Russia-Ukraine conflict, beginning in 2014, represented to many observers a caesura not only in the EU-Russia relationship,[1] but also in German-Russian relations and even more so for Germany's role in Europe: For the first time, Germany engaged at the forefront of a crisis situation with Russia in the immediate neighbourhood of the EU, assuming a leadership role on behalf of the Union. Accredited to German leadership, the EU's response to the Ukraine conflict was stronger and more cohesive than the response to the Russian-Georgian War under the leadership of France in 2008. While in 2008, relations quickly returned to business as usual, the EU's response to the Russia-Ukraine conflict exceeded the lowest common denominator and, for the first time, the EU imposed significant economic sanctions on Russia which remain in effect.[2] The EU was criticised for not foreseeing that the dispute over the conclusion of the

---

[1] Cf. Haukkala, 'Conflict in Ukraine', 2015; Cristian Nitoiu, 'Towards Conflict or Cooperation?: The Ukraine Crisis and EU-Russia Relations', *Southeast European and Black Sea Studies*, 16.3 (2016), 375–90; Derek Averre, 'The Ukraine Conflict: Russia's Challenge to European Security Governance', *Europe-Asia Studies*, 68.4 (2016), 699–725; Cristian Nitoiu, 'Still Entrenched in the Conflict/Cooperation Dichotomy?: EU–Russia Relations and the Ukraine Crisis', *European Politics and Society*, 18.2 (2016), 148–65; Wilson, *Ukraine Crisis*, 2014.

[2] Cf. Helene Sjursen and Guri Rosén, 'Arguing Sanctions: On the EU's Response to the Crisis in Ukraine', in *Europe's Hybrid Foreign Policy: The Ukraine-Russia Crisis*, ed. by Mai'a

---

© The Author(s), under exclusive license to Springer Nature Switzerland AG 2021

L. Fix, *Germany's Role in European Russia Policy*, New Perspectives in German Political Studies,

https://doi.org/10.1007/978-3-030-68226-2_5

EU-Ukraine Association Agreement could turn into a conflict with Russia over Ukraine's territorial integrity and future foreign policy orientation.[3] The response, however—spearheaded by Germany and, to a lesser extent, France—was generally lauded as swift crisis management and a demonstration of unity in the face of a severe crisis with Russia.[4]

Germany's role in the Russia-Ukraine conflict is often referred to as the climax of German leadership, or even hegemony, in Europe.[5] Germany's leadership in the Russia-Ukraine conflict resembled a role reversal with France's leadership role in the Russian-Georgian War 2008, but Germany lacked the institutional legitimacy France had at hand with the Council Presidency. Without the "power of the chair",[6] how was Germany able to exert significant influence on the EU policy formation process and to create followers among other member states? In addition, how did Germany gain legitimacy for a leadership role within the EU? [7] Which instruments of power were applied, especially given the salience of the crisis, and is this evidence of a more assertive German approach?

In contrast to the Russian-Georgian War in 2008, where the active conflict phase spanned a mere two months, the active phase of the Russia-Ukraine conflict has lasted much longer. The analysis will therefore include a longer period of EU policy formation, structured along the following

K. Davis Cross and Ireneusz Pawel Karolewski (= *Journal of Common Market Studies*, 55 (2017)), pp. 20–36 (p. 26).

[3] Cf. Hiski Haukkala, 'A Perfect Storm: Or What Went Wrong and What Went Right for the EU in Ukraine', *Europe-Asia Studies*, 68.4 (2016), 653–64.

[4] Cf. Ireneusz P. Karolewski and Mai'a K. D. Cross, 'The EU's Power in the Russia-Ukraine Crisis: Enabled or Constrained?', in *Europe's Hybrid Foreign Policy: The Ukraine-Russia Crisis*, ed. by Mai'a K. Davis Cross and Ireneusz Pawel Karolewski (= *Journal of Common Market Studies*, 55 (2017)), pp. 137–52.

[5] Fix, 'Different 'Shades'', 2018; Cf. also: Siddi, 'Contested Hegemon', 2018; Elizabeth Pond, *Merkel's Leadership in the Ukraine Crisis*, American Institute for Contemporary German Studies (AICGS) (Washington, DC, 2014) https://www.aicgs.org/publication/merkels-leadership-in-the-ukraine-crisis/ [accessed 9 March 2018]; Elizabeth Pond and Hans Kundnani, 'Germany's Real Role in the Ukraine Crisis: Caught Between East and West', *Foreign Affairs*, March/April 2015; Ulrich Speck, *German Power and the Ukraine Conflict*, Carnegie Europe (Brussels, 2015) http://carnegieeurope.eu/2015/03/26/german-power-and-ukraine-conflict [accessed 30 October 2015].

[6] Cf. Tallberg, 'Power of the Chair', 2010.

[7] Cf. Siddi, 'German Foreign Policy', 2016.

three phases:[8] (1) From February to March 2014, which marks the internationalisation of domestic crisis to an inter-state conflict between Russia and Ukraine, including the annexation of Crimea and the first political EU sanctions; (2) from April to August 2014, including the destabilisation and outbreak of violence in Eastern Ukraine and the introduction of economic sanctions by the EU; (3) from September 2014 to March 2015, including the conclusion of the first and second Minsk agreements and their linkage to the EU sanctions regime. The conclusion will address how the lack of a conflict resolution until today has impacted Germany's role and power within the European Union.

GERMAN POSITIONS AND PREFERENCES

Germany's positions and preferences towards the Russia-Ukraine conflict have to be seen in the broader context of Germany's stance towards the Eastern Partnership, beginning with the negotiations for the EU-Ukraine Association Agreement up to the Euromaidan protests in the winter of 2013/2014. This pre-conflict phase demonstrates that Germany's leadership during the conflict was not the result of a similarly strong engagement towards Ukraine within the Eastern Partnership before the outbreak of the conflict.

Germany and the Eastern Partnership

Germany's policy towards the Eastern Partnership before the Ukraine conflict was characterised by support in general, but also by a reluctance to embrace a leadership role.[9] The Eastern Partnership grew out of the European Neighbourhood Policy, which focused on Eastern and Southern member states. Although the German Foreign Office proposed a "European Neighbourhood Policy Plus" initiative in 2006 in order to place a special emphasis on Eastern neighbours, it has refrained from becoming involved in the initiation of the Eastern Partnership, which was first proposed by Poland and Sweden in May 2008.[10] The Eastern

[8] Cf. also with the conflict phases identified by Wolfgang Seibel, 'Arduous Learning or New Uncertainties?: The Emergence of German Diplomacy in the Ukrainian Crisis', *Global Policy*, 6.10 (2015), 56–72 and Sakwa, *Frontline Ukraine*, 2016.

[9] Cf. Fix and Kirch, *Germany and the EaP*, 2016.

[10] Cf. Iris Kempe, *From a European Neighbourhood Policy towards a New Ostpolitik: The Potential Impact of German Policy*, CAP Policy Analysis 6 (2006) https://www.files.ethz.ch/isn/44156/CAP-Analyse-2006-03_en.pdf [accessed 14 April 2019].

Partnership policy was eventually adopted by the European Council in March 2009.[11] While Germany supported the Eastern Partnership in general, it strongly opposed a membership perspective for these countries. Furthermore, Germany made an effort to balance the EU's increased engagement with the Eastern neighbourhood with renewed policy initiatives towards Russia, in an attempt to build a neighbourhood policy not against, but with Russia.[12]

Together with Georgia and Moldova, Ukraine has been among the frontrunners in the Eastern Partnership. While the technocratic process of negotiating EU Association Agreements with Eastern Partnership countries was predominantly led by EU institutions, Germany played a role in setting the conditions for the political pace of the association process. Although the negotiations for an EU-Ukraine Association Agreement were finalised in December 2011 and initiated by March the next year, the agreement's signature was postponed due to concerns about the rule of law and human rights in Ukraine. Both the EU and Germany criticised the prosecution of former Prime Minister Yulia Tymoshenko as a case of selective justice and considered her release the most important precondition for the conclusion of the Association Agreement. Then-German Foreign Minister Guido Westerwelle met Tymoshenko's daughter on several occasions and proposed medical treatment in Germany in September 2013 as a potentially face-saving solution to the Ukrainian government.[13] Ukraine, for its part, demanded the prospect of EU membership to be formally mentioned in the Agreement.

At the same time, Russia increased pressure on Armenia and Ukraine not to sign their negotiated Association Agreements. After a visit to Moscow in September 2013, the Armenian president announced his decision to join the Russian-led Eurasian Economic Union in exchange for a reduction in Russian gas prices.[14] To Ukraine, Russia offered a loan of

---

[11] Katrin Böttger, 'Deutschland, die Östliche Partnerschaft und Russland', in *Handbuch zur deutschen Europapolitik*, ed. by Böttger and Jopp, pp. 407–20 (p. 411).

[12] Fix and Kirch, *Germany and the EaP*, 2016, p. 10; Böttger, *Deutschland, die Östliche Partnerschaft und Russland*, 2016, p. 407.

[13] 'Westerwelle macht sich für Timoschenko stark', *Die Welt*, 21 June 2013.

[14] 'EU Officials Warn Yerevan over "U-Turn"', *RadioFreeEurope/RadioLiberty*, 4 September 2013.

€750 million alongside a one-time price reduction for Russian gas.[15] In October, Russia imposed new customs regulations as well as trade sanctions on select Ukrainian goods. In a statement, Chancellor Angela Merkel warned Russia against interfering in the affairs of Eastern Partnership countries and pledged solidarity with Ukraine through additional market opportunities for Ukrainian products in case of Russian retaliation.[16]

The Euromaidan Protests

Following an unsuccessful vote in the Ukrainian parliament and a week before the envisaged signing of the Association Agreement, Ukrainian President Yanukovych announced on 28 November in Vilnius that Yulia Tymoshenko would not be released and that Ukraine would not sign the Association Agreement. He instead proposed a joint commission to improve relations between Ukraine, Russia and the EU. Despite the numerous warning signs, Ukraine's withdrawal from the Association Agreement came as surprise to the EU and Germany, as did the subsequent protests that erupted in Kyiv and across the country in reaction to Yanukovych's announcement.[17]

The German government initially adopted a reserved position towards the Euromaidan protests. The new Foreign Minister Frank-Walter Steinmeier, inaugurated on 17 December, rejected a mediator role for Germany in Ukraine, deferring instead to the EU.[18] In a speech, he criticised Russia for exerting pressure on Ukraine, but also the EU for ignoring Ukraine's dependency on Russia.[19] The Coordinator for Intersocietal Cooperation with Russia, Central Asia and the Eastern Partnership Countries, Gernot

---

[15] Cf. Katerina Malygina, *Die Ukraine vor dem EU-Gipfel in Vilnius: Einflussversuche externer Akteure, abrupter Kurswechsel der Regierung und die Volksversammlung zugunsten der europäischen Integration*, Ukraine-Analysen 124 (2013) http://www.laender-analysen.de/ukraine/pdf/UkraineAnalysen124.pdf [accessed 14 April 2019].

[16] Angela Merkel, *Regierungserklärung von Bundeskanzlerin Merkel zum EU-Gipfel "Östliche Partnerschaft" am 28./29. November 2013 in Vilnius, 18. November* (Berlin, 2013) https://archiv.bundesregierung.de/ContentArchiv/DE/Archiv17/Regierungserklaer ung/2013/2013-11-18-merkel-oestl-partnerschaften.html [accessed 9 March 2018].

[17] 'EU-Abkommen mit Ukraine endgültig geplatzt', *Wall Street Journal*, 29 November 2013.

[18] 'Steinmeier lehnt eine Vermittlerrolle ab', *Die Welt*, 19 December 2013.

[19] Cf. Liana Fix and Andrea Gawrich, *Niemiecka polityka zagraniczna a rewolucja na Ukrainie*, Biuletyn Niemiecki 46 (2014) http://fwpn.org.pl/assets/Publikacje/Biuletyn_Niemiecki/2014/BIULETYN_NIEMIECKI_NR_46.pdf [accessed 19 April 2019].

Erler, argued for restraint in Germany's engagement and criticised former Foreign Minister Westerwelle for his surprise visit to Kyiv in the final weeks of his term in office. He also criticised the EU High Representative Catherine Ashton, who attempted to mediate on behalf of the EU between the government and the opposition, as well as for her appearance at the Euromaidan protests, arguing that the EU should avoid being perceived as taking sides.[20] The situation reached its zenith after Yanukovych tightened demonstration laws, leading to violent clashes with dozens of casualties in February 2014. While Germany's position was initially characterised by a reluctance to assume a prominent role, the escalation of the crisis in February 2014 led Germany to step up its presence and resulted in an internationalisation of the conflict.[21]

CRISIS MEDIATION

Conflict Phase I: Mediating in Kyiv

While EU High Representative Catherine Ashton initially lead negotiations in Kyiv between the government and opposition,[22] the outbreak of violence on the Euromaidan on 19/20 February led to the involvement of the Weimar Triangle (Germany, France and Poland) in crisis mediation efforts.[23] The Weimar Triangle format was activated on Germany's initiative for crisis mediation purposes in Ukraine. Foreign Minister Steinmeier proposed a joint trip to Kyiv for 20 February.[24] While Poland immediately supported Germany's initiative, France—traditionally less involved in Eastern affairs than Poland—was convinced by Germany to join efforts during the German-French consultations which took place a few days before in Paris.[25] Although French Foreign Minister

---

[20] Gernot Erler, '"In Sachen Ukraine gibt es in der EU zu viele Fehleinschätzungen": Interview mit Gernot Erler', *Internationale Politik*, 12 December 2013.

[21] Cf. Fix and Kirch, *Germany and the EaP*, 2016.

[22] Damien McElroy, 'Ukraine Opposition Asks EU to Intervene in Talks as Viktor Yanukovych "Wastes Time"', *The Telegraph*, 5 February 2014.

[23] Cf. Dominik P. Jankowski, Tobias Bunde and Martin Michelot, *Reassurance First: Goals for an Ambitious Weimar Triangle*, Center for European Policy Analysis (Washington, DC, 2014) http://cepa.org/index/?id=8f0ba28049c871e3c7f552a32affdbe5 [accessed 9 March 2018].

[24] Interview with former Polish diplomat in Warsaw, 17.05.2016.

[25] Cf. Andreas Rinke, 'Wie Putin Berlin verlor: Moskaus Annexion der Krim hat die deutsche Russland-Politik verändert', *Internationale Politik*, 2014, pp. 33–45.

Laurent Fabius eventually joined the trip to Kyiv, he had a visit to China planned and departed early, leaving the heavy lifting in Kyiv to Germany and Poland.[26] The result of the visit of the three foreign ministers to Kyiv was the brokerage of a deal together with the Russian envoy Vladimir Lukin signed on 21 February between the opposition and Ukrainian President Yanukovych to hold new presidential elections in 2014 as well as to pursue constitutional reforms and initiate an independent investigation into the violence.

Bringing together other member states' foreign ministers for the purpose of assuming a mediation role in the crisis and building a coalition on this issue within the EU added legitimacy and weight to Germany's involvement in crisis mediation and elevated the crisis in Ukraine to a new level of importance: The involvement of the Weimar Triangle signalled that the situation was considered severe enough to require the intervention of member states beyond the engagement of EU High Representative Ashton. Her role was taunted by US Assistant Secretary of State for European and Eurasian Affairs Victoria Nuland, who disparaged the EU as a crisis mediator in a leaked audio of a phone call.[27] Germany thereafter quickly took over the wheel from EU representatives. However, the agreement between the Ukrainian president and the opposition did not last long. The disappearance of President Yanukovych on 22 February in an unclear security situation resulted in an interim government under Arseniy Yatsenyuk, which was not considered legitimate by Russia.[28] Over the following weeks, Russian troop movements in Crimea, the annexation of the peninsula as well as the separatist takeover of cities in Eastern Ukraine made clear that the conflict had changed from a domestic crisis to an interstate conflict between Russia and Ukraine.

[26] Seibel, 'Arduous Learning', 2015, p. 64.

[27] Doina Chiacu and Arshad Mohammad, 'Leaked Audio Reveals Embarrassing U.S. Exchange on Ukraine, EU', *Reuters*, 7 February 2014.

[28] Presidential Executive Office, *Vladimir Putin Answered Journalists' Questions on the Situation in Ukraine, 4 March* (2014) http://en.kremlin.ru/events/president/news/20366 [accessed 10 March 2018].

Conflict Phase II: Building Crisis Mediation Structures

The annexation of Crimea took German officials and policy makers entirely by surprise,[29] although experts from the German Institute for International and Security Affairs, a research institute advising the German government, cautioned against Crimea evolving into a potential new conflict zone following the Russia-Georgia War already in 2008.[30] Unlike Georgia, where secessionist conflicts and conflict management structures have a long pedigree from (post-)Soviet times, Ukraine had not seen secessionist or territorial conflicts prior to Russia's intervention in 2014 and therefore lacked any pre-existing structures and mechanisms. This required the set-up of entirely new crisis mediation and conflict management structures in the following months at the highest international level.

After the formal annexation of Crimea on 18 March by Russia and the outbreak of clashes in Eastern Ukraine, the OSCE turned into the main platform for conflict mediation with significant support from Germany.[31] From the outset, Germany advocated for a strong role for the OSCE and was closely involved in the shuttle diplomacy of the Swiss OSCE chairman Didier Burkhalter for the establishment of an international contact group.[32] Although the idea of a formalised international contact group under the OSCE's leadership never materialised, the Swiss government offered Geneva as a location for an international crisis mediation meeting with Ukraine, Russia, the US and the EU.

In the first round of the Geneva talks on 17 April, the participants agreed on the disarmament of all illegal military formations in Ukraine and their withdrawal from occupied buildings.[33] Yet the agreement was not implemented in the weeks that followed. While Germany was not

---

[29] Interview with German diplomat in Berlin, 09.08.2016.

[30] Cf. Rainer Lindner, 'Die Krim als neuer "Frozen Conflict"?', in *Der bewaffnete Konflikt um Südossetien und internationale Reaktionen*, ed. by Heiko Pleines and Hans-Henning Schröder, Forschungsstelle Osteuropa (Bremen: Forschungsstelle Osteuropa, 2008), pp. 27–28.

[31] Cf. Andrea Gawrich, 'Emerging from the Shadows—The Ukrainian-Russian Crisis and the OSCE's Contribution to the European Security Architecture', *Die Friedens-Warte*, 89.1/2 (2014), 59–80 https://www.jstor.org/stable/24868488 [accessed 19 April 2019].

[32] Cf. Christian Nünlist, 'Testfall Ukraine-Krise: Das Konfliktmanagement der OSZE unter Schweizer Vorsitz', in *Bulletin 2014 zur schweizerischen Sicherheitspolitik*, ed. by Christian Nünlist and Oliver Thränert, Center for Security Studies der ETH Zürich (Zurich, 2014), pp. 35–61 (p. 44).

[33] 'Deal Struck to Calm Ukraine Crisis', *BBC News*, 17 April 2014.

involved in the talks—the EU was represented by High Representative Ashton—Steinmeier participated in talks in Kyiv prior to the Geneva meeting[34] and called for renewed talks after the agreement failed to be implemented.[35] His work behind the scenes to secure a second meeting did not succeed after Russia refused to meet without the participation of the Ukrainian separatists.

Foreign Minister Sergey Lavrov called the Geneva format a closed chapter and criticised the vagueness of the agreement as well as the involvement of the US and the EU in the talks, arguing that the conflict should be negotiated directly between the Ukrainian government and separatists.[36] The Geneva talks remained the only crisis mediation format with the explicit involvement of EU representatives, that is, High Representative Ashton. In the following, the role of EU representatives faded into the background in comparison to the OSCE, partly because the EU was considered by Russia to be a party to the conflict,[37] but also because of the prominent role assumed by member states, especially Germany and France, and the immediate availability of OSCE instruments on the ground, such as contingency plans for the quick deployment of observers.[38]

Germany played an instrumental role for the deployment of an OSCE observer mission, which Steinmeier had already proposed in February during his visit to Moscow.[39] The idea of international observation and mediation and a possible OSCE fact-finding mission was subsequently also supported in the EU Foreign Affairs Council (FAC) conclusions on 3 March as an instrument to facilitate de-escalation.[40] After three weeks of negotiations by the Swiss OSCE chairmanship, an agreement was reached on 21 March on the establishment of an unarmed Special Monitoring Mission in Ukraine, which was later also tasked with monitoring the

[34] 'Kyiv Announces First 'Round Table' Talks, Without Separatists, on Steinmeier Visit', *Deutsche Welle*, 13 May 2014.

[35] 'Ukraine: Germany Calls for Second Geneva Conference', *Deutsche Welle*, 4 May 2014.

[36] 'Lawrow: Nur Kiew und Separatisten können Lösung aushandeln', *Frankfurter Allgemeine Zeitung*, 19 November 2014.

[37] Interview with German diplomat in Berlin, 15.07.2016.

[38] Nünlist, *Testfall*, 2014, p. 50.

[39] Robin Alexander and Daniel F. Sturm, 'Steinmeier begleitet Lawrow nicht mal bis vor die Tür', *Die Welt*, 9 March 2014.

[40] Council of the European Union, Foreign Affairs Council, *Council Conclusions on Ukraine: Foreign Affairs Council Meeting 3 March* (Brussels, 2014) http://www.consilium.europa.eu/media/28853/141291.pdf [accessed 17 March 2019].

implementation of the Minsk agreements.[41] Furthermore, a former German diplomat, Wolfgang Ischinger, assumed the position as the "Representative of the OSCE Chairperson-in-Office for National Dialogue Roundtables in Ukraine", organised in the run-up to the early presidential elections on 25 May.[42] Together with the OSCE, Germany took over as the main actor developing a crisis mediation framework on behalf of the EU and negotiating in the following together with the OSCE ceasefire agreements between the conflict parties.

Conflict Phase III: Negotiating Ceasefire Agreements

The road to the two ceasefire agreements—from the first Minsk agreement on 5 September 2014 to the second agreement on 12 February 2015—was paved by two crisis mediation formats. The Normandy format, consisting of Germany, France, Russia and Ukraine, was born out of situational pragmatism:[43] The first discussions between Merkel, François Hollande, Vladimir Putin and Petro Poroshenko took place at the margins of the 70th anniversary of the Normandy landings in June 2014, and continued with follow-up meetings at the level of heads of state and governments as well as foreign ministers in the following months. Under the auspices of the Normandy format, the OSCE Trilateral Contact Group between Ukraine, Russia and the OSCE, represented by the OSCE Special Representative Heidi Tagliavini, was established.

The Trilateral Contact Group provided a link to the separatists, who attended the meetings, although they were not a formal party to it.[44] The Normandy format and the Trilateral Contact Group facilitated the first

---

[41] Nünlist, *Testfall*, 2014, p. 48.

[42] Interview with former German diplomat in Berlin, 28.08.2016. Heidi Grau, 'The 2014 Swiss OSCE Chairmanship: Between "Routine" and "Crisis"', in *OSCE Yearbook 2014: Yearbook on the Organization for Security and Co-operation in Europe (OSCE)*, ed. by Institute for Peace Research and Security Policy at the University of Hamburg (IFSH), 1st edn (Baden-Baden: Nomos, 2015), pp. 25–40 (p. 30).

[43] Interview with German official in Berlin, 15.07.2016.

[44] Cf. Fred Tanner, 'The OSCE and the Crisis in and around Ukraine: First Lessons for Crisis Management', in *OSCE Yearbook 2015: Yearbook on the Organization for Security and Co-operation in Europe (OSCE)*, ed. by Institute for Peace Research and Security Policy at the University of Hamburg (IFSH), 1st edn (Baden-Baden: Nomos, 2016), pp. 241–50 (p. 245).

ceasefire agreement on 5 September 2014 in Minsk,[45] which was negotiated by OSCE Special Representative Tagliavini after a Ukrainian offensive into Eastern Ukraine was pushed back by Russian forces. The agreement was signed by Russia, Ukraine and the separatists. Yet the ceasefire broke down shortly afterwards, which forced a follow-up memorandum on 19 September, including certain clarifications on the unclear conditions of the 5 September agreement.[46]

Within the Normandy format, Germany assumed a prominent agenda-setting role and gathered the consensual support of the EU and member states behind its crisis mediation efforts. Although EU representatives and institutions did not play a role in the "minilateral format"[47] of the Normandy negotiations, the EU was loosely associated: The European Council in its July 2014 conclusions expressed support from member states for the diplomatic efforts within this format.[48] Germany relied on this association with the EU, which strengthened its own position by having the institutional power and support of the EU behind it. Germany continuously informed access points in EU institutions and member states in bilateral talks about the state of the negotiations.[49] According to Michal Natorski and Karolina Pomorska, this intense "information-sharing practice" contributed to trust building towards the format, reassuring member states that Germany was "acting in good faith".[50] This added legitimacy to Germany's leadership role in crisis mediation, which it assumed without a

---

[45] Organisation for Security and Co-operation in Europe (OSCE), *Protocol on the Results of Consultations of the Trilateral Contact Group, 5 September* (Minsk, 2014) https://www.osce.org/home/123257 [accessed 14 April 2019].

[46] Organisation for Security and Co-operation in Europe (OSCE), *Memorandum of 19 September 2014 Outlining the Parameters for the Implementation of Commitments of the Minsk Protocol of 5 September 2014* (Minsk, 2014) https://www.osce.org/home/123806 [accessed 14 April 2019].

[47] Niklas Helwig, 'Germany in European Diplomacy: Minilateralism as a Tool for Leadership', *German Politics*, 45.1 (2019), 1–17 (p. 10).

[48] European Council, *European Council Conclusions on External Relations (Ukraine and Gaza), 16 July* (Brussels, 2014) https://www.consilium.europa.eu/uedocs/cms_Data/docs/pressdata/en/ec/143990.pdf [accessed 14 April 2019].

[49] Interview with German diplomat in Brussels, 09.03.2016.

[50] Michal Natorski and Karolina Pomorska, 'Trust and Decision-Making in Times of Crisis: The EU's Response to the Events in Ukraine', in *Europe's Hybrid Foreign Policy: The Ukraine-Russia Crisis*, ed. by Mai'a K. Davis Cross and Ireneusz Pawel Karolewski (= *Journal of Common Market Studies*, 55 (2017)), pp. 54–70 (p. 64).

formal mandate, as France had during the Russian-Georgian War through its Council Presidency.

While France was part of the Normandy format from the start, it played a less prominent role than Germany, described by a French official as "leading from behind", with Germany drafting and coordinating the agendas and main talking points.[51] The Normandy format thus reflected the traditional format of the German-French tandem as the "engine" of EU policy formation, yet in a role reversal compared to the Georgia War, with France as junior partner. It is not entirely clear why Poland left the centre stage of crisis mediation after the involvement of the Weimar Triangle mediation; it may be due to Russia's expected opposition or due to concerns about the impact of such a role on its domestic audience.[52] Criticism of the lack of a role for EU institutions and representatives in the Normandy format was voiced for instance by former Polish Foreign Minister Radosław Sikorski, who complained that "on Ukraine, the EU is not even at the negotiating table".[53] For some observers this raised questions of "legitimacy and mandate" of member states,[54] yet this criticism did not affect or initiate a discussion about the composition of the Normandy format in the EU.

Despite the Minsk agreement from September, full-scale fighting in Eastern Ukraine resumed by January 2015. For the second Minsk agreement, the role of the Normandy format was even more important: Merkel, Hollande, Poroshenko and Putin negotiated in a marathon session a "Package of Measures for the Implementation of the Minsk Agreements" which was agreed upon by the representatives of the Trilateral Contact Group on 11 February 2015. The thirteen-point agreement entailed a more detailed and sequenced commitment towards the full implementation of a ceasefire and local elections as well as steps towards

---

[51] Interview with French official in Paris, 23.11.2016.

[52] Cf. Piotr Buras, *Has Germany Sidelined Poland in Ukraine Crisis Negotiations?*, ECFR Commentary (2014) http://www.ecfr.eu/article/commentary_has_germany_sidelined_poland_in_ukraine_crisis_negotiations301 [accessed 10 March 2018].

[53] Radosław Sikorski, 'Member States Must Back Their Jointly Chosen EU Leaders', *Financial Times*, 16 August 2015.

[54] Cf. Kristi Raik, *No Zero-Sum Game among EU Foreign Policy Actors: Germany's Leadership in the Ukraine Crisis has Strengthened the Union*, Comment, Finnish Institute of International Affairs 8/2015 (Helsinki, 2015) https://www.fiia.fi/en/publication/no-zero-sum-game-among-eu-foreign-policy-actors?read [accessed 10 March 2018].

decentralisation.[55] Additionally, the four heads of state and government issued a declaration in support of these measures.[56] Yet shortly after the conclusion, Russian forces regained significant territory in the Battle of Debaltseve and demanded Ukrainian forces surrender, significantly weakening the second Minsk agreement, which remains unfulfilled to this day.[57] In autumn 2016, Foreign Minister Steinmeier in his role as OSCE Chairman at that time proposed a "Steinmeier formula" to solve the problem of sequencing the thirteen points in the second Minsk agreement. Although new Ukrainian President Volodymyr Zelenskyy, elected in April 2019, eventually agreed to the implementation of the Steinmeier formula in principle, no significant steps have been undertaken by the conflict parties towards its implementation, despite progress with regard to prisoner exchanges and humanitarian assistance.[58]

[55] Organisation for Security and Co-operation in Europe (OSCE), *Package of Measures for the Implementation of the Minsk Agreements, 12 February* (Minsk, 2015) https://www.osce.org/cio/140156 [accessed 14 April 2019].

[56] Federal Government of Germany, *Erklärung des Präsidenten der Russischen Föderation, des Präsidenten der Ukraine, des Präsidenten der Französischen Republik und der Bundeskanzlerin der Bundesrepublik Deutschland zur Unterstützung des Maßnahmenpakets zur Umsetzung der Minsker Vereinbarungen angenommen am 12. Februar 2015 in Minsk* (2015) https://www.bundesregierung.de/Content/DE/Pressemitteilungen/BPA/2015/02/2015-02-12-erklaerung-minsk.html [accessed 10 March 2018].

[57] Cf. for critical assessment of the Minsk agreements: International Crisis Group, *The Ukraine Crisis: Risks of Renewed Military Conflict after Minsk II*, Crisis Group Europe Briefing 73 (Kiev, Brussels, 2015) https://www.crisisgroup.org/europe-central-asia/eastern-europe/ukraine/ukraine-crisis-risks-renewed-military-conflict-after-minsk-ii [accessed 10 March 2018]; Balázs Jarábik, *What Did Minsk II Actually Achieve?*, Carnegie Moscow Center (Moscow, 2015) http://carnegie.ru/commentary/59059 [accessed 10 March 2018]; Regina Heller, *Minsk II: neues Spiel, neues Glück?*, Ukraine-Analysen 146 (2015) http://www.laender-analysen.de/ukraine/pdf/UkraineAnalysen146.pdf [accessed 10 March 2018]; Iryna Ivashko and Anton Krut, *Warum sind die Vereinbarungen von Minsk so fragil?*, Ukraine-Analysen 146 (2015) http://www.laender-analysen.de/ukraine/pdf/UkraineAnalysen146.pdf [accessed 14 April 2019]; Stefan Meister, *Warum Minsk II nicht funktionieren wird*, Ukraine-Analysen 146 (2015) http://www.laender-analysen.de/ukraine/pdf/UkraineAnalysen146.pdf [accessed 10 March 2018]; Heiko Pleines, *Trennlinien in der Ostukraine*, Ukraine-Analysen 146 (2015) http://www.laender-analysen.de/ukraine/pdf/UkraineAnalysen146.pdf [accessed 10 March 2018]; Naja Bentzen, *Ukraine and the Minsk II Agreement: On a Frozen Path to Peace?*, Briefing, European Parliamentary Research Service (2016) http://www.europarl.europa.eu/RegData/etudes/BRIE/2016/573951/EPRS_BRI(2016)573951_EN.pdf [accessed 10 March 2018].

[58] Sabine Fischer, *The Donbas Conflict. Opposing Interests and Narratives, Difficult Peace Process*, SWP Research Paper 5 (Berlin, April 2019) https://www.swp-berlin.org/fileadmin/contents/products/research_papers/2019RP05_fhs.pdf [accessed 22 July 2020].

In sum, Germany assumed between 2014 and 2016 a prominent agenda-setting role throughout the negotiation of agreements which was uncontested by other member states, and no alternative crisis mediation claims or proposals were put forward—as in the Russian-Georgian War— despite divergent member states' reactions to the crisis.[59] Germany was able to gather consensual support from member states for its crisis mediation efforts conducted in tandem with France as junior partner, and to build trust and legitimacy for its leadership role. The fact that at the moment when the EU's neighbourhood policy and Russia policy collided, Germany prioritised a common EU stance over its bilateral relations with Russia[60] contributed to "dynamics of mutual trust-building" in the EU.[61] The lack of contestation of Germany's role can also be partly be explained by limited leadership alternatives, given a lengthy transition period after European Parliament elections in May 2014, which created a power vacuum until the appointments of Donald Tusk as European Council President, Jean-Claude Juncker as Commission President and Federica Mogherini as the new High Representative in November 2014.[62] Mogherini adopted a primarily coordinating role but damaged her credibility with a non-paper on Russia, published in January 2015, criticised as being too soft on Russia.[63]

While the institutional power and weight of the EU's backing behind Germany's crisis mediation efforts strengthened its role, this did not correspondingly strengthen the power of the EU as an institution itself: Apart from High Representative Ashton's participation in the Geneva talks, EU representatives remained on the sidelines and were excluded from the main platforms for crisis mediation, in contrast to the OSCE. The US was not part of the Normandy format, but the US established in mid-2015 a bilateral back channel between US and Russian representatives—the Surkov-Nuland talks—to support the Normandy format, however

---

[59] Joerg Forbrig, *A Region Disunited?: Central European Responses to the Russia-Ukraine Crisis*, Europe Policy Paper, The German Marshall Fund of the United States (Washington, DC, 2015) http://www.gmfus.org/publications/region-disunited-central-european-responses-russia-ukraine-crisis [accessed 9 March 2018].

[60] Interview with Polish diplomat in Brussels, 23.03.2016.

[61] Natorski and Pomorska, 'Trust', 2017, p. 62.

[62] Cf. Speck, *German Power*, 2015.

[63] Cf. Kadri Liik, *The Real Problem with Mogherini's Russia*, ECFR Commentary (2015) http://www.ecfr.eu/article/commentary_the_real_problem_with_mogherinis_russia_paper402 [accessed 10 March 2018].

these only played a minor role in crisis mediation efforts.[64] Germany thus not only emerged as the most influential actor within the EU, but in international crisis mediation efforts on the whole.

This dynamic within the EU—with Germany in the lead and France as junior partner—only changed after the election of French President Emmanuel Macron in April 2017. Shortly afterwards, he invited the Russian president to Versailles for their first bilateral meeting. After a steady deterioration of the security situation in Eastern Ukraine in 2018, including an escalation in the Kerch Strait, Macron launched in mid-2019 a new initiative towards Russia, designed to improve bilateral relations and to revive the—by that time dormant—Normandy format.[65] The first meeting of the Normandy format since 2016 took place in Paris in December 2019 with the new Ukrainian President Volodymyr Zelenskyy, yet without concrete results. Despite France's efforts, no progress in conflict mediation has so far been achieved.

SANCTIONS POLICY

In contrast to the Russian-Georgian War, the EU adopted a comprehensive three-tiered sanctions regime in the Russia-Ukraine conflict. These sanctions were put in place in part as reaction to the annexation of Crimea and in part as reaction to the destabilisation in Eastern Ukraine. Throughout the conflict, sanctions were dealt with at the highest political level of heads of state and government and foreign ministers, demonstrating the importance of such decisions for EU and member state policy towards Russia.[66] This analysis will also take into account as contextual

[64] Cf. Vladimir Socor, *Surkov-Nuland Talks on Ukraine: A Nontransparent Channel (Part One)*, Eurasia Daily Monitor, The Jamestown Foundation 103 (Washington, DC, 2016) https://jamestown.org/program/surkov-nuland-talks-on-ukraine-a-nontransparent-channel-part-one/ [accessed 10 March 2018]. From 2017 until 2019, Kurt Volker assumed the role of US special representative for Ukraine negotiations in the Trump administration.

[65] Liana Fix, *Fast Lane to Moscow*, Berlin Policy Journal (Berlin, 2020) https://berlinpolicyjournal.com/fast-lane-to-moscow/ [accessed 22 July 2020].

[66] Specialised media reports, such as Euractiv, EUobserver and the "EuroComment" briefing notes by EU scholar Peter Ludlow, help to gather evidence for the decision-making process in the European Council. The briefing notes "EuroComment" are compiled as extensive commentary on each formal meeting of the European Council since 2002. Cf. Peter Ludlow, http://www.eurocomment.eu/. Cf. Wolfgang Wessels, *The European Council*, The European Union Series (Oxford: Macmillan Education, 2015); Daniel Naurin and Helen Wallace (eds), *Unveiling the Council of the European Union: Games Governments Play in Brussels*, Palgrave Studies in European Union Politics (Basingstoke, New York, NY: Palgrave Macmillan, 2008).

factor US policy including the debates on (military) measures within NATO. Further sanctions beyond the EU-context, such as the G8 suspension or the suspension of Russian voting rights in the Parliamentary Assembly of the Council of Europe, were also adopted (Table 5.1).[67]

Conflict Phase I: Political Sanctions

The first set of restrictive measures against Russian and Crimean officials was instituted against the backdrop of Russia's annexation of the Crimean Peninsula on 18 March 2014. The annexation was an unexpected external shock to the EU and its member states and thereby significantly contributed to the EU policy formation on sanctions. In reaction to the takeover of strategic positions on the Crimean peninsula by Russian forces, a special meeting of EU foreign ministers took place on 3 March.[68] Firstly, the foreign ministers' conclusions framed a common narrative on the interpretation of events as a "clear violation of Ukraine's sovereignty and territorial integrity by acts of aggression by the Russian armed forces". The response thus clearly identified Russia's involvement and responsibility for the proceedings in Crimea. Secondly, the Foreign Affairs Council (FAC) conclusions outlined two possible courses of action: either a negotiated solution of the conflict through a contact group, or "[in] the absence of de-escalating steps by Russia", restrictive measures in the form of a suspension of talks on a new Partnership and Cooperation Agreement with Russia, as well as "further targeted measures". By outlining these courses of action, the FAC was already preparing a roadmap for the European Council meeting on 6 March.

On 5 March on the sidelines of an international meeting on Lebanon, US Secretary of State John Kerry, High Representative Ashton and key

---

[67] Cf. Andrea Gawrich, 'A Bridge with Russia? The Parliamentary Assemblies of the OSCE and of the Council of Europe in the Russia-Ukraine Crisis', in *Parliamentary Diplomacy in European and Global Governance*, ed. by Stelios Stavridis and Davor Jančić, Diplomatic Studies, 13 (Leiden, Boston, MA: Brill, 2017), 156-173.

[68] Council of the European Union, Foreign Affairs Council, *Council Conclusions 3 March*, 2014.

Table 5.1   Overview of sanctions policy towards Russia (2014–2015)

Overview of sanctions policy towards Russia (2014–2015):

EU measures:
• Political sanctions:
   – Negotiations on a new Partnership and Cooperation Agreement and bilateral summits put on hold
   – Asset freezes and travel restrictions for targeted individuals
• Economic sanctions:
   – Limited access to EU primary/secondary capital markets for certain banks and companies
   – Export and import bans on trade in arms
   – Export ban on dual-use goods for military use
   – Denied access to certain sensitive technologies for oil production and exploration
   – Restrictions on economic cooperation (European Bank for Reconstruction and Development, European Investment Bank)
NATO measures:
   – Freezing of working relations in the NATO-Russia Council
   – Establishment of the NATO Very High Readiness Joint Task Force in 2014; Stationing of four rotating NATO battalions in Poland and the Baltic states
Further measures:
   – Suspension of G8 membership
   – Suspension of Russian voting rights in Parliamentary Assembly of the Council of Europe

Source: Author's table, based on: Council of the European Union, *EU Restrictive Measures in Response to the Crisis in Ukraine* (Brussels) <http://www.consilium.europa.eu/en/policies/sanctions/ukraine-crisis/> [accessed 10 March 2018]; North Atlantic Treaty Organization (NATO), *Topics: Relations with Russia* (Brussels, 2019) <https://www.nato.int/cps/en/natolive/topics_50090.htm> [accessed 14 April 2019].

member states attempted to gain Russian Foreign Minister Lavrov's approval for the proposed contact group and a negotiated solution as last diplomatic option before the imposition of sanctions.[69] Yet since no agreement was confirmed by the Russian side at this meeting, the scene was set for EU leaders to decide on restrictive measures at the extraordinary meeting of the Council the following day. The Council meeting initially intended to discuss a two-tiered sanctions regime stopping short of

---

[69] Haroon Siddique and others, 'Ukraine Crisis: Diplomacy Fails to Yield Result as Russia Stays Put in Crimea', *The Guardian*, 5 March 2014.

economic sanctions.[70] However, the incoming news of the decision to bring forward the referendum in Crimea to 16 March presented EU leaders with a fait accompli: The annexation of Crimea was indeed imminent.[71] This created a sense of "urgency" in a crisis "getting worse by the hour".[72] The first draft on restrictive measures was provided by UK Prime Minister David Cameron in a meeting with Tusk, Merkel, Hollande and Matteo Renzi in advance of the Council session, proposing the immediate implementation of stage one of its political sanctions amidst a three-tiered plan for further economic measures.[73] According to Peter Ludlow, Merkel quickly approved of the restrictive measures and contributed additional input, for instance on the need for a dialogue process with Ukraine.[74] Subsequently, the European Council agreed on a three-tiered sanctions regime, including economic sanctions as a last possible option if Russia further escalated the conflict.[75]

As first step, EU leaders suspended bilateral talks with Russia on visa matters as well as on a new Partnership and Cooperation Agreement, and tasked the Foreign Affairs Council to initiate stage two of the sanctions process on 17 March which would include individual travel restrictions.[76] The next meeting of the European Council on 20–21 March would then discuss the possibility of a third stage of economic sanctions and the signing of the political parts of the Association Agreement with Ukraine. The conclusions from 6 March presented a strong and cohesive outcome at a time when the US was still preparing restrictive measures.[77] The

---

[70] Barney Henderson, Arron Merat and David Millward, 'Ukraine Crisis: March 6 as It Happened', *The Telegraph*, 6 March 2014.

[71] Cf. Peter Ludlow, *The Extraordinary European Council of 6 March 2014: The EU Stakes out Its Ground on Ukraine and the Media Do Not Listen*, Preliminary Evaluation (Brussels, 2014), p. 9 http://www.eurocomment.eu/wp-content/uploads/downloads/2014/03/Preliminary-Evaluation-2014.1.pdf [accessed 15 March 2018].

[72] Ludlow, *Extraordinary Council*, 2014, p. 9.

[73] Ibid.

[74] Ibid.

[75] European Council, *Statement of the Heads of State or Government on Ukraine, 6 March* (Brussels, 2014) http://www.consilium.europa.eu/media/29285/141372.pdf [accessed 13 March 2018].

[76] Ibid.

[77] Cf. Simond de Galbert, *A Year of Sanctions against Russia—Now What?: A European Assessment of the Outcome and Future of Russia Sanctions* (Washington DC, Lanham, MD: Rowman & Littlefield, 2015).

conclusions also reaffirmed a common narrative of the conflict as an "unprovoked violation of Ukrainian sovereignty and territorial integrity".[78] Ten days later, in reaction to Crimea's declaration of independence on 16 March, the Foreign Affairs Council on 17 March introduced individual travel restrictions.[79] The next European Council meeting on 20 and 21 March, despite being traditionally a date for discussing economic policy, was also dominated by the conflict in Ukraine and the formal annexation of Crimea on 18 March. The discussions focused mainly on the implementation of the previously agreed list of sanctioned individuals. Invoking historical references and European norms and values, the conclusions of 20 and 21 March described in length this breach of international law as inadequate for the twenty-first century.[80]

When it comes to Germany's role in the sanctions process, both Merkel and Steinmeier were constantly in touch with their Russian counterparts throughout February and March. In particular Merkel's assessment that the Russian president was lying to her about the presence of Russian troops in Crimea and seems to be "in another world", as quoted from her phone conversation with the US president, made global headlines and was regarded as a turning point in the perception of Moscow's intentions.[81] At the Council session, Germany reinforced scepticism with regard to the trustworthiness of the Russian president and underlined the need for solidarity with Ukraine.[82] The fact that Germany was making such an assessment—at the expense of its political and economic relations with Russia—added credibility to Germany's position, advocating for a common sanctions policy.[83] In addition, Merkel and Steinmeier were outspoken in speeches and media appearances about the annexation of Crimea as

---

[78] European Council, *Statement*, 2014.

[79] Council of the European Union, Foreign Affairs Council, *Council Conclusions on Ukraine: Foreign Affairs Council Meeting 17 March* (Brussels, 2014) http://www.consilium.europa.eu/media/28727/141601.pdf [accessed 17 March 2019].

[80] European Council, *EUCO 7/1/14: European Council Conclusions, 20/21 March* (Brussels, 2014) https://www.consilium.europa.eu/media/29198/141749.pdf [accessed 17 March 2018] (p. 14).

[81] Cf. Peter Baker, 'Pressure Rising as Obama Works to Rein in Russia', *The New York Times*, 2 March 2014; Marvin Kalb, *Is Putin "in Another World?"*, The Brookings Institution (2014) https://www.brookings.edu/blog/up-front/2014/03/04/is-putin-in-another-world/ [accessed 15 March 2018].

[82] Ludlow, *Extraordinary Council*, 2014, p. 5.

[83] Cf. Rinke, 'Wie Putin Berlin verlor', 2014.

a clear violation of international law,[84] rejecting alternative interpretations of the situation as a "right to self-determination" by the Crimean people or a "responsibility to protect" the Russian speaking population.[85]

Germany contributed to the establishment of a normative and legalist narrative on the conflict: In a government statement on 13 March, Merkel described the character of the conflict as "a conflict over spheres of influence and territorial claims, as we actually knew them in the nineteenth and twentieth century, a conflict we thought we had overcome". She argues "it remains a breach of international law in central Europe, after which we must not and did not go back to business as usual".[86] The crisis was hence from a German view not primarily perceived as a security threat to Germany itself, but as an unlawful revision of borders—a particularly strong argument in the context of Germany's own history. According to Helene Sjursen and Guri Rosén, this normative force of arguments, especially over a fundamental breach of Ukraine's right to self-determination, played a significant role in the formation of a common EU response on sanctions policy.[87]

EU institutions and representatives, in particular Council President Herman Van Rompuy, played an important role behind the scenes in building consensus among member states on sanctions policy. Van Rompuy designated this particular Council session on 6 March an informal meeting, meaning that EU leaders had no means to consult with their advisors and that the so-called Antici protocols—regular updates to

---

[84] Angela Merkel, Bannas Günter and Berthold Kohler, *Für gemeinsame Werte eintreten: Interview der Frankfurter Allgemeinen Zeitung mit Angel Merkel, 16. Mai* (2014) https://www.bundesregierung.de/Content/DE/Interview/2014/05/2014-05-16-merkel-faz.html [accessed 17 March 2018]; Frank-Walter Steinmeier, *Rede von Außenminister Steinmeier anlässlich der Mitgliederversammlung des Deutsch-Russischen Forums e.V., 19. März* (Berlin, 2014) https://www.auswaertiges-amt.de/de/newsroom/140319-bm-dtrus-forum/260874 [accessed 15 March 2018].

[85] Liana Fix and Evgeniya Bakalova, 'Krise um die Ukraine—Krise internationaler Normen?', in *Ukraine. Krisen. Perspektiven: Interdisziplinäre Betrachtungen eines Landes im Umbruch*, ed. by Evgeniya Bakalova, Tobias Endrich and Khrystyna Shlyakhtovska, Impulse. Studien zu Geschichte, Politik und Gesellschaft, 6 (Berlin: Wissenschaftlicher Verlag Berlin, 2015), pp. 261–83.

[86] Translation by the author. Angela Merkel, *Regierungserklärung von Bundeskanzlerin Merkel, 13. März* (Berlin, 2014) https://www.bundeskanzlerin.de/bkin-de/aktuelles/regierungserklaerung-von-bundeskanzlerin-merkel-443682 [accessed 17 March 2018].

[87] Sjursen and Rosén, 'Arguing Sanctions', 2017, p. 26.

member states' officials during Council meetings—were not recorded.[88] This "mise-en-scène" led to a policy formation process described as a "political pressure cooker" wherein "considerable pressure built up within a confined space amongst a limited number of people".[89] According to Jeffrey Checkel, "more insulated, in-camera" settings are more conducive to suasion in small groups,[90] which is what occurred at this session. While a draft of the Council conclusions was prepared in advance, the passage on restrictive measures had to be decided upon and formulated by EU leaders, contributing to a sense of ownership.[91] In sum, according to Peter Ludlow, "Germany's importance in determining the pace and character of Europe's response (…) was evident before and during both the March Councils".[92] However, the analysis also demonstrated the importance of contextual factors (the annexation of Crimea) and the role of EU representatives (Council President Van Rompuy).

Conflict Phase II: Economic Sanctions

The political sanctions regime was gradually stepped up throughout the following months in light of further external shocks such as the destabilisation in Eastern Ukraine and the kidnapping of OSCE observers, including four Germans. However, Russia's recognition of the election of President Poroshenko in May 2015 was interpreted as a positive sign. It was only on 29 July 2014 that the European Council initiated stage three of the sanctions regime, economic sanctions, after the downing of flight MH17 and further military escalation in Eastern Ukraine. Discussions about whether and when to proceed with economic sanctions were however less consensual than the initiation of political sanctions in March, given that the economic interests of individual member states were affected. In particular, the question of which economic areas to target led to divergent member state preferences.

---

[88] Ludlow, *Extraordinary Council*, 2014, p. 10.

[89] Ibid.

[90] Cf. Jeffrey T. Checkel, 'International Institutions and Socialization in Europe: Introduction and Framework', *International Organization*, 59.04 (2005), 191 (p. 813).

[91] Ludlow, *Extraordinary Council*, 2014, p. 10.

[92] Cf. Peter Ludlow, *The European Council of 20–21 March 2014: The European Semester, Energy Policy, Ukraine and Africa*, Preliminary Evaluation (Brussels, 2014) http://www.eurocomment.eu/preliminary-evaluation-20142/ [accessed 17 March 2018].

In the early stages, Germany was initially reluctant to advocate for economic sanctions, especially given domestic divergences between Merkel's CDU and the SPD of Foreign Minister Steinmeier.[93] However, with the kidnapping of OSCE observers in April, among them four Germans, and the deterioration in Eastern Ukraine, Germany ultimately adopted a supportive stance towards economic sanctions.[94] Together with France, Germany engaged in an agenda-setting role for the introduction of stage-three sanctions. On 27 June 2014, Germany and France presented a draft proposal in close coordination with Ukrainian President Poroshenko to the European Council that called for an immediate move to stage three if certain conditions were not met by the end of June.[95] This draft was blocked, however, by Council President Van Rompuy who did not consider the time to be ripe as consensus on economic sanctions was not yet established.[96] Instead, the conclusions stated the Council would "assess the situation and, should it be required, adopt necessary decisions [and] reconvene at any time for further significant restrictive measures".[97] The Council conclusions therefore stopped short of moving to stage three sanctions. Instead, they focused on increased economic support for Ukraine, coinciding with the signing of the full EU-Ukraine Association Agreement in Brussels.[98]

Given that the conditions outlined in the June Council conclusions were not met by 30 June and further attempts at negotiating a ceasefire were also unsuccessful, a special meeting of the European Council took place on 16 July, at which six further restrictive measures were approved,

---

[93] Cf. Tuomas Forsberg, 'From Ostpolitik to "Frostpolitik"?: Merkel, Putin and German Foreign Policy towards Russia', *International Affairs*, 92.1 (2016), 21–42 https://www. chathamhouse.org/sites/files/chathamhouse/publications/ia/INTA92_1_02_Forsberg. pdf [accessed 18 March 2018].

[94] Seibel, 'Arduous Learning', 2015, p. 64.

[95] Peter Ludlow, *June, July and August 2014: Appointing New Leaders and Dealing with the Ukrainian Crisis*, Preliminary Evaluation (Brussels, 2014), p. 39 http://www.eurocomment.eu/preliminary-evaluation-20144/ [accessed 14 April 2019].

[96] Ibid.

[97] European Council, *EUCO 79/14: European Council Conclusions, 26/27 June* (Brussels, 2014) https://www.consilium.europa.eu/uedocs/cms_Data/docs/pressdata/en/ec/143478.pdf [accessed 17 March 2018] (p. 13).

[98] The political part of the Association Agreement has already been signed before. Cf. Steven Pifer, *Poroshenko Signs EU-Ukraine Association Agreement*, The Brookings Institution (2014) https://www.brookings.edu/blog/up-front/2014/06/27/poroshenko-signs-eu-ukraine-association-agreement/ [accessed 17 March 2018].

including the suspension of cooperation by the European Bank for Reconstruction and Development and the European Investment Bank with Russia.[99] The following day on 17 July, the headlines were dominated by the downing of MH17 over Eastern Ukraine. This event was interpreted by observers as a significant external shock and a game changer for the imposition of economic sanctions:[100] On 22 July, the Foreign Affairs Council asked the Commission and the European External Action Service (EEAS) to finalise the preparations for economic sanctions in four sectors,[101] which were officially enacted on 29 July by a statement in the name of the EU, without further discussion.[102] The contextual factor of the downing of MH17 and especially Russia's response—rejecting any involvement and not permitting access to the crash site in the immediate aftermath—undoubtedly contributed to the swift imposition of sectoral economic sanctions and the establishment of an EU consensus. According to Michał Natorski and Karolina Pomorska, the distrust in the Russian government correspondingly led to an increase in mutual trust and cohesiveness among EU member states.[103]

Against the backdrop of continuous violence and increased Russian troop movements in Eastern Ukraine, the Council meeting on 30 August harshly criticised the "aggression of Russian armed forces on Ukrainian soil" and called on the Commission and the EEAS to present proposals for bolstered economic sanctions within a week.[104] On 5 September, further measures were discussed at EU ambassadorial level, but the implementation was postponed to 8 September, since the first Minsk agreement was

---

[99] European Council, *EUCO 147/14: Special Meeting of the European Council, 16 July* (Brussels, 2014) https://www.consilium.europa.eu/media/25640/143992.pdf [accessed 12 March 2019].

[100] Seibel, 'Arduous Learning', 2015, p. 66; Andreas Rinke, 'Vermitteln, verhandeln, verzweifeln: Wie der Ukraine-Konflikt zur westlich-russischen Dauerkrise wurde', *Internationale Politik*, 2015, pp. 8–21.

[101] Council of the European Union, Foreign Affairs Council, *Press Release, Presse 421, 3330th Council Meeting 22 July* (Brussels, 2014) https://www.consilium.europa.eu/media/25367/144098.pdf [accessed 12 March 2019].

[102] European Council, *EUCO 158/14*, 2014.

[103] Natorski and Pomorska, 'Trust', 2017, p. 57.

[104] European Council, *EUCO 163/14: Special Meeting of the European Council, 30 August* (Brussels, 2014) https://www.consilium.europa.eu/media/25612/144538.pdf [accessed 13 April 2019].

signed under the auspices of the OSCE on the same day.[105] On 8 September, a statement in Van Rompuy's name announced the deepening of existing economic sanctions to take effect "in the next few days" in order to "leave time for an assessment of the implementation of the ceasefire agreement". The statement thus allowed some flexibility in case the situation on the ground improved.[106] Yet, as no improvement on the ground has been reached, the so far strongest economic sanctions package was imposed on Russia on 12 September 2015, together with further measures imposed by the US.[107]

Merkel explained in a speech in the German Bundestag[108] her reasoning behind supporting another economic sanctions package, despite the fact that the ceasefire agreement had been signed. She argued that the violation of Ukraine's territorial integrity and the destabilisation in the East require economic sanctions, but that Germany would be among the first to lift sanctions if the ceasefire agreement were to be fully implemented.[109] Merkel applied primarily normative and legalist arguments regarding the territorial integrity of Ukraine and the necessity to uphold the European security order. She further advocated not to forget the lessons from history, mentioning the anniversaries of the end of WWI, the beginning of WWII and the fall of the Berlin Wall, especially with regard to the violation of borders.[110] Thereby, she once again framed the Russia-Ukraine conflict within a historic dimension explicitly linked to Germany's own historical experience and national identity. This framing of the conflict paradigm as a normative and legalist challenge of historic proportions

[105] Andrei Makhovsky, 'Pro-Russian Rebels Reach Ceasefire Deal', *Reuters*, 5 September 2014.

[106] European Council, *EUCO 179/14: Statement by the President of the European Council Herman Van Rompuy on Further EU Restrictive Measures against Russia, 11 September* (Brussels, 2014) http://www.consilium.europa.eu/uedocs/cms_data/docs/pressdata/en/ec/144867.pdf [accessed 17 March 2018].

[107] Cf. Dan Roberts, 'Sweeping New US and EU Sanctions Target Russia's Banks and Oil Companies', *The Guardian*, 12 September 2014.

[108] Angela Merkel, *Rede von Bundeskanzlerin Merkel vor dem Deutschen Bundestag zum Haushaltsgesetz 2015, 10. September* (Berlin, 2014) https://www.bundesregierung.de/breg-de/service/bulletin/rede-von-bundeskanzlerin-dr-angela-merkel-796638 [accessed 14 April 2019].

[109] Ibid.

[110] Ibid.

added further credibility to Germany's position both domestically and on the European level.[111]

In the following months, due to a lack of progress on the ground, the level of sanctions was upheld and linked to the full implementation of the second Minsk agreement in March 2015, which was signed under the mediation of Germany and France in Minsk in February. This meant that sanctions would only be revoked once the conditions of the second Minsk agreement had been fully met. Again, it was Germany that was setting the agenda and advocated for this linkage of the sanctions regime with the Minsk agreements, for instance during a joint press conference with President Poroshenko in March.[112] Subsequently, the European Council decided that the current level of sanctions would remain in force until all commitments under Minsk II were fully implemented.[113]

In contrast to crisis mediation efforts, EU institutions and representatives played an important role in the preparation and implementation of sanctions,[114] primarily the European Commission and the European Council President Van Rompuy. The European Commission created a sense of shared burden by accounting for the individual interests of member states[115] and distributing fiches with projected affectedness and costs to each member state in advance of the establishment of the final sanctions list.[116] Council President Van Rompuy contributed with his procedural expertise to the "mise-en-scène" and a conducive setting for building consensus among member states. Alongside Germany, France played a supporting role for a common EU sanctions policy, despite French preferential

---

[111] Cf. Marco Siddi, *National Identities and Foreign Policy in the European Union: The Russia Policy of Germany, Poland and Finland* (Colchester: ECPR Press, 2017), pp. 141–43.

[112] Angela Merkel and Petro Poroschenko, *Pressestatements von Bundeskanzlerin Merkel und dem ukrainischen Präsidenten Poroschenko, 16. März* (Berlin, 2015) https://www.bundeskanzlerin.de/Content/DE/Mitschrift/Pressekonferenzen/2015/03/215-03-16-merkel-poroschenko.html [accessed 17 March 2018].

[113] European Council, *EUCO 11/15: European Council Meeting 19 and 20 March* (Brussels, 2015) https://www.consilium.europa.eu/media/21888/european-council-conclusions-19-20-march-2015-en.pdf [accessed 17 March 2018].

[114] Cf. Natorski and Pomorska, 'Trust', 2017.

[115] Cf. Marcin Szczepański, *Economic Impact on the EU of Sanctions over Ukraine Conflict*, Briefing, European Parliamentary Research Service October 2015 (2015), p. 3 http://www.europarl.europa.eu/RegData/etudes/BRIE/2015/569020/EPRS_BRI(2015)569020_EN.pdf [accessed 17 March 2018].

[116] Sjursen and Rosén, 'Arguing Sanctions', 2017, p. 26.

interests in a Mistral warship deal with Russia.[117] Most importantly, however, were Russia's actions in Ukraine, leading to a significant decline in trust not only in Berlin, but among Brussels and member state capitals.

Germany not only supported a three-tiered sanctions regime towards Russia but also assumed an agenda-setting role among member states, advocating for the initiation of the next level of sanctions in reaction to developments in Ukraine. Thereby, Germany exerted a major influence on the formation of EU sanctions policy using instruments such as agenda setting and paradigm framing to contribute to consensus among EU member states on the introduction and reinforcement of sanctions. Particularly noteworthy is Germany's strong emphasis on normative and legalist arguments, thereby advancing a conflict narrative which referred not only to an inter-state conflict between Russia and Ukraine, but to Russia's violation of commonly shared European norms and values.[118] By appealing to norm-guided behaviour instead of individual preferences, Germany's role was perceived as contributing to European "meta-norms" such as "consistency and coherence in policy making" and "joint action as an intrinsic value, including support for functionality and credibility of EU as global actor".[119] This in turn strengthened the legitimacy and credibility of Germany's leadership.

Despite regular rhetorical contestations from member states, the EU's sanctions regime against Russia continued to be extended, with economic sanctions prolonged every six months. Given that the sanctions regime was linked to a full implementation of the Minsk agreements, the lack of progress in conflict resolution gave little leeway for a loosening of sanctions.[120] Furthermore, the EU's sanctions policy was continuously supported by Germany and France. Even in the context of his new Russia initiative, President Macron quickly clarified that lifting sanctions without progress on the ground was very unlikely. In addition, the economies of

---

[117] The Mistral deal was exempted from sanctions due to the exception that existing contracts were not affected. Cf. Sénat, *Les relations avec la Russie. Comment sortir de l'impasse?: Part B. La crise ukrainienne marque un tournant* (Paris, 2015) http://www.senat.fr/rap/r15-021/r15-0212.html [accessed 18 December 2018].

[118] Cf. Siddi, *National Identities*, 2017, pp. 141–43.

[119] Thomas, *Negotiation of EU Foreign Policy*, 2008, p. 8.

[120] Council of the European Union, *EU Restrictive Measures in Response to the Crisis in Ukraine* (Brussels) http://www.consilium.europa.eu/en/policies/sanctions/ukraine-crisis/ [accessed 10 March 2018].

member states and Russia adapted to the fallout of sanctions,[121] which makes the political cost of breaking EU unity, especially against France's and Germany's will, higher than the economic cost of upholding sanctions for member states.

However, Germany's credibility was partially undermined by the decision in 2015 to proceed with the construction of Nord Stream 2, connecting Germany and Russia with a twin pipeline to transport natural gas in addition to the existing Nord Stream pipeline. In June 2015, an agreement was signed between Gazprom, E.ON, Royal Dutch Shell, Engie and OMV. This led to a questioning of Germany's credibility in sanctions policy: Italy delayed the extension of economic sanctions against Russia in December 2015, accusing Germany of double standards.[122] While sanctions were eventually extended, Germany's continuous political backing of the project resulted in divisions among especially Eastern EU member states and with the European Commission. In September 2017, the Commission brought the project under its regulatory rules, supporting the separation of gas ownership from transmission. Despite continuous opposition, Germany granted permission to begin construction at the receiving terminal in Greifswald. Although initially described by the German government as a purely commercial project, Chancellor Merkel acknowledged in April 2018 the risk of bypassing the Ukrainian transit route for the conflict in Eastern Ukraine and supported a Russian-Ukrainian transit agreement. The dispute transcended the European to a transatlantic context when the US approved sanctions against companies and governments working on the pipeline in December 2019, siding with Eastern European member states against Germany.

Conflict Phase III: Military Measures

As a contextual factor, the role of the US including the debate within NATO about military measures will be taken into account as a potential influence on the EU policy formation process. Measures taken or

---

[121] Henry Foy, 'Russia: adapting to sanctions leaves economy in robust health', *Financial Times*, 30 January 2020 https://www.ft.com/content/a9b982e6-169a-11ea-b869-0971bf-fac109 [accessed 22 July 2020].

[122] James Kanter, 'E.U. to Extend Sanctions Against Russia, but Divisions Show', *The New York Times*, 18 December 2015.

discussed within NATO on the initiative of the US were the freezing of working relations in the NATO-Russia Council (NRC), the establishment of the NATO Very High Readiness Joint Task Force and, eventually, the stationing of rotating NATO battalions in Eastern member states.

The suspension of meetings in the NATO-Russia Council was decided upon quickly after the annexation of Crimea and on a consensual basis: In April 2014, NATO members decided to suspend all practical working-level cooperation both civilian and military, arguing that Russia violated among other treaties the NATO-Russia Founding Act.[123] Yet, as lesson learned from the Russian-Georgian War, the suspension did not include the political level, that is, meetings of ambassadors which should "continue as necessary" to keep channels of dialogue open. During the Russian-Georgian War, the opposite was the case, that is, cooperation had been suspended at the political level.[124] Yet in fact, the first meeting of ambassadors reconvened only in 2016.

Furthermore, after the annexation of Crimea, Poland and the Baltic states—supported by the US—argued vehemently for a strengthened NATO presence in their countries as a "tripwire" against a Russian security risk.[125] From a German view, the stationing of permanent NATO troops in Eastern member states would unnecessarily violate the NATO-Russia Founding Act,[126] which from the point of view of Poland and the Baltic states Russia had already been violated with the annexation of Crimea. Despite Polish and Baltic demands, Germany insisted upon the validity of the Founding Act and opposed the stationing of permanent NATO troops.[127] Instead, a compromise was found: The NATO Very High Readiness Joint Task Force (VJTF) was agreed upon at the NATO

[123] North Atlantic Treaty Organization (NATO), *Press Release 062: Statement by NATO Foreign Ministers, 1 April* (Brussels, 2014) https://www.nato.int/cps/en/natohq/news_108501.htm [accessed 14 April 2019].

[124] Interview with German diplomat in Brussels, 08.03.2016.

[125] Cf. 'Trip-Wire Deterrence', *The Economist*, 2 July 2016.

[126] North Atlantic Treaty Organization (NATO), *Founding Act on Mutual Relations, Cooperation and Security between NATO and the Russian Federation* (Paris, 1997) https://www.nato.int/cps/en/natohq/official_texts_25468.htm?selectedLocale=en [accessed 18 March 2018].

[127] 'Merkel Sceptical of NATO Deployments in Eastern Europe', *Euractiv*, 3 July 2014.

Summit in Wales in September 2014, which could be deployed within two days, thereby alleviating the concerns of Eastern NATO member states.[128] As a framework nation, Germany took a leading role in the build-up of the VJTF.[129] Two years later—at the NATO summit in Warsaw in 2016—despite Germany's initial resistance, member states agreed upon the stationing of four NATO battalions in Poland and the Baltic states, yet on a rotational, non-permanent basis in line with the wording of the NATO-Russia Founding Act.[130] This included a German-led battalion in Lithuania.

Last but not least, the question of lethal defensive weapon deliveries to Ukraine was advanced at the beginning of 2015 in particular by the US and through calls of members of Congress to allow Ukraine to better defend itself. In reaction to these demands, Merkel stated publicly that she opposed arming the Ukrainian army against Russian-backed separatists.[131] She reiterated this stance at the Munich Security Conference in February 2015, arguing there was no military solution to the conflict as Russia could always increase its supply of weapons and soldiers.[132] Interestingly, she did not principally question the applicability of military instruments, but argued against the effectiveness of such measures in this specific situation. Heading directly afterwards to Washington, Merkel received support from President Barack Obama for her stance.[133] Germany was hence able to keep the issue of lethal defensive weapon deliveries off the agenda. The

---

[128] North Atlantic Treaty Organization (NATO), *Wales Summit Declaration Issued by the Heads of State and Government Participating in the Meeting of the North Atlantic Council, 5 September* (Wales, 2014) https://www.nato.int/cps/ic/natohq/official_texts_112964.htm [accessed 18 March 2018].

[129] Federal Ministry of Defence, *VJTF—Speerspitze der NATO: Dossier* https://www.bmvg.de/de/themen/dossiers/die-nato-staerke-und-dialog/vjtf-speerspitze-der-nato [accessed 22 April 2019].

[130] North Atlantic Treaty Organization (NATO), *Warsaw Summit Communiqué: Issued by the Heads of State and Government Participating in the Meeting of the North Atlantic Council, 8-9 July* (Warsaw, 2016) https://www.nato.int/cps/en/natohq/official_texts_133169.htm [accessed 18 March 2018].

[131] Spencer Kimball, 'Proposed US Weapons Deliveries to Ukraine Raise Fears of Further Escalation', *Deutsche Welle*, 5 February 2015.

[132] Angela Merkel, *Rede von Bundeskanzlerin Merkel anlässlich der 51. Münchner Sicherheitskonferenz, 7. Februar* (Munich, 2015) https://www.bundesregierung.de/Content/DE/Rede/2015/02/2015-02-07-merkel-sicherheitskonferenz.html [accessed 18 March 2018].

[133] Cf. Michael Kofman and Matthew Rojansky, *U.S. and German Views on Ukraine: The Risks of Trans-Atlantic Misunderstanding*, Friedrich-Ebert-Stiftung Perspective, (Berlin, 2015) https://library.fes.de/pdf-files/id/11456.pdf [accessed 14 April 2019].

fact that Germany secured the support of the US bolstered the perception of Germany's leading role during the conflict. The contextual factor of the US role and the debate within NATO thereby contributed to a strengthening of Germany's leadership role both in Europe as well as across the Atlantic.[134] Germany was able to follow through with its preferences—no violation of the NATO-Russia Founding Act and no lethal weapon deliveries to Ukraine. It is noteworthy that despite its "culture of military restraint"[135] and the formulaic "no military solution", which Germany frequently evoked during the Russia-Ukraine conflict, Germany did engage within NATO in military measures, such as leading the VJTF and later agreeing and contributing to a rotating presence of NATO troops. Yet, preference was given to political and economic measures. This corresponds with a policy of "leading from behind" by the US administration at the time.

After the election of President Donald Trump in 2016, US sanctions policy was expanded in reaction to Russian election interference and detached from the hitherto in lockstep agreed upon EU sanctions regime. In addition, the US Congress passed in December 2019 a sanctions bill related to the construction of the Nord Stream 2 pipeline, which severely strained relations between the US and Germany. Furthermore, the US shifted its policy towards supplying Ukraine with defensive lethal weaponry. This included the sale of Javelin portable anti-tank missiles, to be stored away from the frontline.[136] While Congress and the Trump administration continued to express their commitment to Ukraine's sovereignty and territorial integrity, relations with Ukraine became an issue of toxic domestic debate after the House of Representatives initiated an impeachment inquiry over the White House's withholding of security assistance funds to Ukraine in exchange for compromising information on

[134] Cf. Liana Fix, *Has Germany Led the West's Response toward Russia…and Will It Stay the Course?*, American Institute for Contemporary German Studies (AICGS) (Washington, DC, 2015) https://www.aicgs.org/publication/has-germany-led-the-wests-response-toward-russia [accessed 14 April 2019].

[135] Cf. Rainer Baumann and Gunther Hellmann, 'Germany and the Use of Military Force: 'Total War', the 'Culture of Restraint' and the Quest for Normality', *German Politics*, 10.1 (2010), 61–82.

[136] Cory Welt, *Ukraine: Background, Conflict with Russia, and U.S. Policy*, Congressional Research Service (Washington, DC, 2020) https://fas.org/sgp/crs/row/R45008.pdf [accessed 22 July 2020].

Vice President Joe Biden ahead of the 2020 US elections.[137] US policy shifted from "leading from behind" to a stronger involvement in the conflict, but domestic actors within the US were pulling in different directions, at times even in juxtaposition to Germany's and the EU's approach towards the conflict.

Explaining the Final Outcome

How can Germany's major influence be explained, and what kind of instruments did Germany apply? Do they signify a more assertive German approach in shaping EU policy towards Russia? Which other factors have contributed to this outcome? (Table 5.2)

German Influence

During the Russia-Ukraine conflict, Germany exerted a major influence in both crisis mediation and sanctions policy within the EU. In crisis mediation, Germany was the key actor on behalf of the EU: The mediation of the Weimar Triangle in Kyiv was based on a German initiative. Germany supported the Geneva talks and worked closely together with OSCE mediation efforts including the establishment of a Special Monitoring Mission. Germany was a leading actor in the Normandy format, which together with the Trilateral Contact Group contributed to the conclusion of the first and second Minsk agreements in September 2014 and February 2015. Throughout crisis mediation, Germany used the institutional power instruments of coalition building, agenda setting and access points to influence the final outcome of EU policy.

In sanctions policy, Germany contributed to EU consensus by setting the agenda and advancing a conflict paradigm that was strongly based on normative and legalist arguments, that is, the violation of common European norms and values. On this basis, Germany advocated for norm-guided behaviour and the necessity of sanctions despite economic losses, and was therefore perceived by others as subordinating its own relations with Russia to the greater good. This in turn added legitimacy to Germany's leadership role.[138] Germany's leading role was further

---

[137] Ibid.
[138] Natorski and Pomorska, 'Trust', 2017, p. 62.

Table 5.2 Instruments of power in the Russia–Ukraine conflict

EU policy formation process	Key MS/ EU actors	Contextual variables	Instruments of power applied by Germany			Empirical evidence
			Compulsory power	Institutional power	Productive power	
Crisis mediation						
Conflict Phase I: Weimar Triangle	GER, FR, PL	– Outbreak of violence on Maidan	–	– Coalition building		– German initiative for mediation in Kyiv
Conflict Phase II: Geneva talks and OSCE	GER EU Actors	– Separatist takeovers in Eastern Ukraine	–	– Agenda setting		– Support of Geneva Talks and OSCE conflict mediation
Conflict Phase III: Minsk agreements	GER FR	– Military escalation in Eastern Ukraine	–	– Agenda setting – Access points		– Meetings in Normandy format; information sharing with EU and member states
Sanctions policy						
Conflict Phase I: Political sanctions	GER UK EU Actors	– Crimea annexation	–		– Arguing and suasion – Paradigm framing	– Consensus on economic sanctions – Normative legalist conflict narrative
Conflict Phase II: Economic sanctions	GER FR EU Actors	– Downing of MH17 – Further military escalation	–	– Agenda setting	– Paradigm framing	– Draft proposal on stage three sanctions – Linkage of sanctions to Minsk agreements
Conflict Phase III: Military measures	GER PL Baltic states	– US debate on weapon deliveries – NATO stationing in Eastern MS	–		– Arguing and suasion	– Alignment of US-German positions – Temporary instead of permanent NATO stationing in MS

bolstered by the fact that Germany's positions and preferences were accepted within NATO and by the US.

Germany engaged for the first time in a security crisis with Russia, a policy area in which Germany is traditionally a reluctant actor.[139] With its major influence throughout the Russia-Ukraine conflict, Germany assumed an "informal" Council Presidency role within the EU similar to France during the Russian-Georgian War. The "power of the chair"[140] is therefore not necessarily tied to the formal mandate of a Council Presidency, but also works informally through the weight and legitimacy of the actor assuming the chair.

Alternative Influences I (EU Actors and Member States)

Although France was Germany's closest partner in crisis mediation, it assumed the "back seat"[141] in primarily German-led efforts, for instance in the Normandy format. When it came to economic sanctions, France was more reluctant to approve of stronger sanctions due to French interest in the deal on Mistral warships.[142] France's influence on the EU policy formation process was thus mainly supportive. This resembled a role reversal compared to the Russian-Georgian War, with France as the junior partner in German-led efforts. Only after 2016 and the election of the new Ukrainian president did France assume a more prominent role in crisis mediation efforts.

Poland was involved in the first crisis mediation format—the Weimar Triangle—but left the centre stage of crisis mediation efforts afterwards. Instead, Poland focused on its own security and military reassurances through NATO,[143] similar to the Baltic states. The UK played a role in brokering an agreement in the first conflict phase but did not uphold this involvement throughout the conflict. Although further countries, such as Italy, were questioning the EU's sanctions policy against the backdrop of the construction of Nord Stream 2, the consensus was upheld.

---

[139] Cf. Miskimmon, *Germany and the Common Foreign and Security Policy of the EU*, 2007; Harnisch and Wolf, *Germany's Changing*, 2009; Helwig, *Europe's Engine*, 2016.

[140] Tallberg, 'Power of the Chair', 2010

[141] Interview with French official in Paris, 23.11.2016.

[142] Cf. Sénat, *Relations avec la Russie I*, 2015.

[143] Cf. Grzegorz Gromadzki, *Perception of the Russia-Ukraine Conflict in Germany and in Poland: An Evaluation*, Heinrich Böll Stiftung (Warsaw, 2015), p. 10 https://pl.boell.org/sites/default/files/perception_ru_ua_gromadzki.pdf [accessed 18 March 2018].

In sum, no alternative crisis mediation framework to Germany's had been put forward by other member states, and in contrast to the Russian-Georgian War, the overall policy formation was consensual and exceeded the lowest common denominator. This can also be explained by the strong normative dimension that was prescribed to the conflict by Germany and others. The contextual variables, such as the external shock of the annexation of Crimea, the destabilisation of Eastern Ukraine and the downing of flight MH17, facilitated consensus-building among member states and contributed to the formation of a more cohesive European stance. Germany remained in the lead in crisis mediation from 2014 until 2016. Afterwards, negotiations stalled, and the attempts of President Macron from 2017 onwards to improve relations with Russia and breathe new life into the Normandy format remained unsuccessful.

The role of EU institutions and representatives as alternative influences was varied. In crisis mediation, the lack of a role for EU representatives and institutions was evident: The engagement of the High Representative for instance in Kyiv and during the Geneva talks was quickly taken over by Germany's engagement together with the Weimar Triangle and the Normandy format. The Normandy format was only informally related to EU institutions and representatives through information sharing. The EU was hence not institutionally represented in crisis mediation efforts. In sanctions policy, it was European Council President Van Rompuy and the European Commission who played a greater role behind the scenes by providing information on the fallout of sanctions and maintaining contact with each member state as well as brokering agreements to build consensus.

Having the institutional power of the EU behind its efforts therefore strengthened Germany's role, but the power of the EU as an institution was not strengthened correspondingly. Therefore, according to Jolyon Howorth, "a clear distinction has to be made in terms of the exercise of power, between the EU per se and its Member States. (…) Their impact on major events cannot automatically be credited to the EU itself".[144] He continues that, "even if they ostensibly refer to the European framework (…) the most influential actors during the crisis turned out to be the heads of state or government and the foreign ministers of Germany

---

[144] Jolyon Howorth, "Stability on the Borders': The Ukraine Crisis and the EU's Constrained Policy Towards the Eastern Neighbourhood', in *Europe's Hybrid Foreign Policy: The Ukraine-Russia Crisis*, ed. by Mai'a K. Davis Cross and Ireneusz Pawel Karolewski (= *Journal of Common Market Studies*, 55 (2017)), pp. 121–36 (pp. 121–23).

and France. No EU official—President of the Council, President of the Commission, High Representative—exercised the same degree of influence over events".[145] The EU's role in the conflict is thus not the result of a greater influence of its representatives and institutions, but the result of member states—in particular Germany—wielding institutional power within the EU.

Alternative Influences II (Russia, US, External Shocks)

The EU's policy formation was strongly influenced by external shocks such as the unexpected Euromaidan protests and the outbreak of violence in February 2014, leading to an internationalisation of the conflict and the first crisis mediation efforts. Further external shocks were primarily related to Russia's role in the conflict: The annexation of Crimea, the outbreak of fighting in Eastern Ukraine and the downing of the MH17 were the main factors contributing to the introduction of the sanctions regime. Furthermore, Russia's unconstructive role in the Normandy format and in implementing the Minsk agreements also led to a reinforcement of sanctions. Despite Russian overtures to individual member states,[146] no member state broke EU consensus on sanctions, which demonstrated that the political costs of stepping out of line were judged to be higher than the costs of a continued sanctions policy.

The role of the US as a contextual variable was minor compared to Russia's role, since crisis mediation efforts were primarily outsourced to European actors, in particular Germany. Only by mid-2015 was a bilateral channel introduced to supplement the Normandy format. In sanctions policy, the EU and the US proceeded in lockstep and closely coordinated.[147] On the question of lethal defensive weapon deliveries and the stationing of permanent NATO troops, Germany exerted influence in line with its preferences, agreeing and contributing eventually to a stationing

---

[145] Howorth, 'Stability on the Borders', 2017, pp. 121–23.

[146] Cf. Kadri Liik, *Winning the Normative War with Russia: An EU-Russia Power Audit*, European Council on Foreign Relations (2018) https://www.ecfr.eu/publications/summary/winning_the_normative_war_with_russia_an_eu_russia_power_audit [accessed 14 April 2019]; Mitchell A. Orenstein and R. D. Kelemen, 'Trojan Horses in EU Foreign Policy', in *Europe's Hybrid Foreign Policy: The Ukraine-Russia Crisis*, ed. by Mai'a K. Davis Cross and Ireneusz Pawel Karolewski (= *Journal of Common Market Studies*, 55 (2017)), pp. 87–102.

[147] Cf. Galbert, *Year of Sanctions*, 2015.

of rotating troops in line with the NATO-Russia Founding Act. This changed after 2016, when the Trump administration expanded its sanctions regime towards Russia, including sanctions on Nord Stream 2, and shifted policy towards lethal defensive weapon deliveries. Despite stepping up its involvement under President Trump, US policy towards the conflict remained conflicted due to domestic entanglements.

CONCLUSION: GERMANY AS A LEADING POWER

During the Russia-Ukraine conflict, Germany demonstrated a hitherto unseen leadership role in a crisis situation with Russia, indicating a new German readiness to engage.[148] This leadership role extended beyond the EU-context across the Atlantic. Germany's role is thus often referred to as the height of Germany's influence and one of the most prominent examples of German leadership in Europe.[149] According to a Polish diplomat, Germany underwent a significant development throughout the Russia-Ukraine conflict:[150] From a "watchguard and controller" of the Eastern Partnership, opposing a membership perspective for participating countries, to a "creator" of policy, designing the EU's crisis mediation framework.

Contrary to the fears of Eastern Europeans that an elevated German role in EU Russia policy potentially runs against their interests, the case of the Russia-Ukraine conflict demonstrated that "being an EU leader became more important for Germany than positioning itself as the principled partner of Russia in Europe", according to a Polish diplomat.[151] Although Germany's general position on a membership perspective for Eastern Partnership countries did not change, Germany prioritised crisis mediation in Ukraine over its bilateral relations with Russia and did not shy away from economic sanctions. Thereby, Germany developed a significant cohesive power within the EU and a followership among member states for a policy outcome that exceeded the lowest common denominator, facilitated by the contextual factor of Russia's actions in Crimea and Eastern Ukraine. In particular, Germany's legalist and normative

---

[148] Cf. Jörg Lau and Michael Thumann, 'Tief im Osten, weit voraus', *Zeit Online*, 11 December 2015.

[149] Cf. Bulmer and Paterson (eds), *Germany and the EU*, 2019, p. 231.

[150] Interview with Polish diplomat in Brussels, 23.03.2016.

[151] Ibid.

arguments provided legitimacy and credibility to Germany's role. By appealing to norm-guided behaviour and framing its own preferences as in line with commonly shared norms and values, Germany contributed to the convergence of member state preferences.

In comparison to the August war, the Russia-Ukraine conflict provided less ambiguity about the course of the conflict and Russia's responsibility. The conflict in Ukraine was perceived as a European conflict that was newly created by Russia, out of thin air and without the pedigree from (post-)Soviet times as in Georgia.[152] This contributed to a shift in Germany's Russia policy:[153] It was no longer possible to interpret the conflicts with Georgia and Ukraine as aberrant events unrelated to an otherwise cooperative relationship with Russia. Instead, the Ukraine conflict led to a fundamental reconfiguration of European and Western relations with Russia. Germany contributed to this new paradigm of a genuine caesura in the relationship by framing the conflict as a challenge to European norms and values and evoking historical lessons learned from the twentieth century. Thereby, Berlin steered the EU's Russia policy to be defined primarily through the prism of Ukraine and Russia's actions. This in turn led to a substantial and lasting shift in the EU-Russia relationship: The Ukraine conflict has come to define the paradigm of EU-Russia relations as adversarial instead of based on partnership, which prevented a quick return to business as usual.

Despite this norm-guided approach,[154] Germany continued to support the construction of the Nord Stream 2 pipeline. This controversial project was perceived by some member states as undermining and contradicting Germany's stance towards Russia after 2014 and questioning European solidarity. Nord Stream 2 has become a serious burden for Germany's role in European Russia policy and also for the transatlantic relationship, as the German government underestimated the political and economic fallout of the project.

Furthermore, the lack of conflict resolution in the long term resulted in a partial contestation of Germany's leadership role.[155] After 2016, the situation in Eastern Ukraine steadily deteriorated, with continuous fighting in

---

[152] Interview with German diplomat in Berlin, 09.08.2016.

[153] Ibid.

[154] Cf. Sjursen and Rosén, 'Arguing Sanctions', 2017.

[155] Liana Fix, *Fast Lane to Moscow*, Berlin Policy Journal (Berlin, 2020) https://berlinpolicyjournal.com/fast-lane-to-moscow/ [accessed 22 July 2020].

the Donbas. At the same time, conflict resolution efforts remained stalled, and the Normandy format did not meet on the level of heads of state and government after 2016. Under President Macron, France stepped in with a new initiative to improve relations with Russia. Despite France initiating a Normandy meeting in December 2019 in Paris, its efforts in conflict mediation did not prove successful. At the same time, a deteriorating transatlantic relationship under President Trump's administration led to a decoupling of European and US conflict responses. The politicisation of relations with Ukraine as a US domestic issue complicated a common transatlantic policy towards the Ukraine conflict, thus weakening Germany's leadership role. In sum, the first years of the Russia-Ukraine conflict represented the height of Germany's influence on EU Russia policy. In the end, however, Germany demonstrated how to manage a crisis—based on previous experiences in the Russian-Georgian War—but not how to solve a conflict with Russia.

CHAPTER 6

Conclusion

From Hope to Disillusionment

In April 2001, then-German Chancellor Gerhard Schröder published an article in the German newspaper *Die Zeit* titled "German Russia Policy—European Eastern Policy".[1] He argued that due to its geographic location and history, Germany should assume the role of initiator and motor of the EU's Russia policy. This aspiration for a prominent German role in the EU's Russia policy reflects the decade-old tradition of a special relationship between Germany and Russia as well as Schröder and Russian President Vladimir Putin's "man-to-man" friendship.[2] However, there is more to it: The relations of the last twenty years suggest there is indeed truth in the special role Schröder foresaw for Germany in the EU: Germany

---

[1] Translation by the author. Gerhard Schröder, 'Deutsche Russlandpolitik—europäische Ostpolitik: Gegen Stereotype, für Partnerschaft und Offenheit—eine Positionsbestimmung', *Die Zeit*, 5 April 2001.

[2] Cf. on the German-Russian special relationship: Alexander Rahr, 'Germany and Russia: A Special Relationship', *The Washington Quarterly*, 30.2 (2007), 137–45; Graham Timmins, 'German Ostpolitik under the Red-Green Coalition and EU-Russian Relations', *Debatte: Journal of Contemporary Central and Eastern Europe*, 14.3 (2008), 301–14; Graham Timmins, 'German–Russian Bilateral Relations and EU Policy on Russia: Between Normalisation and the "Multilateral Reflex"', *Journal of Contemporary European Studies*, 19.2 (2011), 189–99.

© The Author(s), under exclusive license to Springer Nature Switzerland AG 2021
L. Fix, *Germany's Role in European Russia Policy*, New Perspectives in German Political Studies,
https://doi.org/10.1007/978-3-030-68226-2_6

assumed a preeminent role and significantly shaped the EU's Russia policy after the EU's Eastern enlargement in 2004—partly along, partly against the interests of new Eastern member states.

Regardless of its successes or failures, Germany continuously attempted to shape the EU's Russia policy in a more diverse playing field of actors after the enlargement in 2004. Even if it was not in the front row of proceedings such as in Georgia 2008, Germany remained the most consistently engaged actor initiating policies and shaping the paradigm of EU-Russia relations: From "more, not less" cooperation with Russia after the low point of the August War in 2008 to the modernisation enthusiasm of the Medvedev era, EU Russia policy has broadly corresponded with the trajectory of Germany's Russia policy. However, Germany's role in EU Russia policy was more nuanced than a mere "hegemonic leadership"[3] or "geo-economic power":[4] Germany's approach represents a more complex and nuanced "Machtpolitik" (power politics) including different conceptualisations and "shades" of power[5] and was subjected to the same constraints of policy making in a European Union "designed consciously and conspicuously to prevent the concentration of power"[6] just like any other member state.

The deterioration of relations, culminating in the Russia-Ukraine conflict, was a major disillusionment for German policy makers. Whereas Eastern European member states were drawing a direct line from the Russian-Georgian War to the Russia-Ukraine conflict, this line was for German policy makers neither immediately evident nor predetermined. According to a German diplomat, drawing a line in hindsight constitutes an "ahistorical" understanding.[7] The question of which direction Russia would take in the future was for German policy makers still open-ended in 2008, and could thus be positively affected—towards a relationship with Russia based on cooperation and mutual trust. This is why Germany

---

[3] Marco Siddi, 'A Contested Hegemon?: Germany's Leadership in EU Relations with Russia', *German Politics*, 94 (2018), 1–18; Simon Bulmer and William E. Paterson (eds), *Germany and the European Union: Europe's Reluctant Hegemon?*, The European Union Series, 1st edn (Oxford: Macmillan Education, 2019).

[4] Stephen F. Szabo, *Germany, Russia and the Rise of Geo-Economics*, 1st edn (London: Bloomsbury, 2015).

[5] Liana Fix, 'The Different "Shades" of German Power: Germany and EU Foreign Policy during the Ukraine Conflict', in *Germany's Eastern Challenge: A 'Hybrid Ostpolitik' in the Making?*, ed. by Patricia Daehnhardt and Vladimír Handl (= *German Politics*, 27 (2018)), pp. 498–515.

[6] Della Sala, *Leaders and Followers*, 2012, p. 307.

[7] Interview with German diplomat in Berlin, 09.08.2016.

engaged extensively in new policy initiatives towards Russia: in order to avoid missing out on an opportunity for a better future relationship. This hope ended, however, at latest in 2014 in bitter disappointment.[8] The Ukraine conflict was the culmination of a long-term crisis in EU-Russia relations,[9] but also the end of a long-term German attempt to shape the EU's Russia policy towards a cooperative relationship, with a different outcome than expected.

Berlin was continuously embedding its Russia policy in a European dimension, for instance with the Modernisation Partnership or the Meseberg initiative. However, this should not be accredited to a "multi-lateral reflex"[10] in Germany's foreign policy: Instead, it represented a conscious effort of exerting influence and steering EU Russia policy towards a direction that conformed with Germany's preferences and flowed naturally from Germany's understanding of its leading role in EU Russia policy. From a German viewpoint, initiatives such as the Modernisation Partnership represented a "Europeanization" of Germany's Russia policy.[11] In a long-term perspective, Germany's continuous attempts at shaping EU Russia policy could also be described as a "Germanification" rather than a "Europeanization" of Russia policy.[12]

At the same time, Germany continued to keep certain policy areas with Russia firmly on a bilateral track, especially the construction of the Nord Stream 2 pipeline. This controversial project was perceived by some member states as undermining and contradicting Germany's stance towards Russia after 2014 and questioned European solidarity. Germany was criticised as disregarding the concerns of Eastern European members, who doubted the economic necessity of the project and warned against the geopolitical consequences of circumventing Ukraine in the process. Initially described by the German government as a purely commercial project, Chancellor Angela Merkel implicitly acknowledged in April 2018 the

---

[8] Cf. Forsberg, 'From Ostpolitik to 'Frostpolitik'', 2016.

[9] Cf. Haukkala, 'Conflict in Ukraine', 2015.

[10] Graham Timmins, 'German–Russian Bilateral Relations and EU Policy on Russia: Between Normalisation and the "Multilateral Reflex"', *Journal of Contemporary European Studies*, 19.2 (2011), 189–99.

[11] Manfred Huterer, 'Strategie ist möglich: Diplomat Huterer über Deutschlands Ostpolitik', in *Zeit im Spiegel: Das Jahrhundert der Osteuropaforschung*, ed. by Manfred Sapper and Volker Weichsel (= *Osteuropa*, 2-3 (2013)), pp. 269–76 (p. 270).

[12] Fix, 'Different 'Shades'', 2018.

destabilising effects of bypassing the Ukrainian transit route and advocated for a Russian-Ukrainian transit agreement.

Nord Stream 2 represents the only bilateral policy with Russia that was "Europeanized" not by Germany, but against Germany's wish. It was put on the European agenda by member states and the European Commission, which brought the project in September 2017 under its regulatory rules and thereby made it part of the EU's Russia policy. The dispute transcended the European to a transatlantic context when the US approved sanctions against companies and governments working on the pipeline in December 2019. Nord Stream 2 has become a serious burden for Germany's role in European Russia policy and also for the transatlantic relationship, since the German government initially underestimated the political and economic fallout of the project. The attempt to separate political from energy relations—based on Cold War experiences that energy relations with the Soviet Union remained reliable throughout crises—proved unrealistic in times of weaponised interdependence.

What were other misjudgements in Germany's Russia policy—or put differently, what did other actors including Eastern Europeans perhaps understand better about Russia—and which elements of Germany's Russia approach proved wise in hindsight? Firstly, German policy makers underestimated Russian domestic politics and Russia's increasingly authoritarian trajectory before and after the return of Vladimir Putin to the presidency in 2012, although the issue was addressed prominently for instance by the German Green Party. The Modernisation Partnership demonstrated that German policy makers hoped to contribute to a transformation and societal liberalisation in Russia, based on the lessons of "Ostpolitik" and the "change through trade" approach that proved successful in Cold War times. This represented a significant overestimation of Germany's leverage and a misjudgement of the preferences of the Russian elite and leadership, interested primarily in consolidating their domestic hold on power through economic opportunities within the Modernisation Partnership. At the same time, Germany also underestimated Russia's claim to a sphere of influence in the neighbourhood—with Eastern Europeans much more clear-eyed in light of their historical experiences—and overestimated both Russia's wish for a cooperative security relationship as well as its willingness to solve protracted conflicts in the neighbourhood, for instance in Transnistria. From a Russian perspective, this conflict represented a valuable instrument of influence in the neighbourhood. To give it up, equally significant concessions would have been necessary from Europeans to manifest Russia's predominance in the neighbourhood. This was principally inacceptable for Germany and Europe. Russia thus maintains this conflict and when necessary, creates new ones, such as in Eastern Ukraine, to increase its leverage on European security.

Germany's guiding principle towards Russia, despite the setback of the Georgia War, remained for many years "more, not less cooperation". In contrast, Eastern European member states argued that this approach might be perceived as weakness by the Russian side and could embolden Russia to take further actions. Their guiding principle can be summarised as hoping for the best, but expecting the worst, in contrast to Germany's approach of expecting the best and hoping the worst will not materialise. What proved wise in hindsight was Germany's approach to form a common position towards Russia and level out differences among member states—especially with Poland in the so-called Weimar Triangle alongside France—in the years from 2010 to 2012. While this was only partially fruitful, it prevented Russia from adopting a divide and rule approach, especially in the Ukraine conflict. In addition, Germany's tough stance towards Russia on sanctions gained credibility by having all of the EU behind it.

Russia's actions in Ukraine led to a more realistic German assessment of Russian interests which shifted closer to the position of Eastern Europeans. At the time, Eastern Europeans were no longer the "Cassandras"[13] in European Russia policy, but the realists. This triggered a soul-searching among German diplomats: Why did it all go wrong, despite Germany's best intentions? What was overlooked, where could one have acted differently?[14] Germany has to be credited for using every room for manoeuvre to influence the relationship with Russia for the better. At least, from a German perspective, there was no remorse about not having tried hard enough, given that Germany had done more than any other member state to advance a cooperative relationship with Russia—regardless of the sobering outcome.

Although German domestic dynamics were not included in this research, it is worth noting the duality in approaches of the Foreign

---

[13] Interview with former Polish diplomat in Warsaw, 17.05.2016.
[14] Interview with German diplomat in Warsaw, 20.05.2016.

Ministry and the Chancellery, led by the respective coalition partners SPD and CDU: During the first (2005–2009) and second Grand Coalition (2013–2017), Foreign Minister Frank-Walter Steinmeier of the Social Democratic Party (SPD) alongside Chancellor Merkel and the Christian Democratic Union (CDU) presented different emphases in policy making. While the Modernisation Partnership was an initiative from the Foreign Ministry, the Meseberg initiative was conceptualised in the Chancellery, resulting in two different approaches in designing a policy initiative and initiating it within the EU. Furthermore, slightly divergent approaches could be observed between both institutions and party representatives in the Russian-Georgian War and the Russia-Ukraine conflict.[15] The approach of the Chancellery and the CDU has been described as tougher towards Russia than that of the SPD and the Foreign Office.[16]

European-Russian and German-Russian relations remained stalled after the outbreak of the Ukraine conflict in 2014. Despite attempts by the new French President Emanuel Macron to breathe new life into the relationship with Russia, it has remained a Gordian knot and dominated from a German perspective by sanctions policy on the one hand and Nord Stream 2 on the other hand. In addition, concerns about Russian interference in European elections, cyber attacks as well as contract killings led to a further deterioration of the relationship. With a broader geopolitical shift underway towards an exacerbating US-China rivalry, relations with Russia have also escaped the European and Transatlantic contexts and are increasingly seen within a broader framework of relations with China.[17] Germany's axiom that dialogue with Russia is necessary on all global issues remains relevant, yet it should be complemented with an Eastern European caveat: That dialogue needs to come from a position of strength and not from weakness.

[15] Cf. Siddi, 'German Foreign Policy', 2016.
[16] Cf. Meister, 'Entfremdete Partner', 2012.
[17] Liana Fix, 'Überholspur nach Moskau', *Internationale Politik*, March/April 2020, pp. 52-55.
Cf. Fix and Kirch, *Germany and the EaP*, 2016.

POLICY INITIATIVES AND CRISIS MEDIATION

What lessons can be drawn from comparing the four case studies of EU Russia policy for the question of Germany's power exertion in Europe? Which patterns are observable that might explain why Germany was influential in the EU's Russia policy in some cases and not in others? The development of the EU's Russia policy and Germany's role demonstrate that Germany's influence was more nuanced and complex than the claim of a hegemonic German role in EU Russia policy would suggest. It included cases of minor as well as major German influence, changing contextual circumstances—especially Russia's domestic developments and resulting foreign policy—and shifting positions, coalitions and role reversals among member states and in Brussels. The EU's Russia policy was constantly in flux and shaping as well as being shaped by various actors' positions and preferences, leading to outcomes as diverse as the EU-Russia Partnership for Modernisation on the one hand and EU sanctions policy in the Ukraine conflict on the other, all within a few short years.

Crisis Situations

In crisis situations, the Russian-Georgian War and the Russia-Ukraine conflict demonstrate two very different German approaches. While Germany acted as junior partner and exerted a minor influence in 2008, it assumed a leading role and exerted a major influence in 2014. Rather than Germany, it was France that assumed a leadership role during the Georgia War when it held the EU Council Presidency. While Germany supported French crisis mediation efforts, it was not in the front row and lacked instruments of institutional power that France had including the legitimising effects of the presidency. Yet Germany still exerted some influence by signalling opposition to further reaching sanctions proposals discussed within the EU and NATO. Thereby, Germany set the boundaries for a—from a German perspective—"pragmatic" response against more forward-leaning member states. Despite an overall minor influence, Germany applied instruments of compulsory power to set these boundaries and to ensure an overlap with German positions and preferences. This approach was also reflected in Germany's opposition to a NATO Membership Action Plan for Georgia. The outcome of the EU's policy represented only the lowest common denominator and EU-Russia relations quickly returned to business as usual without a substantial shift in policy, quite the opposite: The German credo of more, not less cooperation also became the EU's policy in the following years.

In contrast, the Russia-Ukraine conflict demonstrated the height of German influence on EU Russia policy. For the first time, Germany embraced a leading role in a security crisis with Russia, now in a role reversal with France as junior partner. This demonstrated that influence is not necessarily tied to a formal mandate such as the Council Presidency but can also be assumed by an actor without an institutional role. Germany's leadership resulted in a greater cohesive power than France's in 2008, keeping the EU united on sanctions and crisis mediation, triggered by Russia's behaviour in Ukraine. As a result, the EU's response exceeded the lowest common denominator. However, this major German influence was not the result of compulsory power. On the contrary, Germany relied on institutional and productive power instruments to establish a common European stance through agenda setting, coalition building and paradigm framing. The Russia-Ukraine conflict demonstrated the potential of German power, but also the relevance of legitimacy for a leadership role. Of particular importance to other members was the perception of norm-guided German behaviour: By prioritising crisis mediation over bilateral relations with Russia, Germany was perceived as a legitimate leader in a crisis that represented a caesura in the EU-Russian relationship without a quick return to business as usual. Despite this success, Germany's continuous support for Nord Stream 2 undermined its credibility in the years to come.

The overlap of German domestic actors in 2008 and 2014—Chancellor Merkel and Foreign Minister Steinmeier in a grand coalition—suggests a "learning curve"[18] for Germany from the Russian-Georgian War to the Russia-Ukraine conflict on how to shape an EU crisis response. An example for a lesson learned in crisis mediation is the suspension of working level cooperation in the NATO-Russia Council in the Ukraine conflict, whereas the political level—exchanges on ambassadorial level—was upheld. This is a lesson learned from 2008, when working level cooperation was continued, but political cooperation suspended, leading to criticism about the lack of dialogue channels with the Russian side.

---

[18] Interview with Polish diplomat in Brussels, 23.3.2016.

Policy Initiatives

Although both were initiated by Germany, the EU-Russia Partnership for Modernisation and the Meseberg initiative yielded two different outcomes: The EU assumed full ownership of the idea of a modernisation policy and developed its own Partnership for Modernisation followed by bilateral agreements between member states and Russia. In the case of the Meseberg initiative, the EU refused to assume ownership and remained sceptical of the Meseberg memorandum. The Meseberg initiative represented a minor German influence, in contrast to the EU-Russia Partnership for Modernisation. Germany used the window of opportunity under newly elected President Medvedev to set the agenda at an early stage, and successfully advanced the modernisation paradigm to become EU policy. The modernisation paradigm was based on German "Ostpolitik" (Eastern policy) assumptions that Russia could be transformed into a more democratic actor through increased economic interaction. Germany's approach was perceived as a case of constructive bilateralism. Although the modernisation policy lost relevance after President Putin's return to power in 2012, it played a crucial role in defining the EU-Russia relationship during the Medvedev period.

The Meseberg initiative demonstrated the limits of a more assertive approach: Germany was criticised for its bilateral deal-making with Russia without the institutional support of the EU, which was reluctant to assume ownership. Germany concluded a bilateral memorandum on behalf of the EU, encouraged by the context of a seemingly reform-minded Russia and a pro-European government in Moldova. This demonstrated Germany's confidence that it could grasp an opportunity for a win-win situation: solving a conflict in the neighbourhood and proving Russia can be a constructive actor. Germany applied a more assertive approach by linking the issues of conflict resolution and EU-Russia security cooperation as incentives for a joint settlement. The Meseberg initiative was the most ambitious German policy initiative in the area of security policy with Russia. However, it became a case of only minor German influence on EU policy: Neither was the initiative implemented by the EU, nor was the conflict in Transnistria resolved. Instead of advancing the EU-Russia relationship, the initiative contributed to a deterioration and frustration on both sides—a harbinger of the disillusionment to come.

In comparison, Germany's more assertive approach in the Meseberg initiative proved less successful than Germany's more inclusive approach in the EU-Russia modernisation policy. The same applies to crisis situations, where the use of institutional and productive power instruments during the Ukraine conflict proved more successful for a united and common EU response to the crisis than Germany's approach of setting the boundaries in the Georgia War. This suggests that in order for Germany to gain support for its positions and preferences in Russia policy among other member states and EU representatives and institutions, a more inclusive approach and the use of diffuse and indirect instruments of institutional and productive power proved more successful. In contrast, Germany's assertive approach in the Meseberg initiative was met with scepticism by Europeans and led to a reluctance to endorse the initiative. Experimenting with instruments of compulsory power, especially in the area of security policy, can therefore backfire rather than result in more influence.

In all four cases, institutional and productive power instruments were most often chosen as avenues to influence the EU's policy formation towards Russia—demonstrating continuity in the key facets of Germany's European diplomacy,[19] namely the exertion of "soft" or "indirect institutional power" within the EU.[20] However, Germany's readiness to use compulsory power instruments, such as setting the boundaries in the Russian-Georgian War and its "deal-making" in the Meseberg initiative, indicates a willingness to choose from the full menu of available options, including more assertive power instruments, to influence EU policy. This corresponds with the state of research on Germany's European policy, which notes a shift to a more self-confident German approach including a greater willingness to influence EU policy for its own national interests. In Russia policy, more assertive instruments have not become the primary instruments of Germany's power exertion, but Germany's readiness to apply such instruments confirms the proposition that Germany has become a "normalized power"[21] within the European Union (Table 6.1).

The main hypothesis of this study (H1) suggested that *Germany was influential in the formation of the EU's Russia policy after the EU's Eastern*

---

[19] Simon Bulmer, Charlie Jeffery and William E. Paterson, *Germany's European Diplomacy: Shaping the Regional Milieu*, Issues in German Politics (Manchester: Manchester University Press, 2000).

[20] Cf. Katzenstein, 'United Germany', 1997; Anderson, *Hard Interests*, 1997; Bulmer, Jeffery and Paterson, *Germany's European Diplomacy*, 2000.

[21] Bulmer and Paterson, 'Normalized Power', 2010.

Table 6.1 Summary of cases and instruments

Case studies	Instruments of power applied by Germany			German influence
	Compulsory	Institutional	Productive	
Russian-Georgian War 2008	X	X	X	Minor German influence
EU-Russia Partnership for Modernisation 2010		X	X	Major German influence
Meseberg initiative 2010	X	X	X	Minor German influence
Russia-Ukraine conflict 2014		X	X	Major German influence

Source: Author's table

enlargement through the use of instruments of compulsory power, indicating a more assertive German approach. Moreover, the analysis expected *a greater German willingness to engage in security policy and crisis situations with Russia,* and *a correlation between the contexts of policy formation, that is crisis situations and policy initiatives, and the use of certain instruments of power.*

The results of the case studies do not confirm these hypotheses. To the contrary, the use of compulsory power instruments in some cases did not result in a major influence on the EU's policy in these cases. Germany exerted a major influence in the EU's policy formation primarily when applying instruments of institutional and productive power instead of instruments of compulsory power. Put differently: The use of instruments of compulsory power does not necessarily beget major influence. Furthermore, with regard to the sub-hypotheses, the analysis demonstrated indeed a greater willingness to engage in crisis situations with Russia as well as in security policy, demonstrated by the Meseberg initiative and culminating in the Ukraine conflict. However, a correlation of crisis situations and policy initiatives and the use of respective instruments could not be confirmed. As evidenced, the use of specific instruments does not depend on the character of the case.

The most important factor influencing EU Russia policy next to Germany was Russia itself. Firstly, Russia contributed to the outbreak of the two crises in Georgia and Ukraine. Its subsequent actions—hesitating to withdraw Russian troops from Georgia proper as well as escalating the conflict in Eastern Ukraine—significantly shaped member states' positions and the EU response overall. In policy initiatives, Russia on the one hand advanced the modernisation policy by providing templates to EU member states, on the other hand it impeded the implementation of the Meseberg memorandum with its reluctance to take further steps in conflict resolution efforts. Thereby, Russia's actions or non-actions in crises and policies enabled or constrained the influence Germany was able to exert on the EU's Russia policy. The US and NATO played a primarily contextual role in EU Russia policy, such as the NATO Bucharest decision in 2008 and the push for stronger sanctions, the US-Russian reset and the initial lockstep in sanctions policy and military measures in the Ukraine conflict. Another significant intervention by the US was the approval of sanctions against Nord Stream 2.

Among member states, France and Poland played the most prominent roles: France in the traditional tandem with Germany and Poland as a representative of the more Russia-sceptical Eastern member states. Despite the Eastern members' occasional opposition and often reluctance towards German- or French-driven Russia policy, they were seldom able to hinder or exert a major influence on the final outcome of EU policy, at times also going along with initiatives such as the Modernisation Partnerships or acting together with Germany during the Ukraine conflict. The accession of new Eastern member states after the enlargement of 2004 made Germany's attempts at shaping EU Russia policy certainly more complicated but did not necessarily block or overturn these attempts. An exception was Poland's 2006 veto on talks for a new EU-Russia Partnership and Cooperation Agreement unless Russia lifted the ban on Polish meat, which caused criticism rather than solidarity among other member states. According to an Estonian diplomat, it is not easy to "veto Germany", especially when EU unity is perceived as a value in itself.[22] Brussels on the one hand did adopt policy initiatives inspired by Germany, such as the modernisation policy. On the other hand, it partially constrained Germany's exertion of power in the Meseberg initiative, when the reluctance to assume ownership by the High Representative further complicated the implementation of the memorandum. In crisis situations, EU institutions and representatives were most often put in the back seat by member states. However, having the EU behind their policies and using

---

[22] Interview with Estonian diplomat in Berlin, 17.08.2016.

it as a multiplier of influence provided additional weight to member states' efforts, even if not empowering the EU itself.

BETWEEN LEADERSHIP AND HEGEMONY

The innovative methodological contribution of this study was the application of a theoretically-grounded taxonomy of power to the analysis of member states' influence in the EU. This approach assumed firstly, that power is a necessary concept for the EU, and secondly, that power has been tamed but not transcended in the EU,[23] even if there are "no agreed definitions of the forms of influence—or power—available (...) and the ways that these are exercised".[24] Power is per se a difficult framework for analysis considering the epistemological challenges that lead many observers to begin with the caveat that power is an "essentially contested concept".[25] Applying the taxonomy of Barnett and Duvall made use of an existing power-theoretical framework from International Relations for the analysis of EU policy formation. This taxonomy is not a priori excluding a certain form of power but instead includes different conceptualisations. As Vincent Della Sala argues, while realist and intergovernmental approaches suggest member states' influence "would be largely determined by the material resources" they bring to the table, there are "other resources that may affect the capacity of states to influence others that are not necessarily related to size or material resources": influence can also result from the "framing of policy questions, the setting of agendas, and diplomacy" as well as "institutional capacity".[26] These different forms are reflected in the operationalisation of the taxonomy of Barnett and Duvall. Further research focusing on power in the EU and the application of power concepts from International Relations—from (neo-)realist to constructivist notions—could be useful if adapted to the specific EU policy context. Ultimately, this poses the question whether a specific conceptualisation of power is needed for European Studies.

---

[23] Magnette, Bunse and Nicolaïdis, *Big vs Small*, 2007, p. 134.

[24] Wallace, *Exercising Power*, 2005, p. 36.

[25] Cf. Janice B. Mattern, 'The Concept of Power and the (Un)Discipline of International Relations', in *The Oxford Handbook of International Relations*, ed. by Christian Reus-Smit and Duncan Snidal, Oxford Handbooks of Political Science (Oxford, New York, NY: Oxford University Press, 2008), pp. 691–98, Forsberg, 'Power in International Relations', 2014, p. 211; Berenskoetter, *Thinking about Power*, 2007, p. 2.

[26] Della Sala, *Leaders and Followers*, 2012, p. 314-315.

Based on this power-theoretical analysis, where is Germany's power projection in the EU's Russia policy conceptually situated between leadership and hegemony? The research on leadership within the EU has seen numerous new contributions addressing Germany's leadership role, often reflecting Oran Young's categories of leadership.[27] Some of this literature employs role theory to explain temporary, functional and social leadership roles in the EU. According to Lisbeth Aggestam, the "German political elite is engaged in a process of 'role making' as it responds to both profound geostrategic shifts in its external environment, and the role expectations of others".[28] Leadership is implicitly connected to the concepts of power and influence. According to Arild Underdahl, leadership should be defined as a subcategory of influence, in which one actor "directs the behaviour of others towards a certain goal over a certain period of time" to overcome "collective action problems".[29] While this adequately reflects Germany's role in the Ukraine conflict, influence can also be exercised without a leadership role, such as by Germany in the Russian-Georgian War. Furthermore, the literature on temporary, functional and social leadership roles has difficulties to account for and explain a long-term exertion of influence by a member state in a certain policy area, such as Germany's continuous attempts at influencing EU Russia policy. Hegemony, on the other hand, as defined by Charles Kindleberger,[30] does not fit the case either, given the inherent constraints of EU policy making.[31]

Taking the example of EU Russia policy, this study suggests that Germany's continuous attempts of power projection can be more adequately conceptualised by the term *policy dominance* rather

[27] Cf. Harnisch and Schild (eds), *Deutsche Außenpolitik*, 2014; Harnisch, *Myth of German Hegemony*, 2017; Aggestam, *European Foreign Policy*, 2017; Aggestam and Johansson, 'Leadership Paradox', 2017; Oran Young, 'Political leadership and regime formation: On the development of institutions in international society', *International Organization*, 45.3 (1991), 281–308, p. 303.

[28] Lisbeth Aggestam and Adrian Hyde-Price, 'Learning to Lead? Germany and the Leadership Paradox in EU Foreign Policy', *German Politics*, 29.1 (2020), 8-24.

[29] Arild Underdal, 'Leadership Theory: Rediscovering the Arts of Management', in *International Multilateral Negotiation*, ed. by Zartman, 178–97.

[30] Cf. Charles P. Kindleberger, 'Dominance and Leadership in the International Economy: Exploitation, Public Goods, and Free Rides', *International Studies Quarterly*, 25.2 (1981), 242–54.

[31] Cf. Simon Bulmer and William E. Paterson (eds), *Germany and the European Union: Europe's Reluctant Hegemon?*, The European Union Series, 1st edn (Oxford: Macmillan Education, 2019).

than leadership or hegemony. This term designates a continuous engagement over a longer period of time in one policy field with the aim to set policies (or oppose others') and shape the respective paradigm, as demonstrated in EU Russia policy: Germany's influence on the EU's Russia policy transcended temporary leadership roles or issue-specific attempts of influence and represents a continuous engagement and interest in shaping a policy field over a longer period of time. Conceptually, this term could bridge the categories of leadership and hegemony as an "in-between" mode of long-term power exertion specific to EU policy making.

In contrast to leadership, which usually does not have to remain "constant in time and internally coherent" since "even powerful leaders pick and choose their fights",[32] *policy dominance* suggests a continuous and coherent engagement as well as activities aimed at exerting influence and mobilising resources necessary to achieve a defined goal. In this process, a member state becomes the decisive axis of policy making within the EU or between the EU and a third party. *Policy dominance* thus allows for a bigger picture on the question of member state influence in the EU and conceptualises a policy-specific interest by a member state in becoming the dominant actor in a policy area. The analysis of further cases of *policy dominance* in the EU could be an insightful research agenda which would allow to develop the concept of *policy dominance* further. How have other EU member states influenced EU policy in a specific policy field, for instance, France in the EU's southern policy—the Union for the Mediterranean[33]—or Poland with the initiation of the Eastern Partnership? An accumulation of *policy dominance* by a member state in a number of different policy areas could then be an indicator for a hegemonic role of a member state in overall EU policy.

A New German Power?

Does Germany's role in EU Russia policy signify the end of an era of "Machtvergessenheit"[34] (forgetfulness of power) in German politics and the beginning of a "German Europe"?[35] Germany has indeed relearned

---

[32] Della Sala, *Leaders and Followers*, 2012, p. 307.

[33] Cf. Mireia Delgado, 'France and the Union for the Mediterranean: Individualism versus Co-operation', *Mediterranean Politics*, 16.1 (2011), 39–57.

[34] Schwarz, *Gezähmte Deutschen*, 1985.

[35] Cf. Ulrich Beck, *Das deutsche Europa: Neue Machtlandschaften im Zeichen der Krise*, Edition Suhrkamp digital, 1st edn (Berlin: Suhrkamp, 2012).

power politics and applied in Russia policy the full menu of instruments available, representing different "shades" of power—from realist to constructivist notions. This represents a more assertive approach than the traditionally soft exertion of power in German European policy.[36] At the same time, Germany's role in Russia policy demonstrated elements of continuity and was more nuanced and complex than the claim of a hegemonic German role in EU Russia policy would suggest. This points to the difficulties of applying the concept of hegemony to a system of EU governance designed to prevent a concentration of power and to "tame and acknowledge sovereignty at the same time".[37] As Simone Bunse and Kalypso Nicolaïdis argue, "Napoleons and Bismarcks would not do in the halls of Brussels".[38] This applies especially to European foreign policy, where decisions are adopted under unanimity. By applying and combining different instruments of power, Germany engaged to become the central axis of policy making between the EU and Russia. Thereby, it exerted *policy dominance* and demonstrated overall a greater assertiveness in European Russia policy.

However, greater assertiveness does not necessarily lead to greater influence but can result in resistance by other member states as well as EU representatives and institutions, if it is not accompanied by legitimacy. According to Alexander Wendt, achieving legitimate authority, not merely having influence or power, is the key to success for states in advancing their agenda.[39] Legitimacy is thus not an "alternative to power, or distinct from it"—instead, it represents an "essential component part" with the function "to guide, condition, and sometimes constrain" power.[40] This applies equally to EU policy making, which "requires not only leadership, but the consent of the 'followers'".[41] According to Derek Beach, "providing 'acceptable' leadership" is based upon the recognition of the utility of

[36] Cf. Katzenstein, 'United Germany', 1997; Anderson, *Hard Interests*, 1997; Bulmer, Jeffery and Paterson, *Germany's European Diplomacy*, 2000.

[37] Bunse and Nicolaïdis, *Large vs Small States*, 2012, p. 251.

[38] Bunse and Nicolaïdis, *Large vs Small States*, 2012, p. 249.

[39] Alexander Wendt, *Social Theory of International Politics*, Cambridge Studies in International Relations, 67 (Cambridge, New York, NY: Cambridge University Press, 1999), p. 208.

[40] Martin A. Smith, *Power in a Changing Global Order: The US, Russia, and China* (Cambridge: Polity Press, 2012), p. 29.

[41] Bulmer and Paterson (eds), *Germany and the EU*, 2019, p. 4.

the potential leader or his or her legitimacy.[42] The Meseberg initiative provides for a particularly illustrative case study of a lack of legitimacy, when Germany did not receive sufficient followership by others, whereas the Russia-Ukraine conflict demonstrates the opposite: The acceptance of German leadership. Establishing legitimacy was more successful with an inclusive approach in the Ukraine conflict instead of the assertive approach used in the Meseberg initiative. Leadership is accepted when it is perceived by others as being dedicated to solving a "collective action problem",[43] providing public goods as an "authoritative member of the in-group" which "does not lecture or demand but instead, 'acts out principles of serious deliberative argument'".[44] In the Ukraine conflict, Germany's reputation helped increase its legitimacy: The fact that even Germany advocated for sanctions was perceived by some actors as a confirmation that the situation is indeed dire.[45] The necessity to legitimise its role applies to all member states, but even more so for Germany in Russia policy, where the legacy of the German-Russian "special relationship" remains a liability with newer member states.

Germany is thus under a unqiue pressure to justify its legitimacy, the perceived right to use power. A prominent concept to justify German power exertion in the German foreign policy discourse is the notion of German "responsibility",[46] which suggests a more positive, implicitly normative connotation of power.[47] German policy makers often feel uncomfortable with the term "power" and prefer instead "responsibility". This concept "plays a key role for the way in which entrenched norms are used either for the justification or the critical contestation of Germany's political leadership".[48] According to Frank Wendler, the "reference to

[42] Beach and Mazzucelli (eds), *Leadership in the Big Bangs*, 2007, p. 233.

[43] Cf. Christer Karlsson and others, 'The Legitimacy of Leadership in International Climate Change Negotiations', *AMBIO*, 41.S1 (2012), 46–55.

[44] Jeffrey T. Checkel, 'Why Comply?: Social Learning and European Identity Change', *International Organization*, 55.3 (2001), 553–88 (p. 563).

[45] Interview with French expert (2) in Paris, 24.11.2016.

[46] Cf. Giegerich and Terhalle, 'Munich Consensus', 2016; Stiftung Wissenschaft und Politik and The German Marshall Fund of the United States, *Neue Macht, Neue Verantwortung: Elemente einer deutschen Außen- und Sicherheitspolitik für eine Welt im Umbruch* (Berlin, 2013) https://www.swp-berlin.org/fileadmin/contents/products/projekt_papiere/DeutAussenSicherhpol_SWP_GMF_2013.pdf [accessed 30 September 2018].

[47] Forsberg, 'Power in International Relations', 2014, p. 214.

[48] Frank Wendler, 'Recalibrating Germany's Role in Europe: Framing Leadership as Responsibility', *German Politics*, 26.4 (2017), 574-590, p. 574.

responsibility is used as a moral obligation on the part of policy-makers" to redefine and justify leadership by Germany in an enlarged EU.[49]

The positive normative connotation of responsibility has also raised criticism: Responsibility can be used to legitimise power exertion as "altruistic" rather than driven by national interests, according to Wendler. Responsibility has not only been used as a "keyword" for framing Germany's "new, more exposed role" and as a term to "avoid use of semantically problematic terms for leadership" in the German language, but also to understate German interests and influence: "If Germany leads, it has done so because it assumes an obligation to serve the collective interests of member states".[50] In the context of the Eurozone crisis, political action was "justified primarily as a reactive response to a crisis situation, ostensibly downplaying genuinely national interests to collectively benefit European nations". The idea of responsibility towards other member states carries in this case "paternalistic overtones" and raises the question of "who is a responsible European".[51] While the application of this concept by Germany was mostly accepted during the Ukraine conflict, it raised criticism in the case of the Eurozone crisis and remains ambivalent. For analytical purposes, the term *policy dominance* for Germany's role in EU Russia policy is thus more precise than the normatively veiled notion of responsibility. It remains, however, a popular concept in German foreign and security policy[52] and in crisis-management within the EU.[53]

The scepticism towards a prominent German role has diminished under the impression of mounting crises within and outside the EU. For instance, then Polish Foreign Minister Radosław Sikorski argued in 2011 during the Eurozone crisis in Berlin: "I fear German power less than I am

---

[49] Wendler, 'Recalibrating Germany's Role in Europe', p. 585.

[50] Wendler, 'Recalibrating Germany's Role in Europe', p. 582.

[51] Wendler, 'Recalibrating Germany's Role in Europe', p. 585.

[52] Niklas Helwig and Marco Siddi, 'German Leadership in the Foreign and Security Policy of the European Union, *German Politics*, 29.1 (2020), 1-7; Tuomas Iso-Markku and Gisela Müller-Brandeck-Bocquet, 'Towards German leadership? Germany's Evolving Role and the EU's Common Security and Defence Policy', *German Politics*, 29.1 (2020), 59-78; Nicole Koenig, 'Leading Beyond Civilian Power: Germany's Role Re-conception in European Crisis Management', *German Politics*, 29.1 (2020), 79-96.

[53] Wulf Reiners and Funda Tekin, 'Taking Refuge in Leadership? Facilitators and Constraints of Germany's Influence in EU Migration Policy and EU-Turkey Affairs during the Refugee Crisis (2015–2016)', *German Politics*, 29.1 (2020), 115-130.

beginning to fear German inactivity".[54] Yet, the exertion of power and applying a more assertive approach within the EU is for historical reasons more difficult for Germany than it is for France or Great Britain, given its burdened past.[55] A "Machiavellian" use of power by Germany would raise suspicion not only with Eastern, but also Western states that Germany might attempt to "claim a role and influence commensurate with its size and formal power", according to Bunse and Nicolaïdis. The acceptance of Germany's role in the EU is thus dependent on "Germany's behaviour under its new 'biggest of the big' status" and on whether Germany will continue to play a "pivotal role between big and small, old and new member states",[56] especially in light of disintegrative forces in the EU.[57] The crucial question is not whether, but how Germany will exert power, or put differently: Which "shade" of power Germany applies—something resembling domination or (legitimate) authority?[58]

At a time when the international order is in disarray, Germany is "system-relevant" in the EU and Germany's action or non-action matters in almost every conceivable constellation.[59] However, Germany is confronted with a dilemma: While German political elites are mostly converging on the need for a stronger German role, the liberal order in which Germany can exercise leadership is "at risk of crumbling away".[60] As argued by Robert Kagan, "Europe was able to become Venus thanks to historical circumstances—not least the relatively peaceful liberal order

---

[54] Cf. Radosław Sikorski, 'I Fear Germany's Power Less than Her Inactivity', *Financial Times*, 28 November 2008.

[55] Cf. Beverly Crawford and Kim B. Olsen, 'The Puzzle of Persistence and Power: Explaining Germany's Normative Foreign Policy', *German Politics*, 26.4 (2017), 591-608.

[56] Bunse and Nicolaïdis, *Large vs Small States*, 2012, p. 265.

[57] Cf. Erik Jones, 'Towards a Theory of Disintegration', *Journal of European Public Policy*, 25.3 (2018), 440–51; Dermot Hodson and Uwe Puetter, 'Studying Europe after the Fall: Four Thoughts on Post-EU Studies', *Journal of European Public Policy*, 25.3 (2018), 465–74.

[58] Cf. Forsberg, 'Power in International Relations', 2014.

[59] Barbara Lippert, *Deutsche Europapolitik zwischen Tradition und Irritation: Beobachtungen aus aktuellem Anlass*, Arbeitspapier FG EU/Europa, Stiftung Wissenschaft und Politik (2015), p. 4 https://www.swp-berlin.org/fileadmin/contents/products/arbeitspapiere/Deutsche_Europapolitik.pdf [accessed 14 April 2019].

[60] Liana Fix and Steven Keil, *Berlin's foreign policy dilemma: A paradigm shift in volatile times*, Report, U.S.—Europe Analysis Series 58, The Brookings Institution (Washington, DC, 2017) https://www.brookings.edu/wp-content/uploads/2017/02/berlins-foreign-policy-drama.pdf [accessed 30 August 2020].

created and sustained by the United States".[61] If this order vanishes, he assumes nothing would "stop Europeans from returning to the power politics that dominated their continent for millennia"—including Germany. This would in turn lead to a "perfect European storm".[62] While this is without a doubt a worrisome scenario, it is still only one among many scenarios on Germany's future role in Europe. In any scenario addressing the "new German question", Russia policy will constitute an important marker for which path Germany is going to choose.

[61] Cf. Robert Kagan, 'The New German Question: What Happens When Europe Comes Apart?', *Foreign Affairs*, May/June 2019.
[62] Cf. Kagan, 'The New German Question: What Happens When Europe Comes Apart?', 2019.

LIST OF INTERVIEWS

1. Interview with German diplomat in Brussels, 08.03.2016.
2. Interview with German diplomat in Brussels, 09.03.2016.
3. Interview with German diplomat in Warsaw, 20.05.2016.
4. Interview with German diplomat in Brussels, 30.05.2016.
5. Interview with German diplomat in Berlin, 15.07.2016.
6. Interview with German diplomat in Berlin, 09.08.2016.
7. Interview with former German diplomat in Berlin, 28.08.2016.
8. Interview with German official in Berlin, 15.07.2016.
9. Interview with German official in Berlin, 01.08.2016.
10. Interview with German parliamentary policy advisor in Berlin, 02.09.2016.
11. Interview with German expert in Berlin, 16.08.2016.
12. Interviews with current and former experts from the German Institute for International and Security Affairs (SWP) in Berlin, May-July 2016.
13. Interview with French diplomat in Brussels, 31.05.2016.
14. Interview with French diplomat in Paris, 23.11.2016.
15. Interview with French diplomat (2) in Paris, 23.11.2016.
16. Interview with French diplomat in Paris, 24.11.2016.
17. Interview with French diplomat in Paris, 25.11.2016.
18. Interview with French diplomat (2) in Paris, 25.11.2016.

© The Author(s), under exclusive license to Springer Nature Switzerland AG 2021

L. Fix, *Germany's Role in European Russia Policy*, New Perspectives in German Political Studies,
https://doi.org/10.1007/978-3-030-68226-2

19. Interview with French official in Paris, 23.11.2016.
20. Interview with French expert in Paris, 24.11.2016.
21. Interview with French expert (2) in Paris, 24.11.2016.
22. Interview with Polish diplomat in Brussels, 23.03.2016.
23. Interview with Polish diplomat in Warsaw, 17.05.2016.
24. Interview with Polish diplomat in Warsaw, 19.05.2016.
25. Interview with former Polish diplomat in Warsaw, 17.05.2016.
26. Interview with Polish official in Warsaw, 16.05.2016.
27. Interview with Polish expert in Warsaw, 16.05.2016.
28. Interview with Polish expert in Warsaw, 19.05.2016.
29. Interview with Polish expert (2) in Warsaw, 19.05.2016.
30. Interview with Polish expert in Warsaw, 20.05.2016.
31. Interview with Estonian diplomat in Berlin, 17.08.2016.
32. Interview with British expert in Brussels, 08.03.2016.
33. Interview with European Commission official in Brussels, 30.05.2016.
34. Interview with European Council official in Brussels, 31.05.2016.
35. Interview with European Council official in Brussels, 01.06.2016.
36. Interview with European diplomat in Brussels, 31.05.2016.
37. Interview with European diplomat in Brussels, 01.06.2016.
38. Interview with former European diplomat, 28.12.2016.
39. Interview with European parliamentary policy advisor, 01.06.2016.
40. Interview with Moldovan expert in Berlin, 26.05.2016.
41. Interview with former Moldovan official and expert, 06.12.2016.
42. Interview with Russian diplomat in Brussels, 01.06.2016.
43. Interview with US diplomat in Washington, 02.11.2015.
44. Interview with US diplomat in Washington, 11.11.2015.
45. Interview with former US diplomat in Washington, 25.11.2015.

BIBLIOGRAPHY

OFFICIAL DOCUMENTS

Ashton, Catherine. 2010. *A 77/10: Statement by High Representative Catherine Ashton on Moldova/Transnistria*. Brussels, May 17. Accessed September 28, 2017. https://euronest.blogspot.de/2010/05/statement-by-high-representative_18.html.

Barroso, Jose M. 2012. Bringing EU-Russian Relations to a New Level. In *Selected Articles on Modernisation and Innovation in Russia*, ed. Hanna Mäkinen. Turku: Electronic Publications of Pan-European Institute.

Bundesministerium für Wirtschaft und Technologie. 2010. *Erklärung über Schwerpunkte der deutsch-russischen wirtschaftlichen Zusammenarbeit im Rahmen ihrer Modernisierungspartnerschaft*, November 26. Berlin. Accessed April 14, 2019. https://russische-botschaft.ru/wp-content/uploads/2014/11/Erkl%C3%A4rung-%C3%BCber-Moderniserungspartnerschaft.pdf.

Bush, George W.. 2008. *Remarks on the Situation in Georgia*, August 11. Accessed October 30, 2018. https://www.gpo.gov/fdsys/pkg/PPP-2008-book2/pdf/PPP-2008-book2-doc-pg1137.pdf.

Council of the European Union. 2008a. *12594/2/08: Extraordinary European Council, Presidency Conclusions*, September 1, Brussels. Accessed March 17, 2019. http://www.consilium.europa.eu/ueDocs/cms_Data/docs/pressData/en/ec/102545.pdf.

———. 2008b. *Council Joint Action 2008/736/CFSP on the European Union Monitoring Mission in Georgia, EUMM Georgia*, September 15, Brussels.

© The Author(s), under exclusive license to Springer Nature
Switzerland AG 2021
L. Fix, *Germany's Role in European Russia Policy*, New Perspectives
in German Political Studies,
https://doi.org/10.1007/978-3-030-68226-2

Accessed March 17, 2019. https://publications.europa.eu/en/publication-detail/-/publication/0babfe13-406a-4fa3-b3a9-3b7aa0fe5236/language-en.
———. 2008c. General Affairs and External Relations. *Press Release, Presse 236, Extraordinary Meeting*, August 13, Brussels. Accessed October 21, 2018. http://eeas.europa.eu/archives/delegations/georgia/documents/eu_georgia/13august2008_en.pdf.
———. 2010. *Joint Statement on the Partnership for Modernisation EU-Russia Summit 31 May–1 June*, Rostov-on-Don. Accessed March 17, 2019. http://europa.eu/rapid/press-release_PRES-10-154_en.htm.
———. 2014a. Foreign Affairs Council. *Council Conclusions on Ukraine: Foreign Affairs Council Meeting*, March 17, Brussels. Accessed March 17, 2019. http://www.consilium.europa.eu/media/28727/141601.pdf.
———. 2014b. *Council Conclusions on Ukraine: Foreign Affairs Council Meeting*, March 3, Brussels. Accessed March 17, 2019. http://www.consilium.europa.eu/media/28853/141291.pdf.
———. 2014c. *Press Release, Presse 421, 3330th Council Meeting*, July 22, Brussels. Accessed March 12, 2019. https://www.consilium.europa.eu/media/25367/144098.pdf.
Council of the European Union. *EU Restrictive Measures in Response to the Crisis in Ukraine*. Brussels. Accessed March 10, 2018. http://www.consilium.europa.eu/en/policies/sanctions/ukraine-crisis/.
European Council. 2014a. *EUCO 147/14: Special Meeting of the European Council*, July 16, Brussels. Accessed March 12, 2019. https://www.consilium.europa.eu/media/25640/143992.pdf.
———. 2014b. *EUCO 158/14: Statement by the President of the European Council Herman Van Rompuy and the President of the European Commission in the name of the European Union on the agreed additional restrictive measures against Russia*, July 29, Brussels. Accessed March 17, 2018. http://www.consilium.europa.eu/media/22015/144158.pdf.
———. 2014c. *EUCO 163/14: Special Meeting of the European Council*, August 30, Brussels. Accessed April 13, 2019. https://www.consilium.europa.eu/media/25612/144538.pdf.
———. 2014d. *EUCO 179/14: Statement by the President of the European Council Herman Van Rompuy on Further EU Restrictive Measures against Russia*, September 11, Brussels. Accessed March 17, 2018. http://www.consilium.europa.eu/uedocs/cms_data/docs/pressdata/en/ec/144867.pdf.
———. 2014e. *EUCO 7/1/14: European Council Conclusions*, March 20/21, Brussels. Accessed March 17, 2018. https://www.consilium.europa.eu/media/29198/141749.pdf.
———. 2014f. *EUCO 79/14: European Council Conclusions*, June 26/27, Brussels. Accessed March 17, 2018. https://www.consilium.europa.eu/uedocs/cms_Data/docs/pressdata/en/ec/143478.pdf.

————. 2014g. *European Council Conclusions on External Relations (Ukraine and Gaza)*, July 16, Brussels. Accessed April 14, 2019. https://www.consilium.europa.eu/uedocs/cms_Data/docs/pressdata/en/ec/143990.pdf.

————. 2014h. *Statement of the Heads of State or Government on Ukraine*, March 6, Brussels. Accessed March 13, 2018. http://www.consilium.europa.eu/media/29285/141372.pdf.

————. 2015. *EUCO 11/15: European Council Meeting*, March 19 and 20, Brussels. Accessed March 17, 2018. https://www.consilium.europa.eu/media/21888/european-council-conclusions-19-20-march-2015-en.pdf.

European Council, The President. 2010. *PCE 110/10: Remarks by Herman Van Rompuy, President of the European Council, at the EU-Russia Summit*, June 1, Rostov-on-Don. Accessed March 9, 2018. https://www.consilium.europa.eu/media/27756/114736.pdf.

European Parliament. 2010. *New Momentum in EU-Moldova Relations*, October 21, Brussels. Accessed September 28, 2017. http://www.europarl.europa.eu/news/en/press-room/20101020IPR89508/new-momentum-in-eu-moldova-relations.

————. 2011. *Parliamentary Questions, Reply*, January 25, Brussels. Accessed September 28, 2017. http://www.europarl.europa.eu/sides/getAllAnswers.do?reference=E-2010-8055&language=MT.

European Union. 2008. *MEMO/08/678, Review of EU-Russia Relations*, November 5, Brussels. Accessed April 14, 2019. https://www.europa.eu/rapid/press-release_MEMO-08-678_en.pdf.

Federal Chancellor. 2008. *Merkel Fordert Schnellen Rückzug Russischer Truppen*, August 17, Tbilisi. Accessed December 16, 2018. https://www.bundeskanzlerin.de/bkin-de/merkel-fordert-schnellen-rueckzug-russischer-truppen-609458.

————. 2012. *Erste Schritte in Richtung EU: Staatsbesuch in der Republik Moldau*, August 22, Chisinau. Accessed September 29, 2017. https://www.bundeskanzlerin.de/ContentArchiv/DE/Archiv17/Reiseberichte/moldau-2012-08-22-merkel.html.

Federal Foreign Office. 2008. *Statement on Georgia of Foreign Ministers of Canada, France, Germany, Italy, Japan, the United States and the United Kingdom*, August 27. Accessed December 16, 2018. https://www.auswaertiges-amt.de/en/newsroom/news/080827-g7-erklaerung-georgien/234804.

————. 2009. *Steinmeier Commends the Work of the Tagliavini Commission*, September 30, Berlin. Accessed October 24, 2018. https://www.auswaertiges-amt.de/en/newsroom/news/090930-tagliavini/233248.

————. 2012. *German, Polish and Russian Foreign Ministers Meet in Berlin*, March 20, Berlin. Accessed December 16, 2018. https://www.auswaertiges-amt.de/en/newsroom/news/120320-trialog/249316.

Federal Government of Germany. 2015. *Erklärung des Präsidenten der Russischen Föderation, des Präsidenten der Ukraine, des Präsidenten der Französischen Republik und der Bundeskanzlerin der Bundesrepublik Deutschland zur Unterstützung des Maßnahmenpakets zur Umsetzung der Minsker Vereinbarungen angenommen am 12. Februar 2015 in Minsk.* Accessed March 10, 2018. https://www.bundesregierung.de/Content/DE/Pressemitteilungen/BPA/2015/02/2015-02-12-erklaerung-minsk.html.

Federal Ministry of Defence. 2015. *VJTF—Speerspitze der NATO: Dossier.* Accessed April 22, 2019. https://www.bmvg.de/de/themen/dossiers/die-nato-staerke-und-dialog/vjtf-speerspitze-der-nato.

German Bundestag. 2011. *Drucksache 17/8239: Antwort der Bundesregierung auf die Kleine Anfrage der Abgeordneten Viola von Cramon-Taubadel, Volker Beck (Köln), Marieluise Beck (Bremen), weiterer Abgeordneter und der Fraktion BÜNDNIS 90/DIE GRÜNEN, Stand des Meseburg-Memorandums,* Dezember 21. Accessed September 27, 2017. http://dipbt.bundestag.de/dip21/btd/17/082/1708239.pdf.

———. 2014. *Drucksache 18/1745: Antwort der Bundesregierung auf die Kleine Anfrage der Abgeordneten Sevim Dağdelen, Dr. Alexander S. Neu, Heike Hänsel, weiterer Abgeordneter und der Fraktion DIE LINKE, 12. Juni,* Berlin. Accessed April 13, 2019. https://www.bundesanzeiger-verlag.de/fileadmin/Betrifft-Recht/Dokumente/edrucksachen/pdf/1801745.pdf.

Hoop Scheffer, Jaap de. 2008. *Press Conference by NATO Secretary General after the Meeting of the North Atlantic Council at the Level of Foreign Ministers,* August 19, Brussels. Accessed December 16, 2018. https://www.nato.int/docu/speech/2008/s080819c.html.

Kaczyński, Lech and others. 2008. *Joint Statement by Presidents of Poland, Estonia, Latvia and Lithuania,* August 9. Accessed October 21, 2018. https://halldor2.wordpress.com/2008/08/09/joint-statement-by-presidents-of-poland-estonia-latvia-and-lithuania/.

Medvedev, Dmitry. 2008a. *Presidential Decree of the Russian Federation "About Recognition of the Republic of Abkhazia",* No. 1260, August 26. Accessed December 16, 2018. http://cis-legislation.com/document.fwx?rgn=24164.

———. 2008b. *Presidential Decree of the Russian Federation "About Recognition of the Republic South Ossetia",* No. 1261, August 26. Accessed December 16, 2018. http://cis-legislation.com/document.fwx?rgn=24165.

———. 2008c. *Speech at Meeting with German Political, Parliamentary and Civic Leaders,* June 5. Accessed September 28, 2017. http://en.kremlin.ru/events/president/transcripts/320.

———. 2009a. *Go Russia!* September 10, Moscow. Accessed April 13, 2019. http://en.kremlin.ru/events/president/news/5413.

———. 2009b. *The Draft of the European Security Treaty,* November 29. Accessed March 12, 2019. http://en.kremlin.ru/events/president/news/6152.

————. 2009c. *Россия, вперёд!* September 10, Moscow. Accessed April 13, 2019. http://www.kremlin.ru/news/5413.

Medvedev, Dmitry, and Nicolas Sarkozy. 2008. *Press Conference Following Talks with President of France Nicolas Sarkozy*, September 8. Accessed December 16, 2018. http://en.kremlin.ru/events/president/transcripts/1330.

Merkel, Angela. 2008a. *Rede von Bundeskanzlerin Dr. Angela Merkel im Rahmen ihres Besuchs in Estland*, August 26, Tallinn. Accessed December 16, 2018. https://www.bundesregierung.de/breg-de/service/bulletin/rede-von-bundeskanzlerin-dr-angela-merkel-796320.

————. 2008b. *Regierungserklärung von Bundeskanzlerin Merkel zum Europäischen Rat in Brüssel am 11./12. Dezember 2008 vor dem Deutschen Bundestag, 4. Dezember*, Berlin. Accessed December 16, 2018. https://www.bundesregierung.de/breg-de/service/bulletin/regierungserklaerung-von-bundeskanzlerin-dr-angela-merkel-zum-europaeischen-rat-in-bruessel-am-11-12-dezember-2008-796120.

————. 2010a. *Memorandum (Meeting of Chancellor Angela Merkel and President Medvedev*, June 4–5, Meseberg. Accessed September 27, 2017. https://archiv.bundesregierung.de/resource/blob/656928/389532/da09e7a21880fb55dfd2d868996295ce/2010-06-05-meseberg-memorandum-data.pdf.

————. 2010b. *Memorandum (Treffen zwischen Bundeskanzlerin Angela Merkel und Präsident Dmitri Medwedew, 4. und 5. Juni)*, Meseberg. Accessed March 12, 2019. https://archiv.bundesregierung.de/resource/blob/656928/452948/9e765ba1c0f63f45787cd6eb06a28968/2010-06-07-meseberg-memorandum-deutsch-data.pdf.

————. 2010c. *Pressestatements von Bundeskanzlerin Angela Merkel und dem Präsidenten der Russischen Föderation, Dmitri Medwedew, 5. Juni*, Meseberg. Accessed April 13 2019. https://archiv.bundesregierung.de/archiv-de/dokumente/pressestatements-von-bundeskanzlerin-angela-merkel-und-dem-praesidenten-der-russischen-foederation-dmitri-medwedew-am-5-juni-2010-in-meseberg-846802.

————. 2010d. *Меморандум по итогам встречи Президента России Д.Медведева и Федерального канцлера Германии А.Меркель, 4–5 июня*, Meseberg. Accessed April 13, 2019. http://www.kremlin.ru/supplement/575.

————. 2010e. *Совместная пресс-конференция с Федеральным канцлером Германии Ангелой Меркель по итогам российско-германских переговоров, 5 июня*, Meseberg. Accessed April 13, 2019. http://kremlin.ru/events/president/transcripts/7973.

————. 2010f. *Pressekonferenz Merkel, Sarkozy und Medwedew, 19. Oktober*, Deauville. Accessed September 28, 2017. https://www.bundeskanzlerin.de/ContentArchiv/DE/Archiv17/Mitschrift/Pressekonferenzen/2010/10/2010-10-19-pk-deauville.html.

———. 2013. *Regierungserklärung von Bundeskanzlerin Merkel zum EU-Gipfel "Östliche Partnerschaft" am 28./29. November 2013 in Vilnius,* November 18, Berlin. Accessed March 9, 2018. https://archiv.bundesregierung.de/ContentArchiv/DE/Archiv17/Regierungserklaerung/2013/2013-11-18-merkel-oestl-partnerschaften.html.

———. 2014a. *Rede von Bundeskanzlerin Merkel vor dem Deutschen Bundestag zum Haushaltsgesetz 2015,* September 10, Berlin. Accessed April 14, 2019. https://www.bundesregierung.de/breg-de/service/bulletin/rede-von-bundeskanzlerin-dr-angela-merkel-796638.

———. 2014b. *Regierungserklärung von Bundeskanzlerin Merkel, 13. März,* Berlin. Accessed March 17, 2018. https://www.bundeskanzlerin.de/bkin-de/aktuelles/regierungserklaerung-von-bundeskanzlerin-merkel-443682.

———. 2015. *Rede von Bundeskanzlerin Merkel anlässlich der 51. Münchner Sicherheitskonferenz, 7. Februar,* Munich. Accessed March 18, 2018. https://www.bundesregierung.de/Content/DE/Rede/2015/02/2015-02-07-merkel-sicherheitskonferenz.html.

Merkel, Angela, and Emil Boc. 2010. *Pressestatements von Bundeskanzlerin Angela Merkel und dem Premierminister von Rumänien, Emil Boc, 12. Oktober,* Bucharest. Accessed September 28, 2017. https://www.bundeskanzlerin.de/ContentArchiv/DE/Archiv17/Mitschrift/Pressekonferenzen/2010/10/2010-10-12-pk-bk-bukarest.html.

Merkel, Angela, and Vladimir Filat. 2010. *Pressestatement Bundeskanzlerin Merkel und der Ministerpräsident der Republik Moldau, Vladimir Filat, 12. Mai,* Berlin. Accessed September 28, 2017. https://www.bundesregierung.de/ContentArchiv/DE/Archiv17/Mitschrift/Pressekonferenzen/2010/05/2010-05-12-filat-merkel.html.

Merkel, Angela, and Dmitry Medvedev. 2010. *Joint News Conference with German Federal Chancellor Angela Merkel following Russian-German Talks,* June 5, Meseberg. Accessed September 28, 2017. http://en.kremlin.ru/events/president/transcripts/7973.

Merkel, Angela, and Petro Poroschenko. 2015. *Pressestatements von Bundeskanzlerin Merkel und dem ukrainischen Präsidenten Poroschenko, 16. März,* Berlin. Accessed March 17, 2018. https://www.bundeskanzlerin.de/Content/DE/Mitschrift/Pressekonferenzen/2015/03/215-03-16-merkel-poroschenko.html.

Merkel, Angela, and Nicolas Sarkozy. 2009. *"Wir Europäer müssen mit einer Stimme sprechen": Süddeutsche Zeitung, 4. Februar.* Accessed September 28, 2017. http://www.sueddeutsche.de/politik/sicherheitskonferenz-merkel-und-sarkozy-wir-europaer-muessen-mit-einer-stimme-sprechen-1.473581.

Merkel, Angela, Nicolas Sarkozy, and Dmitry Medvedev. 2010. *Déclaration finale: Rencontre Allemagne-France-Russie, 19 Octobre,* Deauville. Accessed April 13, 2019. https://uk.ambafrance.org/Rencontre-Allemagne-France-Russie.

Merkel, Angela, Bannas Günter, and Berthold Kohler. 2014. *Für gemeinsame Werte eintreten: Interview der Frankfurter Allgemeinen Zeitung mit Angel Merkel, 16. Mai.* Accessed March 17, 2018. https://www.bundesregierung. de/Content/DE/Interview/2014/05/2014-05-16-merkel-faz.html.

Mingarelli, Hugues, and Andrei Slepnev. 2010. *Progress Report Agreed by the Coordinators of the EU-Russia Partnership for Modernisation for Information to the EU-Russia Summit of 7 December.* Accessed April 13, 2019. http://eeas. europa.eu/archives/docs/russia/docs/eu_russia_progress_report_2010_en.pdf.

Ministry of Foreign Affairs of Romania. 2010. *Romania and Republic of Moldova sign Treaty on State Border Regime, Cooperation and Mutual Assistance in Border Matters*, November 8. Accessed March 13, 2019. https://mae.ro/en/node/5904.

North Atlantic Treaty Organization. 1997. *Founding Act on Mutual Relations, Cooperation and Security between NATO and the Russian Federation*, Paris. Accessed March 18, 2018. https://www.nato.int/cps/en/natohq/official_texts_25468.htm?selectedLocale=en.

———. 2008a. *Bucharest Summit Declaration: Issued by the Heads of State and Government Participating in the Meeting of the North Atlantic Council*, April 3, Bucharest. Accessed October 21, 2018. https://www.nato.int/cps/us/natohq/official_texts_8443.htm.

———. 2008b. *NATO Decisions on Open-Door Policy.* Accessed October 21, 2018. https://www.nato.int/docu/update/2008/04-april/e0403h.html.

———. 2008c. *NATO's Foreign Ministers Reiterate Their Support to Georgia*, August 19. Accessed December 16, 2018. https://www.nato.int/docu/update/2008/08-august/e0819a.html.

———. 2008d. *Statement: Meeting of the North Atlantic Council at the level of Foreign Ministers held at NATO Headquarters*, August 19, Brussels. Accessed December 16, 2018. https://www.nato.int/cps/en/natolive/official_texts_29950.htm.

———. 2014a. *Press Release 062: Statement by NATO Foreign Ministers*, April 1, Brussels. Accessed April 14, 2019. https://www.nato.int/cps/en/natohq/news_108501.htm.

———. 2014b. *Wales Summit Declaration Issued by the Heads of State and Government Participating in the Meeting of the North Atlantic Council*, September 5, Wales. Accessed March 18, 2018. https://www.nato.int/cps/ic/natohq/official_texts_112964.htm.

———. 2016. *Warsaw Summit Communiqué: Issued by the Heads of State and Government Participating in the Meeting of the North Atlantic Council*, July 8–9, Warsaw. Accessed March 18, 2018. https://www.nato.int/cps/en/natohq/official_texts_133169.htm.

———. 2019. *Topics: Relations with Russia*, Brussels. Accessed April 14, 2019. https://www.nato.int/cps/en/natolive/topics_50090.htm.

Organisation for Security. 2010. *Restoring Trust: The Corfu Process*, December 1. Accessed April 13, 2019. http://www.osce.org/mc/87193.

———. 2014. *Protocol on the Results of Consultations of the Trilateral Contact Group*, September 5, Minsk. Accessed April 14, 2019. https://www.osce.org/home/123257.

———. 2015. *Package of Measures for the Implementation of the Minsk Agreements*, February 12, Minsk. Accessed April 14, 2019. https://www.osce.org/cio/140156.

Organisation for Security and Co-operation in Europe (OSCE). 2014. *Memorandum of 19 September 2014 Outlining the Parameters for the Implementation of Commitments of the Minsk Protocol of 5 September 2014*, Minsk. Accessed April 14, 2019. https://www.osce.org/home/123806.

Petersburger Dialog. 2008. *Gemeinsame Erklärung des Deutschen und des Russischen Lenkungsausschusses des Petersburger Dialoges zur Gestaltung der Modernisierungspartnerschaft*, 2. *Oktober*, St. Petersburg. Accessed March 8, 2018. http://www.petersburger-dialog.de/files/Unterzeichnung%20 Modernisierungspartnerschaft%20dt.pdf.

Presidential Executive Office. 2014. *Vladimir Putin Answered Journalists' Questions on the Situation in Ukraine*, March 4. Accessed March 10, 2018. http://en.kremlin.ru/events/president/news/20366.

Sarkozy, Nicolas. 2008. L'Union européenne et la Russie dans la gouvernance mondiale. *Politique étrangère* 4: 723–732. https://doi.org/10.3917/pe.084.0723.

Sénat. 2015a. *Les relations avec la Russie. Comment sortir de l'impasse?: Part A: L'histoire récente et ses occasions manquées*. Paris. Accessed December 18, 2018. http://www.senat.fr/rap/r15-021/r15-0214.html.

———. 2015b. *Les relations avec la Russie. Comment sortir de l'impasse?: Part B. La crise ukrainienne marque un tournant*. Paris. Accessed December 18, 2018. http://www.senat.fr/rap/r15-021/r15-0212.html.

Steinmeier, Frank-Walter. 2008a. *Rede von Außenminister Steinmeier zur gesamteuropäischen Sicherheitspartnerschaft*, Dezember 11. Accessed December 16, 2018. https://www.auswaertiges-amt.de/de/newsroom/081210-schwarzkopf/219814.

———. 2008b. *"Tackling Global Challenges Together—Prospects for the German-Russian Modernization Partnership": Speech by Federal Minister Steinmeier at the meeting of the Bilateral Steering Committee of the Petersburg Dialogue*, July 3. Accessed April 13, 2019. https://www.auswaertiges-amt.de/en/newsroom/news/080703-petersburger-rede-bm/232866.

———. 2008c. *"Time for a German-Russian Modernization Partnership": Frank-Walter Steinmeier, Federal Minister for Foreign Affairs, at the Department of*

International Relations of the Urals State University in Yekaterinburg, May 13. Accessed April 13, 2019. https://www.auswaertiges-amt.de/en/newsroom/news/080513-bm-russland/232842.

———. 2014. *Rede von Außenminister Steinmeier anlässlich der Mitgliederversammlung des Deutsch-Russischen Forums e.V., 19. März*, Berlin. Accessed March 15, 2018. https://www.auswaertiges-amt.de/de/newsroom/140319-bm-dtrus-forum/260874.

Tagliavini, Heidi. 2009. *Report of the Independent International Fact-Finding Mission on the Conflict in Georgia: Volume I–III*. Accessed April 13, 2019. http://www.mpil.de//files/pdf4/IIFFMCG_Volume_I2.pdf; http://www.mpil.de//files/pdf4/IIFFMCG_Volume_II1.pdf; http://www.mpil.de//files/pdf4/IIFFMCG_Volume_III1.pdf.

The Ministry of Foreign Affairs of the Russian Federation. 2010. *Transcript of Remarks and Response to Media Questions by Russian Foreign Minister Sergey Lavrov at Joint Press Conference after Meeting of Weimar Triangle Foreign Ministers*, June 23, Paris. Accessed March 13, 2019. http://www.mid.ru/en/web/guest/posledniye_dobavlnenniye/-/asset_publisher/MCZ7HQuMdqBY/content/id/244486.

———. 2014. *Foreign Minister Sergey Lavrov Makes a Speech and Answers Questions Following His Talks with German Foreign Minister Frank-Walter Steinmeier*, November 18, Moscow. Accessed September 28, 2017. http://www.mid.ru/en/press_service/minister_speeches/-/asset_publisher/7OvQR5KJWVmR/content/id/790869.

Wiegand, Gunnar. 2014. *Progress Report Approved by the Coordinators of the EU-Russia Partnership for Modernization for information to the EU-Russia Summit on 28 January*. Accessed April 19, 2019. https://web.archive.org/web/20140705232631/https://eeas.europa.eu/russia/docs/eu_russia_progress_report_2014_en.pdf.

Wiegand, Gunnar, and Alexey Likhachev. 2012. *Progress Report Agreed by the Coordinators of the EU-Russia Partnership for Modernisation for Information to the EU-Russia Summit of 21 December*. Accessed April 14, 2019. http://www.eeas.europa.eu/archives/docs/russia/docs/2012_p4m_progress_report_signed_en.pdf.

Wiegand, Gunnar, and Andrei Slepnev. 2011. *Progress Report Agreed by the Coordinators of the EU-Russia Partnership for Modernisation for Information to the EU-Russia Summit of 9–10 June*. Accessed April 19, 2019. http://www.eeas.europa.eu/archives/delegations/russia/documents/news/20110610_01_en.pdf.

WikiLeaks. 2008a. *Debate on Russian Role in OAE Foreshadows Dividing Lines on NATO-Russia Policy*. August 13. Accessed December 16, 2018. https://wikileaks.org/plusd/cables/08USNATO287_a.html.

———. 2008b. *Germany Carefully Watching Russian Withdrawal*, August 22. Accessed October 24, 2018. https://wikileaks.org/plusd/cables/08BERLIN1176_a.html.

———. 2008c. *Germany/Georgia: Status of EU Observer Mission and Other Initiatives*, September 12. Accessed December 16, 2018. https://wikileaks.org/plusd/cables/08BERLIN1261_a.html.

———. 2008d. *Germany's View of Georgia: Frustration Rising but Awaiting French Results in Moscow*, August 12. Accessed October 24, 2018. https://wikileaks.org/plusd/cables/08BERLIN1101_a.html.

———. 2008e. *GOP Rallies Neighbors, EU to Condemn Russian Actions in Georgia*, August 11. Accessed October 24, 2018. https://wikileaks.org/plusd/cables/08WARSAW947_a.html.

———. 2008f. *Lithuania, The EU, and Russia: Possible Veto on Business-as-Usual*, October 23. Accessed December 16, 2018. https://wikileaks.org/plusd/cables/08VILNIUS903_a.html.

———. 2008g. *Lugar Codel: Germans Emphasize Need for Cooperation with Russians on Energy*, September 10. Accessed December 16, 2018. https://wikileaks.org/plusd/cables/08BERLIN1244_a.html.

———. 2008h. *Merkel "Will Talk Tough" in Sochi: Foreign Office and Bundestag Display Mixture of Resolve and Skepticism*, 15 August. Accessed October 24, 2018. https://wikileaks.org/plusd/cables/08BERLIN1130_a.html.

———. 2008i. *NATO Allies Lack Cohesion during First Meeting on Georgia Crisis*, August 11. Accessed December 16, 2018. https://wikileaks.org/plusd/cables/08USNATO281_a.html.

———. 2008j. *North Atlantic Council Visit to Tbilisi*, September 30. Accessed October 24, 2018. https://wikileaks.org/plusd/cables/08USNATO352_a.html.

———. 2008k. *RFG: NATO-Russia: Maintaining Consensus on "No Business-As-Usual"*. October 29. Accessed December 16, 2018. https://wikileaks.org/plusd/cables/08USNATO402_a.html.

———. 2008l. *Russia, Georgia, Germany, Lithuania and the EU: Threats and Responses*, August 27. Accessed December 16, 2018. https://wikileaks.org/plusd/cables/08VILNIUS708_a.html.

———. 2008m. *TFGG01: Chancellor Merkel Says Russia Has not Fullfilled Six-Point Plan*, August 25. Accessed December 16, 2018. https://wikileaks.org/plusd/cables/08BERLIN1181_a.html.

———. 2012. *National Security Advisor Heusgen on Afghanistan, Middle East, Iran, Detainees, Russia, Nukes and Balkans*, November 12. Accessed March 13, 2019. https://wikileaks.org/plusd/cables/09BERLIN1433_a.html.

Monographies & Edited Volumes

Adomeit, Hannes. 2011. Russlands "Modernisierungspartnerschaften": Ursprünge, Inhalte und Erfolgsaussichten. In *Russland modernisiert sich—oder doch nicht?* Sozialwissenschaftliche Schriftenreihe, 36/37, ed. Hannes Adomeit, 25–72. Vienna: Internationales Institut für Liberale Politik Wien.

Aggestam, Lisbeth. 2017. *European Foreign Policy and the Quest for a Global Role: Britain, France and Germany*, Routledge Advances in European Politics. London: Routledge.

Anderson, Jeffrey J. 1997. Hard Interests, Soft Power, and Germany's Changing Role in Europe. In *Tamed Power: Germany in Europe*, ed. Peter J. Katzenstein, 1st ed., 80–107. Ithaca, NY and London: Cornell University Press.

Ansell, Chris, Arjen Boin, and Paul 't Hart. 2014. Political Leadership in Times of Crisis. In *The Oxford Handbook of Political Leadership*, ed. Rod A.W. Rhodes and Paul 't. Hart, 418–429. Oxford and New York, NY: Oxford University Press.

Åslund, Anders. 2015. *Ukraine: What Went Wrong and How to Fix It*. Washington, DC: Peterson Institute for International Economics.

Asmus, Ronald D. 2010. *A Little War that Shook the World: Georgia, Russia and the Future of the West*. 1st ed. New York: Palgrave Macmillan.

Baldwin, David A. 2013. Power and International Relations. In *Handbook of International Relations*, ed. Walter Carlsnaes, Thomas Risse-Kappen, and Beth A. Simmons, 2nd ed., 273–297. Los Angeles, CA: SAGE Publications.

Baring, Arnulf. 1994. *Germany's New Position in Europe: Problems and Perspectives*, German Historical Perspectives Series, 8. Oxford and Providence, RI: Berg.

Bastian, Katrin. 2006. *Die Europäische Union und Russland*. 1st ed. Wiesbaden: VS Verlag für Sozialwissenschaften.

Beach, Derek. 2007. *Leadership in the Big Bangs of European Integration*, Palgrave Studies in European Union Politics. Basingstoke and New York, NY: Palgrave Macmillan.

Beach, Derek, and Colette Mazzucelli. 2007. Introduction. In *Leadership in the Big Bangs of European Integration*, Palgrave Studies in European Union Politics, ed. Derek Beach and Colette Mazzucelli, 1–21. Basingstoke and New York, NY: Palgrave Macmillan.

Beach, Derek, and Rasmus B. Pedersen. 2013. *Process-Tracing Methods: Foundations and Guidelines*. Ann Arbor, MI: University of Michigan Press.

Beck, Ulrich. 2012. *Das deutsche Europa: Neue Machtlandschaften im Zeichen der Krise*, Edition Suhrkamp Digital. 1st ed. Berlin: Suhrkamp.

Beichelt, Timm. 2013. Germany: In Search of a New Balance. In *The Member States of the European Union*, The New European Union Series, ed. Simon Bulmer and Christian Lequesne, 2nd ed., 85–107. Oxford: Oxford University Press.

Bennett, Andrew, and Jeffrey T. Checkel. 2015. Process Tracing: from Philosophical Roots to Best Practices. In *Process Tracing: From Metaphor to Analytic Tool*, Strategies for Social Inquiry, ed. Andrew Bennett and Jeffrey T. Checkel, 3–37. Cambridge and New York, NY: Cambridge University Press.

Berenskoetter, Felix. 2007. Thinking about Power. In *Power in World Politics*, ed. Felix Berenskoetter and Michael J. Williams, 1–22. London and New York, NY: Routledge.

Bergmann, Julian, and Arne Niemann. 2015. Theories of European Integration. In *The SAGE Handbook of European Foreign Policy*, ed. Knud E. Jørgensen and others, 166–182. Los Angeles, CA: SAGE Publications.

Bieling, Hans-Jürgen, and Marika Lerch. 2013. *Theorien der europäischen Integration*. 3rd ed. Wiesbaden: Springer VS.

Börzel, Tanja A., and Thomas Risse. 2003. Conceptualizing the Domestic Impact of Europe. In *The Politics of Europeanization*, ed. Kevin Featherstone and Claudio M. Radaelli, 57–80. Oxford and New York, NY: Oxford University Press.

Böttger, Katrin. 2016. Deutschland, die Östliche Partnerschaft und Russland. In *Handbuch zur deutschen Europapolitik*, ed. Katrin Böttger and Mathias Jopp, 1st ed., 407–420. Baden-Baden: Nomos.

Böttger, Katrin, and Mathias Jopp. 2016. Grundlinien deutscher Europapolitik. In *Handbuch zur deutschen Europapolitik*, ed. Katrin Böttger and Mathias Jopp, 1st ed., 13–28. Baden-Baden: Nomos.

Bulmer, Simon. 1997. Shaping the Rules?: The Constitutive Politics of the European Union and German Power. In *Tamed Power: Germany in Europe*, ed. Peter J. Katzenstein, 1st ed., 49–79. Ithaca, NY and London: Cornell University Press.

———. 2008. Theorizing Europeanization. In *Europeanization: New Research Agendas*, ed. Paolo Graziano and Maarten P. Vink, 46–58. Basingstoke and New York, NY: Palgrave Macmillan.

———. 2016. Germany's Role in the Handling of the European Monetary and Refugee Crisis. In *Jahrbuch der Europäischen Integration 2016*, ed. Werner Weidenfeld and Wolfgang Wessels, 1st ed., 1–10. Baden-Baden: Nomos.

———. 2019. *Germany and the European Union: Europe's Reluctant Hegemon?* The European Union Series. 1st ed. Oxford: Macmillan Education.

Bulmer, Simon, and William E. Paterson. 2019. From Political Dwarf to Potential Hegemon? German Foreign Policy in Transition. In *Germany and the European Union: Europe's Reluctant Hegemon?* ed. Simon Bulmer, William E. Paterson, and The European Union Series, 1st ed., 201–237. Oxford: Macmillan Education.

Bulmer, Simon, and Claudio M. Radaelli. 2005. The Europeanization of National Policy. In *The Member States of the European Union*, ed. Simon Bulmer and Christian Lequesne, 338–359. Oxford: Oxford University Press.

Bulmer, Simon, Charlie Jeffery, and William E. Paterson. 2000. *Germany's European Diplomacy: Shaping the Regional Milieu*, Issues in German Politics. Manchester: Manchester University Press.

Bunse, Simone, and Kalypso Nicolaïdis. 2012. Large versus Small States: Anti-hegemony and the Politics of Shared Leadership. In *The Oxford Handbook of the European Union*, Oxford Handbooks Online, ed. Erik Jones, Anand Menon, and Stephen Weatherill, 249–266. Oxford: Oxford University Press.

Carlsnaes, Walter. 2015. European Foreign Policy. In *The SAGE Handbook of European Foreign Policy*, ed. Knud E. Jørgensen and others, 545–560. Los Angeles, CA: SAGE Publications.

Cichoki, Bartosz. 2013. Poland. In *National Perspectives on Russia: European Foreign Policy in the Making?* Routledge Advances in European Politics, 94, ed. Maxine David, Jackie Gower, and Hiski Haukkala, 89–100. London and New York, NY: Routledge.

Cornell, Svante E., and S.F. Starr. 2015. *The Guns of August 2008: Russia's War in Georgia*, Studies of Central Asia and the Caucasus. Armonk, NY: M.E. Sharpe.

Crawford, Beverly. 2007. *Power and German Foreign Policy: Embedded Hegemony in Europe*, New Perspectives in German Studies. Basingstoke and New York: Palgrave Macmillan.

Daehnhardt, Patricia. 2011. Germany in the European Union. In *National and European Foreign Policies: Towards Europeanization*, Routledge Advances in European Politics, 74, ed. Reuben Y.-P. Wong and Christopher Hill, 35–56. Abingdon and New York, NY: Routledge.

Dahl, Robert A. 1961. *Who Governs?: Democracy and Power in an American City*, Yale Studies in Political Science, 4. New Haven, CT: Yale University Press.

David, Maxine, Jackie Gower, and Hiski Haukkala. 2013. *National Perspectives on Russia: European Foreign Policy in the Making?* Routledge Advances in European Politics, 94. London and New York, NY: Routledge.

Delcour, Laure, and Elsa Tulmets. 2013. Die deutsch-französischen Beziehungen im russisch-georgischen Konflikt: Parallel laufende diplomatische Initiativen. In *Die Konsenswerkstatt: Deutsch-französische Kommunikations- und Entscheidungsprozesse in der Europapolitik*, Genshagener Schriften—Europa politisch denken, 2, ed. Claire Demesmay, Martin Koopmann, and Julien Thorel, 105–120. Baden-Baden: Nomos.

Della Sala, Vincent. 2012. Leaders and Followers: Leadership Amongst Member States in a Differentiated Europe. In *The Oxford Handbook of the European Union*, Oxford Handbooks Online, ed. Erik Jones, Anand Menon, and Stephen Weatherill, 306–316. Oxford: Oxford University Press.

Dembinski, Matthias and others. 2008. *Nach dem Kaukasus-Krieg: Einbindung statt Eindämmung Russlands*, HSFK-Report, 2008, 6. Frankfurt a. M.: Hessische Stiftung Friedens- und Konfliktforschung.

Devyatkov, Andrey. 2012a. Russia: Relations with Moldova Under a Paradigm of Ambiguity. In *Moldova: Arena of International Influences*, ed. Marcin Kosienkowski and William Schreiber, 183–204. Lanham, MD: Lexington Books.

Duchêne, François. 1972. Europe's Role in World Peace. In *Europe Tomorrow: Sixteen Europeans Look Ahead*, ed. Richard Mayne, 32–47. London: Fontana.

Dyson, Kenneth H.F., and Klaus Goetz. 2003. *Germany, Europe and the Politics of Constraint*, Proceedings of the British Academy, 119. Oxford: Oxford University Press.

Fix, Liana, and Evgeniya Bakalova. 2015. Krise um die Ukraine—Krise internationaler Normen? In *Ukraine. Krisen. Perspektiven: Interdisziplinäre Betrachtungen eines Landes im Umbruch*, Impulse. Studien zu Geschichte, Politik und Gesellschaft, 6, ed. Evgeniya Bakalova, Tobias Endrich, and Khrystyna Shlyakhtovska, 261–283. Wissenschaftlicher Verlag Berlin: Berlin.

Forsberg, Tuomas. 2014. Power in International Relations: An Interdisciplinary Perspective. In *International Studies: Interdisciplinary Approaches*, Palgrave Studies in International Relations, ed. Pami Aalto, Vilho Harle, and Sami Moisio, 207–227. Basingstoke and New York, NY: Palgrave Macmillan.

Forsberg, Tuomas, and Hiski Haukkala. 2016. *The European Union and Russia*, The European Union Series. 1st ed. London and New York, NY: Macmillan Education; Palgrave.

Gawrich, Andrea. 2017. A Bridge with Russia? The Parliamentary Assemblies of the OSCE and of the Council of Europe in the Russia-Ukraine Crisis. In *Parliamentary Diplomacy in European and Global Governance*, Diplomatic Studies, 13, ed. Stelios Stavridis and Davor Jančić, 156–173. Leiden and Boston, MA: Brill.

Gel'man, Vladimir. 2017. *Authoritarian Modernization in Russia: Ideas, Institutions, and Policies*, Studies in Contemporary Russia. London and New York, NY: Routledge.

George, Alexander L., and Andrew Bennett. 2005. *Case Studies and Theory Development in the Social Sciences*, BCSIA Studies in International Security. Cambridge, MA: MIT Press.

Ginsberg, Roy H. 1989. *Foreign Policy Actions of the European Community: The Politics of Scale*, Adamantine Series Studies in International Relations and World Security, 3. Boulder: L. Rienner.

———. 2001. *The European Union in International Politics: Baptism by Fire*, New International Relations of Europe. Lanham, MD: Rowman & Littlefield.

Gower, Jackie. 2009. The European Union's Policy on Russia: Rhetoric or Reality? In *Russia and Europe in the Twenty-First Century: An Uneasy Partnership*, ed. Jackie Gower and Graham Timmins, 111–132. London and New York, NY: Anthem Press.

Gower, Jackie, and Graham Timmins. 2009. *Russia and Europe in the Twenty-First Century: An Uneasy Partnership*. London and New York, NY: Anthem Press.

Grabbe, H. 2006. *The EU's Transformative Power: Europeanization through Conditionality in Central and Eastern Europe*. 1st ed. Basingstoke: Palgrave Macmillan.

Grau, Heidi. 2015. The 2014 Swiss OSCE Chairmanship: Between "Routine" and "Crisis". In *OSCE Yearbook 2014: Yearbook on the Organization for Security and Co-operation in Europe (OSCE)*, Institute for Peace Research and Security Policy at the University of Hamburg (IFSH), 1st ed., 25–40. Nomos: Baden-Baden.

Hacke, Christian. 1988. *Weltmacht wider Willen: Die Aussenpolitik der Bundesrepublik Deutschland*. Stuttgart: Klett-Cotta.

Haftendorn, Helga. 2001. *Deutsche Außenpolitik zwischen Selbstbeschränkung und Selbstbehauptung: 1945–2000*. Stuttgart and Munich: Deutsche Verlags-Anstalt.

Harnisch, Sebastian, and Hanns W. Maull. 2001. *Germany as a Civilian Power?: The Foreign Policy of the Berlin Republic*, Issues in German Politics. Manchester and New York, NY: Manchester University Press.

Harnisch, Sebastian, and Siegfried Schieder. 2006. Germany's New European Policy: Weaker, Leaner, Meaner. In *Germany's Uncertain Power: Foreign Policy of the Berlin Republic*, ed. Hanns W. Maull, 95–108. Basingstoke and New York, NY: Palgrave Macmillan.

Harnisch, Sebastian, and Joachim Schild. 2014. *Deutsche Außenpolitik und internationale Führung: Ressourcen, Praktiken und Politiken in einer veränderten Europäischen Union*, Aussenpolitik und Internationale Ordnung. 1st ed. Baden-Baden: Nomos.

Haukkala, Hiski. 2010. *The EU-Russia Strategic Partnership: The Limits of Post-Sovereignty in International Relations*, Routledge Advances in International Relations and Global Politics, 85. London and New York, NY: Routledge.

Hellmann, Gunther. 2006. *Germany's EU Policy on Asylum and Defence: De-Europeanization by Default?* New Perspectives in German Studies. Basingstoke and New York, NY: Palgrave Macmillan.

Hill, Christopher. 1998. Closing the Capability-Expectations Gap? In *A Common Foreign Policy for Europe?: Competing Visions of the CFSP*, European Public Policy Series, ed. John Peterson and Helene Sjursen, 18–38. London and New York, NY: Routledge.

Hill, William H. 2012. *Russia, the Near Abroad, and the West: Lessons from the Moldova-Transdniestria Conflict*. Washington, DC and Baltimore, MD: Woodrow Wilson Center Press and Johns Hopkins University Press.

Jørgensen, Knud E. 2015. Introduction: Research Traditions. In *The SAGE Handbook of European Foreign Policy*, ed. Knud E. Jørgensen and others, vol. 1, 3–14. Los Angeles, CA: SAGE Publications.

Katzenstein, Peter J. 1997a. *Tamed Power: Germany in Europe*. 1st ed. Ithaca, NY and London: Cornell University Press.

————. 1997b. United Germany in an Integrating Europe. In *Tamed Power: Germany in Europe*, ed. Peter J. Katzenstein, 1st ed., 1–48. Ithaca, NY and London: Cornell University Press.

Kempe, Iris. 2012. Die EU und Russland. In *Jahrbuch der Europäischen Integration 2011*, ed. Werner Weidenfeld and Wolfgang Wessels, 1st ed., 317–322. Baden-Baden: Nomos.

Knodt, Michèle, and Beate Kohler-Koch. 2000. *Deutschland zwischen Europäisierung und Selbstbehauptung*, Mannheimer Jahrbuch für europäische Sozialforschung, 5. Frankfurt a. M. and New York, NY: Campus.

Kosienkowski, Marcin. 2012. Poland: Rediscovering Moldova. In *Moldova: Arena of International Influences*, ed. Marcin Kosienkowski and William Schreiber, 143–158. Lanham, MD: Lexington Books.

Kropatcheva, Elena. 2009. Russia's Response to Georgia's Military Operation in South Ossetia. In *OSCE Yearbook 2008: Yearbook on the Organization for Security and Co-Operation in Europe (OSCE)*, ed. Institute for Peace Research and Security Policy at the University of Hamburg (IFSH), 1st ed., 45–61. Nomos: Baden-Baden.

Krumm, Reinhard, Sergei Medvedev, and Hans-Henning Schröder. 2012. *Constructing Identities in Europe: German and Russian Perspectives*, Internationale Politik und Sicherheit, 66. 1st ed. Baden-Baden: Nomos.

Küchler, Florian. 2008. *The Role of the European Union in Moldova's Transnistria Conflict*, Soviet and Post-Soviet Politics and Society, 78. Stuttgart: Ibidem.

Kundnani, Hans. 2014. *The Paradox of German Power*. 1st ed. London: Hurst.

Lang, Kai-Olaf. 2008a. Polen, Deutschland und die EU-Ostpolitik: Spannungsfelder und Kooperationspotentiale. In *Deutschland und Polen: Die europäische und internationale Politik*, ed. Thomas Jäger and Daria W. Dylla, 123–136. Wiesbaden: VS Verlag für Sozialwissenschaften.

Lašas, Ainius, and D.J. Galbreath. 2013. Estonia, Latvia and Lithuania: Baltic-Russian Relations in the Post-Enlargement Era. In *National Perspectives on Russia: European Foreign Policy in the Making?* Routledge Advances in European Politics, 94, ed. Maxine David, Jackie Gower, and Hiski Haukkala, 149–168. London and New York, NY: Routledge.

Le Noan, Rachel. 2013. France. In *National Perspectives on Russia: European Foreign Policy in the Making?* Routledge Advances in European Politics, 94, ed. Maxine David, Jackie Gower, and Hiski Haukkala, 30–47. London and New York, NY: Routledge.

Ledeneva, Alena V. 2013. *Can Russia Modernise?: Sistema, Power Networks and Informal Governance*. Cambridge: Cambridge University Press.

Lough, John. 2021. *Germany's Russia problem. The struggle for balance in Europe*. Manchester: Manchester University Press.

Lukes, Steven. 1974. *Power: A Radical View*, Studies in Sociology. London and New York, NY: Macmillan.

Maass, Anna-Sophie. 2018. *EU-Russia Relations, 1999–2015: From Courtship to Confrontation*, Routledge Contemporary Russia and Eastern Europe Studies. 1st ed. Abingdon and New York NY: Taylor & Francis.

Magnette, Paul, S. Bunse, and Kalypso Nicolaïdis. 2007. Big versus Small: Shared Leadership in the EU and Power Politics in the Convention. In *Leadership in the Big Bangs of European Integration*, Palgrave Studies in European Union Politics, ed. Derek Beach and Colette Mazzucelli, 134–157. Basingstoke and New York, NY: Palgrave Macmillan.

Mattern, Janice B. 2008. The Concept of Power and the (Un)Discipline of International Relations. In *The Oxford Handbook of International Relations*, Oxford Handbooks of Political Science, ed. Christian Reus-Smit and Duncan Snidal, 691–698. Oxford and New York, NY: Oxford University Press.

Milevschi, Octavian. 2012. Romania: From Brotherly Affection with Moldova to Disillusionment and Pragmatism. In *Moldova: Arena of International Influences*, ed. Marcin Kosienkowski and William Schreiber, 159–182. Lanham, MD: Lexington Books.

Milner, Helen V. 1997. *Interests, Institutions, and Information: Domestic Politics and International Relations*. Princeton, NJ: Princeton University Press.

Milward, Alan S. 1992. *The European Rescue of the Nation-State*, Contemporary European History/Politics. London: Routledge.

Miskimmon, Alister. 2007. *Germany and the Common Foreign and Security Policy of the European Union: Between Europeanisation and National Adaptation*, New Perspectives in German Studies. Basingstoke and New York, NY: Palgrave Macmillan.

Mokken, R.N., and Frans N. Stokman. 1976. Power and Influence as Political Phenomena. In *Power and Political Theory: Some European Perspectives*, ed. Brian Barry, 33–54. London and New York, NY: Wiley.

Moravcsik, Andrew. 1998. *The Choice for Europe: Social Purpose and State Power from Messina to Maastricht*, Cornell Studies in Political Economy. Ithaca, NY: Cornell University Press.

Mouritzen, Hans, and Anders Wivel. 2012. *Explaining Foreign Policy: International Diplomacy and the Russo-Georgian War*. Boulder: L. Rienner.

Naurin, Daniel, and Helen Wallace. 2008. *Unveiling the Council of the European Union: Games Governments Play in Brussels*, Palgrave Studies in European Union Politics. Basingstoke and New York, NY: Palgrave Macmillan.

Neukirch, Claus. 2012. From Confidence Building to Conflict Settlement in Moldova? In *OSCE Yearbook 2011: Yearbook on the Organization for Security and Co-operation in Europe (OSCE)*, Institute for Peace Research and Security Policy at the University of Hamburg (IFSH), 1st ed., 137–150. Nomos: Baden-Baden.

Øhrgaard, Jakob C. 2004. International Relations or European Integration: Is the CFSP Sui Generis? In *Rethinking European Union Foreign Policy*, Europe in Change, ed. Ben Tonra and Thomas Christiansen, 26–44. Manchester and New York, NY: Manchester University Press.

Parmentier, Florent. 2012. France: Unfulfilled Potential as Major Partner. In *Moldova: Arena of International Influences*, ed. Marcin Kosienkowski and William Schreiber, 77–86. Lanham, MD: Lexington Books.

Pijpers, Alfred. 1990. *The Vicissitudes of European Political Cooperation: Towards a Realist Interpretation of the EC's Collective Diplomacy*. Leiden: Rijksuniversiteit te Leiden.

Popescu, Nicu. 2011. *EU Foreign Policy and Post-Soviet Conflicts: Stealth Intervention*, Routledge Advances in European Politics. London: Routledge.

Princen, Sebastiaan. 2009. *Agenda-Setting in the European Union*, Palgrave Studies in European Union Politics. Basingstoke and New York, NY: Palgrave Macmillan.

Radaelli, Claudio M. 2003. The Europeanization of Public Policy. In *The Politics of Europeanization*, ed. Kevin Featherstone and Claudio M. Radaelli, 27–56. Oxford and New York, NY: Oxford University Press.

Reiter, Erich. 2012. *Problemlage und Lösungsansätze im Transnistrienkonflikt*, Schriftenreihe zur internationalen Politik, 5. Vienna; Cologne; Weimar: Böhlau.

Rittberger, Volker. 1999. Deutschlands Außenpolitik nach der Vereinigung: Zur Anwendbarkeit theoretischer Modelle der Außenpolitik: Machtstaat, Handelsstaat oder Zivilstaat? In *Friedenspolitik in und für Europa: Festschrift für Gerda Zellentin zum 65. Geburtstag*, ed. Wolfgang Bergem, Volker Ronge, and Georg Weißeno, 83–108. Wiesbaden: VS Verlag für Sozialwissenschaften.

———. 2001. *German Foreign Policy since Unification: Theories and Case Studies*, Issues in German Politics. Manchester and New York, NY: Manchester University Press.

Rosamond, Ben. 2000. *Theories of European Integration*, The European Union Series. Oxford: Macmillan Education.

Sakwa, Richard. 2016. *Frontline Ukraine*. London and New York, NY: I. B. Tauris.

———. 2017. *Russia Against the Rest: The Cold Peace and the Breakdown of the European Security Order*. Cambridge and New York, NY: Cambridge University Press.

Scharpf, Fritz W. 1997. *Games Real Actors Play: Actor-Centered Institutionalism in Policy Research*, Theoretical Lenses on Public Policy. Boulder: Westview Press.

Schimmelfennig, Frank. 2009. Liberal Intergovernmentalism. In *European Integration Theory*, ed. Antje Wiener and Thomas Diez, 2nd ed., 75–94. Oxford and New York, NY: Oxford University Press.

Schneider, Heinrich, Mathias Jopp, and Uwe Schmalz. 2002. *Eine neue deutsche Europapolitik?: Rahmenbedingungen—Problemfelder—Optionen*, Europäische Schriften des Instituts für Europäische Politik, 77. Bonn: Europa-Union.

Schneider-Deters, Winfried, P.W. Schulze, and H. Timmermann. 2008. *Die Europäische Union, Russland und Eurasien: Die Rückkehr der Geopolitik*. Berlin: BWV.

Schwarz, Hans-Peter. 1985. *Die gezähmten Deutschen: Von der Machtbesessenheit zur Machtvergessenheit.* 2nd ed. Stuttgart: Deutsche Verlags-Anstalt.

———. 1994. *Die Zentralmacht Europas: Deutschlands Rückkehr auf die Weltbühne.* 1st ed. Berlin: Siedler.

Sherr, James. 2015. The Implications of the Russia-Georgia War for European Security. In *The Guns of August 2008: Russia's War in Georgia,* Studies of Central Asia and the Caucasus, ed. Svante E. Cornell and S.F. Starr, 196–224. Armonk, NY: M.E. Sharpe.

Siddi, Marco. 2017. *National Identities and Foreign Policy in the European Union: The Russia Policy of Germany, Poland and Finland.* Colchester: ECPR Press.

Slapin, Jonathan B. 2015. *Veto Power: Institutional Design in the European Union,* New Comparative Politics. Ann Arbor, MI: University of Michigan Press.

Smith, Michael E. 2004a. *Europe's Foreign and Security Policy: The Institutionalization of Cooperation,* Themes in European Governance. Cambridge and New York, NY: Cambridge University Press.

Spanger, Hans-Joachim. 2011. Die deutsche Russlandpolitik. In *Deutsche Außenpolitik: Sicherheit, Wohlfahrt, Institutionen und Normen,* ed. Thomas Jäger, Alexander Höse, and Kai Oppermann, 2nd ed., 648–672. Wiesbaden: VS Verlag für Sozialwissenschaften.

Steininger, Rolf. 2001. The German Question, 1945–95. In *Germany since Unification: The Development of the Berlin Republic,* ed. Klaus Larres, 2nd ed., 9–32. Basingstoke, New York, NY: Palgrave.

Stent, Angela. 2001. *Russia and Germany Reborn: Unification, the Soviet Collapse, and the New Europe.* Princeton, NJ: Princeton University Press.

Stewart, Susan. 2013. Germany. In *National Perspectives on Russia: European Foreign Policy in the Making?* Routledge Advances in European Politics, 94, ed. Maxine David, Jackie Gower, and Hiski Haukkala, 13–29. London and New York, NY: Routledge.

Stöber, Silvia. 2011. The Failure of the OSCE Mission to Georgia—What Remains? In *OSCE Yearbook 2010: Yearbook on the Organization for Security and Co-operation in Europe (OSCE),* ed. Institute for Peace Research and Security Policy at the University of Hamburg (IFSH), 1st ed., 203–220. Nomos: Baden-Baden.

Szabo, Stephen F. 2015. *Germany, Russia and the Rise of Geo-Economics.* 1st ed. London: Bloomsbury.

Tallberg, Jonas. 2006. *Leadership and Negotiation in the European Union.* Cambridge: Cambridge University Press.

Tanner, Fred. 2016. The OSCE and the Crisis in and around Ukraine: First Lessons for Crisis Management. In *OSCE Yearbook 2015: Yearbook on the Organization for Security and Co-operation in Europe (OSCE),* ed. Institute for Peace Research and Security Policy at the University of Hamburg (IFSH), 1st ed., 241–250. Nomos: Baden-Baden.

Tonra, Ben. 2015. Europeanization. In *The SAGE Handbook of European Foreign Policy*, ed. Knud E. Jørgensen and others, 182–195. Los Angeles, CA: SAGE Publications.

Tonra, Ben, and Thomas Christiansen. 2004. The Study of EU Foreign Policy: Between International Relations and European Studies. In *Rethinking European Union Foreign Policy*, Europe in Change, ed. Ben Tonra and Thomas Christiansen, 1–9. Manchester and New York, NY: Manchester University Press.

Underdal, Arild. 1994. Leadership Theory: Rediscovering the Arts of Management. In *International Multilateral Negotiation: Approaches to the Management of Complexity*, The Jossey-Bass Conflict Resolution Series, ed. I.W. Zartman, 1st ed., 178–197. Jossey-Bass: San Francisco.

de Waal, Thomas. 2010. *The Caucasus: An Introduction*. Oxford and New York, NY: Oxford University Press.

Wallace, Helen. 2005. Exercising Power and Influence in the European Union. In *The Member States of the European Union*, ed. Simon Bulmer and Christian Lequesne, 25–44. Oxford: Oxford University Press.

Wendt, Alexander. 1999. *Social Theory of International Politics*, Cambridge Studies in International Relations, 67. Cambridge and New York, NY: Cambridge University Press.

Wessels, Wolfgang. 2015. *The European Council*, The European Union Series. Oxford: Macmillan Education.

White, Brian. 2001. *Understanding European Foreign Policy*. Basingstoke and New York, NY: Palgrave.

Whitman, Richard G., and Stefan Wolff. 2010a. *The European Neighbourhood Policy in Perspective: Context, Implementation and Impact*, Palgrave Studies in European Union Politics. Basingstoke and New York, NY: Palgrave Macmillan.

Wilson, Andrew. 2014. *Ukraine Crisis: What it Means for the West*. New Haven, CT: Yale University Press.

Wong, Reuben Y.-P. 2005. The Europeanization of Foreign Policy. In *International Relations and the European Union*, New European Union Series, ed. Christopher Hill and Michael Smith, 4th ed., 134–153. Oxford and New York, NY: Oxford University Press.

Wong, Reuben Y.-P., and Christopher Hill. 2011. *National and European Foreign Policies: Towards Europeanization*, Routledge Advances in European Politics, 74. Abingdon and New York, NY: Routledge.

Zabarah, Dareg A. 2012. Germany: Increased Attention towards Moldova? In *Moldova: Arena of International Influences*, ed. Marcin Kosienkowski and William Schreiber, 87–104. Lanham, MD: Lexington Books.

Zagorski, Andrei. 2012. Russland und der Transnistrienkonflikt. In *Problemlage und Lösungsansätze im Transnistrienkonflikt*, Schriftenreihe zur internationalen Politik, 5, ed. Erich Reiter, 77–102. Vienna; Cologne; Weimar: Böhlau.

Zartman, I.W. 1994. *International Multilateral Negotiation: Approaches to the Management of Complexity*, The Jossey-Bass Conflict Resolution Series. 1st ed. San Francisco: Jossey-Bass.

Zellner, Wolfgang. 2009. *Die Zukunft konventioneller Rüstungskontrolle in Europa = The Future of Conventional Arms Control in Europe*, Demokratie, Sicherheit, Frieden, 194. 1st ed. Baden-Baden: Nomos.

JOURNAL ARTICLES

Aggestam, Lisbeth, and Markus Johansson. 2017. The Leadership Paradox in EU Foreign Policy. *Journal of Common Market Studies* 55 (6): 1203–1220. https://doi.org/10.1111/jcms.12558.

Allison, Roy. 2008. Russia Resurgent?: Moscow's Campaign to "Coerce Georgia to Peace". *International Affairs* 84 (6): 1145–1171. https://doi.org/10.1111/j.1468-2346.2008.00762.x.

Averre, Derek. 2016. The Ukraine Conflict: Russia's Challenge to European Security Governance. *Europe-Asia Studies* 68 (4): 699–725. https://doi.org/10.1080/09668136.2016.1176993.

Bachrach, Peter, and Morton S. Baratz. 1962. Two Faces of Power. *American Political Science Review* 56 (04): 947–952. https://doi.org/10.2307/1952796.

Bailer, Stefanie. 2010. What Factors Determine Bargaining Power and Success in EU Negotiations?. In *Negotiation Theory and the EU*, ed. Andreas Dür, Gemma Mateo, and Daniel C. Thomas (= *Journal of European Public Policy* 17), pp. 743–757.

Barnett, Michael, and Raymond Duvall. 2005. Power in International Politics. *International Organization* 59 (1): 39–75. https://www.jstor.org/stable/3877878.

Baumann, Rainer. 2002. The Transformation of German Multilateralism: Changes in the Foreign Policy Discourse since Unification. *German Politics & Society* 20 (4): 1–26. https://www.jstor.org/stable/23740512.

Baumann, Rainer, and Gunther Hellmann. 2010. Germany and the Use of Military Force: "Total War", the "Culture of Restraint" and the Quest for Normality. *German Politics* 10 (1): 61–82. https://doi.org/10.1080/0964400041233137394.

Berenskoetter, Felix, and Michael J. Williams. 2004. Editors' Introduction. In *Facets of Power in International Relations: Special Issue*, ed. Felix Berenskoetter and Michael J. Williams (= *Millennium: Journal of International Studies*, 33), pp. i–vi.

Blank, Stephen. 2009. America and the Russo-Georgian War. *Small Wars & Insurgencies* 20 (2): 425–451. https://doi.org/10.1080/09592310902975547.

Blatter, Joachim, and Till Blume. 2008. In Search of Co-Variance, Causal Mechanisms or Congruence?: Towards a Plural Understanding of Case Studies.

   Swiss Political Science Review 14 (2): 315–356. https://doi.org/10.1002/
   j.1662-6370.2008.tb00105.x.
Bowker, Mike. 2011. The War in Georgia and the Western Response. *Central
   Asian Survey* 30 (2): 197–211. https://doi.org/10.1080/0263493
   7.2011.570121.
Bulmer, Simon. 2013. Germany as the EU's Reluctant Hegemon?: Of Economic
   Strength and Political Constraints. *Journal of European Public Policy* 20 (10):
   1387–1405. https://doi.org/10.1080/13501763.2013.822824.
Bulmer, Simon, and William E. Paterson. 2010. Germany and the European
   Union: From "Tamed Power" to Normalized Power? *International Affairs* 86
   (5): 1051–1073. https://doi.org/10.1111/j.1468-2346.2010.00928.x.
Burkhardt, Fabian. 2013. Neopatrimonialisierung statt Modernisierung: Deutsche
   Russlandpolitik plus russischer otkat. *Osteuropa* 63 (8): 95–106.
Casier, Tom. 2017. The Different Faces of Power in European Union–Russia
   Relations. *Cooperation and Conflict* 53 (1): 101–117. https://doi.
   org/10.1177/0010836717729179.
Checkel, Jeffrey T. 2001. Why Comply?: Social Learning and European Identity
   Change. *International Organization* 55 (3): 553–588. https://doi.
   org/10.1162/00208180152507551.
———. 2003. "Going Native" in Europe? *Comparative Political Studies* 36 (1–2):
   209–331. https://doi.org/10.1177/0010414002239377.
———. 2005. International Institutions and Socialization in Europe: Introduction
   and Framework. *International Organization* 59 (04): 191. https://doi.
   org/10.1017/S0020818305050289.
Chivvis, Christopher S., and Thomas Rid. 2009. The Roots of Germany's Russia
   Policy. *Survival* 51 (2): 105–122. https://doi.org/10.1080/
   00396330902860850.
Daehnhardt, Patricia. 2018. German Foreign Policy, the Ukraine Crisis and the
   Euro-Atlantic Order: Assessing the Dynamics of Change. *German Politics* 26
   (4): 1–23. https://doi.org/10.1080/09644008.2018.1448386.
Daehnhardt, Patricia, and Vladimír Handl. 2018. Germany's Eastern Challenge
   and the Russia–Ukraine Crisis: A New Ostpolitik in the Making?. In *Germany's
   Eastern Challenge: A 'Hybrid Ostpolitik' in the Making?*, ed. Patricia Daehnhardt
   and Vladimír Handl (= *German Politics*, 27), pp. 445–459.
David, Maxine, and Tatiana Romanova. 2015. Modernisation in EU–Russian
   Relations: Past, Present, and Future. *European Politics and Society* 16 (1): 1–10.
   https://doi.org/10.1080/15705854.2014.965895.
Delgado, Mireia. 2011. France and the Union for the Mediterranean: Individualism
   Versus Co-operation. *Mediterranean Politics* 16 (1): 39–57. https://doi.org/
   10.1080/13629395.2011.547376.

Devyatkov, Andrey. 2012b. Russian Policy toward Transnistria: Between Multilateralism and Marginalization. *Problems of Post-Communism* 59 (3): 53–62. https://doi.org/10.2753/PPC1075-8216590305.

Dür, Andreas, Gemma Mateo, and Daniel C. Thomas. 2010. Negotiation Theory and the EU: The State of the Art. In *Negotiation Theory and the EU*, ed. Andreas Dür, Gemma Mateo and Daniel C. Thomas (= *Journal of European Public Policy*, 17), pp. 613–618.

Elgström, Ole, and Christer Jönsson. 2000. Negotiation in the European Union: Bargaining or Problem-Solving? *Journal of European Public Policy* 7 (5): 684–704. https://doi.org/10.1080/13501760010014902.

Facon, Isabelle. 2015. La relation France-Russie à l'épreuve. *Annuaire français de relation internationales* 16: 117–131. https://www.frstrategie.org/web/documents/publications/autres/2015/2015-facon-afri-relation-france-russie.pdf.

Fix, Liana. 2018. The Different "Shades" of German Power: Germany and EU Foreign Policy during the Ukraine Conflict. In *Germany's Eastern Challenge: A "Hybrid Ostpolitik" in the Making?*, ed. Patricia Daehnhardt and Vladimír Handl (= *German Politics*, 27), pp. 498–515.

Flenley, Paul. 2014. The Partnership for Modernisation: Contradictions of the Russian Modernisation Agenda. *European Politics and Society* 16 (1): 11–26. https://doi.org/10.1080/15705854.2014.965893.

de Flers, Nicole A., and Patrick Müller. 2012. Dimensions and Mechanisms of the Europeanization of Member State Foreign Policy: State of the Art and New Research Avenues. *Journal of European Integration* 34 (1): 19–35. https://doi.org/10.1080/07036337.2011.566330.

Forsberg, Tuomas. 2016. From Ostpolitik to "Frostpolitik"?: Merkel, Putin and German Foreign Policy towards Russia. *International Affairs* 92 (1): 21–42. https://doi.org/10.1111/1468-2346.12505.

Forsberg, Tuomas, and Graeme P. Herd. 2005. The EU, Human Rights, and the Russo-Chechen Conflict. *Political Science Quarterly* 120 (3): 455–478. https://doi.org/10.1002/j.1538-165X.2005.tb00554.x.

Forsberg, Tuomas, and Graeme Herd. 2015. Russia and NATO: From Windows of Opportunities to Closed Doors. *Journal of Contemporary European Studies* 23 (1): 41–57. https://doi.org/10.1080/14782804.2014.1001824.

Freire, Maria R., and Lícinia Simão. 2013. The EU's Security Actorness: The Case of EUMM in Georgia. *European Security* 22 (4): 464–477. https://doi.org/10.1080/09662839.2013.808191.

Gabanyi, Anneli U. 2012. Der Konflikt in Transnistrien im Kontext der europäischen Sicherheitspolitik. *Strategie und Sicherheit* 2012 (1): 357–368. https://doi.org/10.7767/sus.2012.2012.1.357.

Gawrich, Andrea. 2014. Emerging from the Shadows—The Ukrainian-Russian Crisis and the OSCE's Contribution to the European Security Architecture.

Die Friedens-Warte 89 (1/2): 59–80. Accessed April 19, 2019. https://www. jstor.org/stable/24868488.

Gerring, John. 2010. Causal Mechanisms: Yes, But.... *Comparative Political Studies* 43 (11): 1499–1526. https://doi.org/10.1177/0010414010376911.

Getmanchuk, Alyona, and Sergiy Solodkyy. 2018. German Crisis Management Efforts in the Ukraine–Russia Conflict from Kyiv's Perspective. In *Germany's Eastern Challenge: A 'Hybrid Ostpolitik' in the Making?*, ed. Patricia Daehnhardt and Vladimír Handl (= *German Politics*, 27), pp. 1–18.

Giegerich, Bastian, and Maximilian Terhalle. 2016. The Munich Consensus and the Purpose of German Power. *Survival* 58 (2): 155–166. https://doi.org/1 0.1080/00396338.2016.1161909.

Gomart, Thomas. 2007. France's Russia Policy: Balancing Interests and Values. *The Washington Quarterly* 30 (2): 147–155. https://doi.org/10.1162/ wash.2007.30.2.147.

Guzzini, Stefano. 1993. Structural Power: The Limits of Neorealist Power Analysis. *International Organization* 47 (03): 443–478. https://doi. org/10.1017/S0020818300028022.

de Haas, Marcel. 2010. Medvedev's Alternative European Security Architecture. *Security and Human Rights* 21 (1): 45–48. https://doi.org/10.1163/ 187502310791306070.

Haukkala, Hiski. 2014. Russian Reactions to the European Neighborhood Policy. *Problems of Post-Communism* 55 (5): 40–48. https://doi.org/10.2753/ PPC1075-8216550504.

———. 2015. From Cooperative to Contested Europe?: The Conflict in Ukraine as a Culmination of a Long-Term Crisis in EU–Russia Relations. *Journal of Contemporary European Studies* 23 (1): 25–40. https://doi.org/10.108 0/14782804.2014.1001822.

———. 2016. A Perfect Storm: Or What Went Wrong and What Went Right for the EU in Ukraine. *Europe-Asia Studies* 68 (4): 653–664. https://doi.org/1 0.1080/09668136.2016.1156055.

Hellmann, Gunther. 2009. Fatal Attraction?: German Foreign Policy and IR/ Foreign Policy Theory. *Journal of International Relations and Development* 12 (3): 257–292. https://doi.org/10.1057/jird.2009.11.

Helwig, Niklas. 2019. Germany in European Diplomacy: Minilateralism as a Tool for Leadership. *German Politics* 45 (1): 1–17. https://doi.org/10.108 0/09644008.2018.1563891.

Hill, William H. 2014. The OSCE and the Moldova-Transdniestria Conflict: Lessons in Mediation and Conflict Management. *Security and Human Rights* 24 (3–4): 287–297. https://doi.org/10.1163/18750230-02404015.

Hodson, Dermot, and Uwe Puetter. 2018. Studying Europe after the Fall: Four Thoughts on Post-EU Studies. *Journal of European Public Policy* 25 (3): 465–474. https://doi.org/10.1080/13501763.2017.1411382.

Hoffmann, Stanley. 1966. Obstinate or Obsolete?: The Fate of the Nation-State and the Case of Western Europe. *Daedalus* 95 (3): 862–915. http://www.jstor.org/stable/20027004.

Holzscheiter, Anna. 2004. Discourse as Capability: Non-State Actors' Capital in Global Governance. In *Facets of Power in International Relations: Special Issue*, ed. Felix Berenskoetter and Michael J. Williams (= *Millennium: Journal of International Studies*, 33), pp. 723–746.

Howorth, Jolyon. 2017. "Stability on the Borders": The Ukraine Crisis and the EU's Constrained Policy Towards the Eastern Neighbourhood. In *Europe's Hybrid Foreign Policy: The Ukraine-Russia Crisis*, ed. Mai'a K. Davis Cross and Ireneusz Pawel Karolewski (= *Journal of Common Market Studies*, 55), pp. 121–136.

Hoyer, Werner. 2010. A German View on the OSCE Corfu Process: An Opportunity to Strengthen Cooperative Security in Europe. *Security and Human Rights* 21 (2): 114–118. https://doi.org/10.1163/187502310791305846.

Huterer, Manfred. 2013. Strategie ist möglich: Diplomat Huterer über Deutschlands Ostpolitik. In *Zeit im Spiegel: Das Jahrhundert der Osteuropaforschung*, ed. Manfred Sapper and Volker Weichsel (= *Osteuropa*, 2–3), pp. 269–276.

Jones, Erik. 2018. Towards a Theory of Disintegration. *Journal of European Public Policy* 25 (3): 440–451. https://doi.org/10.1080/13501763.2017.1411381.

Kagan, Robert. 2019. The New German Question: What Happens When Europe Comes Apart?. *Foreign Affairs*, May/June. Accessed April 14, 2019. https://www.foreignaffairs.com/articles/germany/2019-04-02/new-german-question.

Karagiannis, Emmanuel. 2013. The 2008 Russian–Georgian War via the Lens of Offensive Realism. *European Security* 22 (1): 74–93. https://doi.org/10.1080/09662839.2012.698265.

Karlsson, Christer and others. 2012. The Legitimacy of Leadership in International Climate Change Negotiations. *AMBIO* 41 (S1): 46–55. https://doi.org/10.1007/s13280-011-0240-7.

Karolewski, Ireneusz P., and Mai'a K.D. Cross. 2017. The EU's Power in the Russia-Ukraine Crisis: Enabled or Constrained?. In *Europe's Hybrid Foreign Policy: The Ukraine-Russia Crisis*, ed. Mai'a K. Davis Cross and Ireneusz Pawel Karolewski (= *Journal of Common Market Studies*, 55), pp. 137–152.

Kindleberger, Charles P. 1981. Dominance and Leadership in the International Economy: Exploitation, Public Goods, and Free Rides. *International Studies Quarterly* 25 (2): 242–254. https://doi.org/10.2307/2600355.

Kohler-Koch, Beate. 1991. Deutsche Einigung im Spannungsfeld internationaler Umbrüche. *Politische Vierteljahresschrift* 32 (4): 605–620. https://www.jstor.org/stable/24196168.

Laqueur, Walter. 2010. Moscow's Modernization Dilemma: Is Russia Charting a New Foreign Policy? *Foreign Affairs* 89 (6): 153–160. Accessed December 16, 2018. https://www.jstor.org/stable/20788726.

Larionova, Marina. 2014. Can the Partnership for Modernisation Help Promote the EU–Russia Strategic Partnership? *European Politics and Society* 16 (1): 62–79. https://doi.org/10.1080/15705854.2014.965896.

Larsen, Henrik B.L. 2012. The Russo-Georgian War and Beyond: Towards a European Great Power Concert. *European Security* 21 (1): 102–121. https://doi.org/10.1080/09662839.2012.656595.

Lašas, Ainius. 2012. When History Matters: Baltic and Polish Reactions to the Russo-Georgian War. *Europe-Asia Studies* 64 (6): 1061–1075. https://doi.org/10.1080/09668136.2012.691724.

Layton, Samuel. 2013. Reframing European Security: Russia's Proposal for a New European Security Architecture. *International Relations* 28 (1): 25–45. https://doi.org/10.1177/0047117813507734.

Lewington, Richard. 2013. Keeping the Peace in the South Caucasus: The EU Monitoring Mission in Georgia. *Asian Affairs* 44 (1): 51–69. https://doi.org/10.1080/03068374.2012.760787.

Lintonen, Raimo. 2004. Understanding EU Crisis Decision-Making: The Case of Chechnya and the Finnish Presidency. *Journal of Contingencies and Crisis Management* 12 (1): 29–38. https://doi.org/10.1111/j.0966-0879.2004.01201004.x.

Major, Claudia. 2005. Europeanisation and Foreign and Security Policy—Undermining or Rescuing the Nation State? *Politics* 25 (3): 175–190. https://doi.org/10.1111/j.1467-9256.2005.00242.x.

Makarychev, Andrey, and Sergunin Alexander. 2013. The EU, Russia and Models of International Society in a Wider Europe. *Journal of Contemporary European Research* 9 (2): 313–329. https://www.jcer.net/index.php/jcer/article/view/506/408.

Makarychev, Andrey, and Stefan Meister. 2014. The Modernisation Debate and Russian-German Normative Cleavages. *European Politics and Society* 16 (1): 80–94. https://doi.org/10.1080/15705854.2014.965897.

Mäkinen, Sirke, Hanna Smith, and Tuomas Forsberg. 2016. "With a Little Help from my Friends": Russia's Modernisation and the Visa Regime with the European Union. *Europe-Asia Studies* 68 (1): 164–181. https://doi.org/10.1080/09668136.2015.1123223.

Manners, Ian. 2002. Normative Power Europe: A Contradiction in Terms? *Journal of Common Market Studies* 40 (2): 235–258. https://doi.org/10.1111/1468-5965.00353.

Maull, Hanns W. 1990. Germany and Japan: The New Civilian Powers. *Foreign Affairs* 69 (5): 91–106. https://doi.org/10.2307/20044603.

————. 2008. Germany and the Art of Coalition Building. *Journal of European Integration* 30(1):131–152.https://doi.org/10.1080/07036330801959531.

————. 2018. Reflective, Hegemonic, Geo-Economic, Civilian…?: The Puzzle of German Power. *German Politics* 27 (4): 1–19. https://doi.org/10.108 0/09644008.2018.1446520.

McKibben, Heather E. 2010. Issue Characteristics, Issue Linkage, and States' Choice of Bargaining Strategies in the European Union. In *Negotiation Theory and the EU*, ed. Andreas Dür, Gemma Mateo, and Daniel C. Thomas (= *Journal of European Public Policy*, 17), pp. 694–707.

Mearsheimer, John J. 1990. Back to the Future: Instability in Europe after the Cold War. *International Security* 15 (1): 5–56. https://doi.org/10.2307/2538981.

Meckstroth, Theodore W. 1975. "Most Different Systems" and "Most Similar Systems": A Study in the Logic of Comparative Inquiry. *Comparative Political Studies* 8 (2): 132–157. https://doi.org/10.1177/001041407500800202.

Meister, Stefan. 2012. Entfremdete Partner: Deutschland und Russland. *Osteuropa* 62 (6–8): 475–484. Accessed March 8, 2018. https://www.zeitschrift-osteuropa.de/hefte/2012/6-8/entfremdete-partner/.

Michael, Gabriel J. 2015. Who's Afraid of WikiLeaks?: Missed Opportunities in Political Science Research. *Review of Policy Research* 32 (2): 175–199. https://doi.org/10.1111/ropr.12120.

Mikecz, Robert. 2012. Interviewing Elites: Addressing Methodological Issues. *Qualitative Inquiry* 18 (6): 482–493. https://doi.org/10.1177/1077800412442818.

Moravcsik, Andrew. 1993. Preferences and Power in the European Community: A Liberal Intergovernmentalist Approach. *Journal of Common Market Studies* 31 (4): 473–524. https://doi.org/10.1111/j.1468-5965.1993.tb00477.x.

Morisse-Schilbach, Melanie. 2011. "Ach Deutschland!": Greece, the Euro Crisis, and the Costs and Benefits of Being a Benign Hegemon. *Internationale Politik und Gesellschaft* 1: 26–41.

Moumoutzis, Kyriakos. 2011. Still Fashionable Yet Useless?: Addressing Problems with Research on the Europeanization of Foreign Policy. *Journal of Common Market Studies* 49 (3): 607–629. https://doi.org/10.1111/j.1468-5965.2010.02146.x.

Müller, Harald. 2004. Arguing, Bargaining and All That: Communicative Action, Rationalist Theory and the Logic of Appropriateness in International Relations. *European Journal of International Relations* 10 (3): 395–435. https://doi.org/10.1177/1354066104045542.

Natorski, Michal, and Karolina Pomorska. 2017. Trust and Decision-Making in Times of Crisis: The EU's Response to the Events in Ukraine. In *Europe's Hybrid Foreign Policy: The Ukraine-Russia Crisis*, ed. Mai'a K. Davis Cross and Ireneusz Pawel Karolewski (= *Journal of Common Market Studies*, 55), pp. 54–70.

Niemann, Arne, and Jeannette Mak. 2010. (How) Do Norms Guide Presidency Behaviour in EU Negotiations?. In *Negotiation Theory and the EU*, ed. Andreas Dür, Gemma Mateo, and Daniel C. Thomas (= *Journal of European Public Policy*, 17), pp. 727–742.

Nitoiu, Cristian. 2016a. Still Entrenched in the Conflict/Cooperation Dichotomy?: EU–Russia Relations and the Ukraine Crisis. *European Politics and Society* 18 (2): 148–165. https://doi.org/10.1080/23745118.2016.1197875.

———. 2016b. Towards Conflict or Cooperation?: The Ukraine Crisis and EU-Russia Relations. *Southeast European and Black Sea Studies* 16 (3): 375–390. https://doi.org/10.1080/14683857.2016.1193305.

Odell, John S. 2010. Three Islands of Knowledge about Negotiation in International Organizations. In *Negotiation Theory and the EU*, ed. Andreas Dür, Gemma Mateo, and Daniel C. Thomas (= *Journal of European Public Policy*, 17), pp. 619–632.

Olsen, Johan P. 2002. The Many Faces of Europeanization. *Journal of Common Market Studies* 40 (5): 921–952. https://doi.org/10.1111/1468-5965.00403.

Oppermann, Kai. 2018. Between a Rock and a Hard Place?: Navigating Domestic and International Expectations on German Foreign Policy. *German Politics* 95 (4): 1–17. https://doi.org/10.1080/09644008.2018.1481208.

Orenstein, Mitchell A., and R.D. Kelemen. 2017. Trojan Horses in EU Foreign Policy. In *Europe's Hybrid Foreign Policy: The Ukraine-Russia Crisis*, ed. Mai'a K. Davis Cross and Ireneusz Pawel Karolewski (= *Journal of Common Market Studies*, 55), pp. 87–102.

Pollack, Mark A. 1997. Delegation, Agency, and Agenda Setting in the European Community. *International Organization* 51 (1): 99–134. https://www.jstor.org/stable/2703953.

Pond, Elizabeth, and Hans Kundnani. 2015. Germany's Real Role in the Ukraine Crisis: Caught Between East and West. *Foreign Affairs*, March/April. Accessed April 22, 2019. https://www.foreignaffairs.com/articles/eastern-europe-caucasus/germany-s-real-role-ukraine-crisis.

Princen, Sebastiaan. 2007. Agenda-Setting in the European Union: A Theoretical Exploration and Agenda for Research. *Journal of European Public Policy* 14 (1): 21–38. https://doi.org/10.1080/13501760601071539.

———. 2011. Agenda-Setting Strategies in EU Policy Processes. *Journal of European Public Policy* 18 (7): 927–943. https://doi.org/10.1080/1350176 3.2011.599960.

Princen, Sebastiaan, and Paul 't Hart. 2014. Putting Policy Paradigms in Their Place. *Journal of European Public Policy* 21 (3): 470–474. https://doi.org/1 0.1080/13501763.2013.876177.

Princen, Sebastiaan, and Femke van Esch. 2016. Paradigm Formation and Paradigm Change in the EU's Stability and Growth Pact. *European Political Science Review* 8 (03): 355–375. https://doi.org/10.1017/S1755773915000089.

Rahr, Alexander. 2007. Germany and Russia: A Special Relationship. *The Washington Quarterly* 30 (2): 137–145. https://doi.org/10.1162/wash.2007.30.2.137.

Richards, David. 2016. Elite Interviewing: Approaches and Pitfalls. *Politics* 16 (3): 199–204. https://doi.org/10.1111/j.1467-9256.1996.tb00039.x.

Risse, Thomas, and Mareike Kleine. 2010. Deliberation in Negotiations. In *Negotiation Theory and the EU*, ed. Andreas Dür, Gemma Mateo and Daniel C. Thomas (= *Journal of European Public Policy*, 17), pp. 708–726.

Romanova, Tatiana. 2014. The Partnership for Modernisation Through the Three Level-of-Analysis Perspectives. *European Politics and Society* 16 (1): 45–61. https://doi.org/10.1080/15705854.2014.965900.

Romanova, Tatiana, and Elena Pavlova. 2014. What Modernisation?: The Case of Russian Partnerships for Modernisation with the European Union and Its Member States. *Journal of Contemporary European Studies* 22 (4): 499–517. https://doi.org/10.1080/14782804.2014.954530.

Sapper, Manfred. 2008. *Rückblick auf ein Lehrstück: Der Kaukasuskrieg und die Folgen* (= *Osteuropa*, 11).

Schild, Joachim. 2013. Leadership in Hard Times: Germany, France, and the Management of the Eurozone Crisis. *German Politics and Society* 31 (1): 24–47. https://doi.org/10.3167/gps.2013.310103.

Schmidt-Felzmann, Anke. 2008. All for One?: EU Member States and the Union's Common Policy Towards the Russian Federation. *Journal of Contemporary European Studies* 16 (2): 169–187. https://doi.org/10.1080/14782800802309771.

Schoeller, Magnus G. 2015. Providing Political Leadership?: Three Case Studies on Germany's Ambiguous Role in the Eurozone Crisis. *Journal of European Public Policy* 24 (1): 1–20. https://doi.org/10.1080/13501763.2016.1146325.

Seibel, Wolfgang. 2015. Arduous Learning or New Uncertainties?: The Emergence of German Diplomacy in the Ukrainian Crisis. *Global Policy* 6 (10): 56–72. https://doi.org/10.1111/1758-5899.12229.

Siddi, Marco. 2016. German Foreign Policy towards Russia in the Aftermath of the Ukraine Crisis: A New Ostpolitik? *Europe-Asia Studies* 68 (4): 665–677. https://doi.org/10.1080/09668136.2016.1173879.

———. 2018. A Contested Hegemon?: Germany's Leadership in EU Relations with Russia. *German Politics* 94: 1–18. https://doi.org/10.1080/09644008.2018.1551485.

Sinkkonen, Teemu. 2011. A Security Dilemma on the Boundary Line: An EU Perspective to Georgian–Russian Confrontation after the 2008 War. *Southeast European and Black Sea Studies* 11 (3): 265–278. https://doi.org/10.1080/14683857.2011.589152.

Sjursen, Helene, and Guri Rosén. 2017. Arguing Sanctions: On the EU's Response to the Crisis in Ukraine. In *Europe's Hybrid Foreign Policy: The Ukraine-Russia Crisis*, ed. Mai'a K. Davis Cross and Ireneusz Pawel Karolewski (= *Journal of Common Market Studies*, 55), pp. 20–36.

Smith, Karen E. 2003. Understanding the European Foreign Policy System. *Contemporary European History* 12 (2): 239–254. https://doi.org/10.1017/S0960777303001176.

Smith, Michael. 2004b. Toward a Theory of EU Foreign Policy-Making: Multi-Level Governance, Domestic Politics, and National Adaptation to Europe's Common Foreign and Security Policy. *Journal of European Public Policy* 11 (4): 740–758. https://doi.org/10.1080/1350176042000248124.

Spanger, Hans-Joachim. 2012. Modernisierungspartnerschaft zwischen EU und Russland. *Strategie und Sicherheit* 2012 (1): 395–407. https://doi.org/10.7767/sus.2012.2012.1.395.

Stent, Angela. 2012. US–Russia Relations in the Second Obama Administration. *Survival* 54 (6): 123–138. https://doi.org/10.1080/00396338.2012.749635.

Tallberg, Jonas. 2010a. Explaining the Institutional Foundations of European Union Negotiations. In *Negotiation Theory and the EU*, ed. Andreas Dür, Gemma Mateo and Daniel C. Thomas (= *Journal of European Public Policy*, 17), pp. 633–647.

———. 2010b. The Power of the Chair: Formal Leadership in International Cooperation. *International Studies Quarterly* 54 (1): 241–265. https://doi.org/10.1111/j.1468-2478.2009.00585.x.

Timmermann, Heinz. 2008. EU-Russland: Hintergründe und Perspektiven einer schwierigen Beziehung. *Integration* 31: 159–178.

Timmins, Graham. 2008. German Ostpolitik under the Red-Green Coalition and EU-Russian Relations. *Debatte: Journal of Contemporary Central and Eastern Europe* 14 (3): 301–314. https://doi.org/10.1080/09651560601043082.

———. 2011. German–Russian Bilateral Relations and EU Policy on Russia: Between Normalisation and the "Multilateral Reflex". *Journal of Contemporary European Studies* 19 (2): 189–199. https://doi.org/10.1080/14782804.2011.580907.

Tonra, Ben. 2000. Mapping EU Foreign Policy Studies. *Journal of European Public Policy* 7 (1): 163–169. https://doi.org/10.1080/135017600343322.

Wagner, Wolfgang. 2003. Why the EU's Common Foreign and Security Policy Will Remain Intergovernmental: A Rationalist Institutional Choice Analysis of European Crisis Management Policy. *Journal of European Public Policy* 10 (4): 576–595. https://doi.org/10.1080/1350176032000101262.

Waltz, Kenneth N. 1993. The Emerging Structure of International Politics. *International Security* 18 (2): 44. https://doi.org/10.2307/2539097.

Warntjen, Andreas. 2010. Between Bargaining and Deliberation: Decision-Making in the Council of the European Union. In *Negotiation Theory and the EU*, ed.

Andreas Dür, Gemma Mateo, and Daniel C. Thomas (= *Journal of European Public Policy*, 17), pp. 665–679.

White, Brian. 2016. The European Challenge to Foreign Policy Analysis. *European Journal of International Relations* 5 (1): 37–66. https://doi.org/10.117 7/1354066199005001002.

Whitman, Richard G., and Stefan Wolff. 2010b. The EU as a Conflict Manager?: The Case of Georgia and Its Implications. *International Affairs* 86 (1): 87–107. https://doi.org/10.1111/j.1468-2346.2010.00870.x.

Williams, Andrew. 1999. Conflict Resolution after the Cold War: The Case of Moldova. *Review of International Studies* 25 (1): 71–86. https://doi.org/10.1017/S0260210599000716.

Wolff, Stefan, 'A Resolvable Frozen Conflict?: Designing a Settlement for Transnistria', *Nationalities Papers*, 39.6 (2011), 863–870. https://doi.org/1 0.1080/00905992.2011.617363.

Wright, Nicholas. 2018. No Longer the Elephant Outside the Room: Why the Ukraine Crisis Reflects a Deeper Shift Towards German Leadership of European Foreign Policy. In *Germany's Eastern Challenge: A 'Hybrid Ostpolitik' in the Making?*, ed. Patricia Daehnhardt and Vladimír Handl (= *German Politics*, 27), pp. 479–497.

Policy & Working Papers

Barysch, Katinka. 2010. The EU-Russia Partnership for Modernisation. In *The EU-Russia Modernisation Partnership*, The EU-Russia Centre Review, 28–32.
———. 2011. *The EU and Russia: All Smiles and No Action?*. Policy Brief, Centre for European Reform. Accessed April 14, 2019. https://www.cer.eu/sites/default/files/publications/attachments/pdf/2011/pb_russia_april11-157.pdf.

Bentzen, Naja. 2016. *Ukraine and the Minsk II Agreement: On a Frozen Path to Peace?*. Briefing, European Parliamentary Research Service. Accessed March 10, 2018. http://www.europarl.europa.eu/RegData/etudes/BRIE/2016/573951/EPRS_BRI(2016)573951_EN.pdf.

Brzoska, Michael and others. 2008. *Der Kaukasuskrieg 2008: Ein regionaler Konflikt mit internationalen Folgen. Eine Stellungnahme aus dem IFSH*, Hamburger Informationen zur Friedensforschung und Sicherheitspolitik 45, Hamburg. Accessed April 13, 2019. https://ifsh.de/pdf/publikationen/hifs/HI45.pdf.

Buras, Piotr. 2014. *Has Germany Sidelined Poland in Ukraine Crisis Negotiations?*, ECFR Commentary. Accessed March 10, 2018. http://www.ecfr.eu/article/commentary_has_germany_sidelined_poland_in_ukraine_crisis_negotiations301.

Centre for Eastern Studies. 2010. *Ukraine Supports the Russian Position on Transnistria*. Analyses. Accessed September 28, 2017. https://www.osw.waw. pl/en/publikacje/analyses/2010-05-19/ukraine-supports-russian-position-transnistria.

———. 2011. *Russia's Superficial Concession on Transnistria*. Analyses. Accessed March 13, 2019. https://www.osw.waw.pl/en/publikacje/analyses/2011-04-06/russias-superficial-concession-transnistria.

Ćwiek-Karpowicz, Jarosław. 2011. *Polish Foreign Policy Toward its Eastern Neighbors: Is a Close Cooperation with Germany Possible?*. DGAPanalyse kompakt 6, Berlin. Accessed December 18, 2018. https://dgap.org/en/think-tank/publications/dgapanalyse-compact/polish-foreign-policy-toward-its-eastern-neighbors.

Ćwiek-Karpowicz, Jarosław, and Ryszarda Formuszewicz. 2010. *Partnership on Modernisation: The EU's New Initiative towards Russia*. Bulletin, The Polish Institute of International Affairs, Warsaw. Accessed April 14, 2019. http://www.pism.pl/files/?id_plik=2713.

Delcour, Laure. 2011. *The EU and Russia's Modernisation: One Partnership, Two Views*. International Affairs at LSE Blog. Accessed March 8, 2018. http://blogs.lse.ac.uk/ideas/2011/04/the-eu-and-russia%e2%80%99s-modernisation-one-partnership-two-views/.

Di Puppo, Lili. 2009. *The EU Investigation Report on the August 2008 War and the Reactions from Georgia and Russia*. Caucasus Analytical Digest 10. Accessed October 24, 2018. http://www.laender-analysen.de/cad/pdf/CaucasusAnalyticalDigest10.pdf.

Di Puppo, Lili and others. 2008. *Perspectives on the Georgian-Russian War*. Caucasus Analytical Digest 1. Accessed October 24, 2018. http://www.laender-analysen.de/cad/pdf/CaucasusAnalyticalDigest01.pdf.

Fischer, Sabine. 2008. European Policy towards the South Caucasus after the Georgia Crisis. In *Perspectives on the Georgian-Russian War*, ed. Lili Di Puppo and others. Caucasus Analytical Digest, pp. 2–6.

———. 2013. EU-Russia Relations: A Partnership for Modernisation? In *From Cooperation to Partnership: Moving Beyond the Russia-EU Deadlock*, Europe in Dialogue, 1, ed. Bertelsmann-Stiftung, 26–34. Bertelsmann Stiftung: Gütersloh.

Fix, Liana. 2015. *Has Germany Led the West's Response toward Russia…and Will It Stay the Course?* Washington, DC: American Institute for Contemporary German Studies (AICGS). Accessed April 14, 2019. https://www.aicgs.org/publication/has-germany-led-the-wests-response-toward-russia.

Fix, Liana, and Andrea Gawrich. 2014. *Niemiecka polityka zagraniczna a rewolucja na Ukrainie*. Biuletyn Niemiecki 46. Accessed April 19, 2019. http://fwpn. org.pl/assets/Publikacje/Biuletyn_Niemiecki/2014/BIULETYN_NIEMIECKI_NR_46.pdf.

Fix, Liana, and Anna-Lena Kirch. *Germany and the Eastern Partnership after the Ukraine Crisis*, Note du Cerfa, French Institute of International Relations (Paris, Brussels, 2016). Accessed March 9, 2018. https://www.ifri.org/sites/default/files/atoms/files/ndc_128_kirch_fix_en.pdf.

Fleckenstein, Knut. 2012. The EU-Russia Modernisation Partnership—What's in It? In *Selected Articles on Modernisation and Innovation in Russia*, ed. Hanna Mäkinen, 3. Turku: Electronic Publications of Pan-European Institute.

Forbrig, Joerg. 2015. A Region Disunited?: Central European Responses to the Russia-Ukraine Crisis. Europe Policy Paper, The German Marshall Fund of the United States, Washington, DC. Accessed March 9, 2018. http://www.gmfus. org/publications/region-disunited-central-european-responses-russia-ukraine-crisis.

de Galbert, Simond. 2015. *A Year of Sanctions against Russia—Now What?: A European Assessment of the Outcome and Future of Russia Sanctions*. Washington, DC and Lanham, MD: Rowman & Littlefield.

Gallis, Paul. 2008. *The NATO Summit at Bucharest*. Washington, DC: Congressional Research Service. Accessed October 21, 2018. https://fas.org/sgp/crs/row/RS22847.pdf.

Goltz, Alexander and others. 2010. *Russia in the 21st Century: Vision for the Future*. Moscow: Institute of Contemporary Development (INSOR). Accessed April 14, 2019. http://www.riocenter.ru/files/INSOR%20Russia%20in%20the%2021st%20century_ENG.pdf.

Gotkowska, Justyna. 2010. *The German-Russian Modernisation Partnership—Failing to Meet Great Expectations*. Warsaw: OSW Analyses. Accessed March 9, 2018. https://www.osw.waw.pl/en/publikacje/analyses/2010-07-21/german-russian-modernisation-partnership-failing-to-meet-great.

Gromadzki, Grzegorz. 2015. *Perception of the Russia-Ukraine Conflict in Germany and in Poland: An Evaluation*. Warsaw: Heinrich Böll Stiftung. Accessed March 18, 2018. https://pl.boell.org/sites/default/files/perception_ru_ua_gromadzki.pdf.

Grund, Manfred. 2011. *Transnistrien und die künftige Sicherheitsarchitektur in Europa*. KAS Auslandsinformationen 9/10. Accessed September 27, 2017. http://www.kas.de/wf/doc/kas_28726-544-1-30.pdf?110908153915.

Grund, Manfred, Hans M. Sieg, and Kristin Wesemann. 2011. Transnistria and the Future Security Architecture in Europe: KAS International Reports, pp. 60–90.

Guzzini, Stefano. 2009. On the Measure of Power and the Power of Measure in International Relations. DIIS Working Paper, Danish Institute for International Studie 28, Copenhagen.

Harnisch, Sebastian. 2017. The Myth of German Hegemony: Assessing International Leadership Roles of the Merkel Governements. Paper Presented at the 2017 Annual Conference of the International Studies Association,

Baltimore, February 21–25. Accessed September 30, 2018. https://www.uni-heidelberg.de/md/politik/harnisch/person/publikationen/harnisch__isa_2017_germany_and_leadership_roles_final.pdf.

———. 2018. *Germany and EU Foreign Policy: Preliminary Chapter for Oxford Handbook of German Politics*. Heidelberg: Universität Heidelberg. Accessed March 13, 2019. https://www.uni-heidelberg.de/md/politik/harnisch/person/publikationen/harnisch_2018_germany_and_eu_foreign_policy_8.1.2018.pdf.

Harnisch, Sebastian, and Raimund Wolf. 2009. *Germany's Changing Security Culture and Governance*. Accessed March 2, 2019. https://www.uni-heidelberg.de/md/politik/harnisch/person/publikationen/harnisch__wolf_2009_germany____s_changing_security_culture_and_governance.pdf.

Heller, Regina. 2015. *Minsk II: neues Spiel, neues Glück?*. Ukraine-Analysen 146. Accessed March 10, 2018. http://www.laender-analysen.de/ukraine/pdf/UkraineAnalysen146.pdf.

Hellmann, Gunther. 2014. *Die Deutschen und die Russen: Über Neigungen und machtpolitische Sozialisierungen*. WeltTrends 96. Accessed March 2, 2019. www.fb03.uni-frankfurt.de/50290123/WeltTrends2014_final.pdf.

Helwig, Niklas. 2016. *Europe's New Political Engine: Germany's Role in the EU's Foreign and Security Policy*. Report, Finnish Institute for International Affairs 44, Helsinki. Accessed April 14, 2019. https://www.fiia.fi/wp-content/uploads/2017/01/fiiareport44_europes_new_political_engine.pdf.

Huterer, Manfred. 2010. The Russia Factor in Transatlantic Relations and New Opportunities for U.S.-EU-Russia Cooperation. Working Paper, The Brookings Institution 4, Washington, DC. Accessed April 14, 2019. https://www.brookings.edu/wp-content/uploads/2016/06/06_us_eu_russia_huterer.pdf.

Institut für Friedensforschung und Sicherheitspolitik an der Universität Hamburg. 2016. *Protracted Conflicts in the OSCE Area: Innovative Approaches for Co-Operation in the Conflict Zones*. Hamburg: OSCE Network of Think Tanks and Academic Institutions. Accessed April 14, 2019. http://osce-network.net/file-OSCE-Network/documents/Protracted_Conflicts_OSCE_WEB.pdf.

International Crisis Group. 2008. Russia vs Georgia: The Fallout. Europe Report 195. Tbilisi, Brussels. Accessed April 14, 2019. https://www.crisisgroup.org/europe-central-asia/caucasus/georgia/russia-vs-georgia-fallout.

———. 2015. The Ukraine Crisis: Risks of Renewed Military Conflict after Minsk II. Crisis Group Europe Briefing 73, Kiev, Brussels. Accessed March 10, 2018. https://www.crisisgroup.org/europe-central-asia/eastern-europe/ukraine/ukraine-crisis-risks-renewed-military-conflict-after-minsk-ii.

Ischinger, Wolfgang. 2016. Das Russland-Paradox: Vom (richtigen und falschen) Umgang mit Moskau, Munich Security Conference (MSC) Blog. Accessed October 21, 2018. https://www.securityconference.de/news/article/monthly-mind-juli-2016-das-russland-paradox-vom-richtigen-oder-falschen-umgang-mit-moskau/.

Ivashko, Iryna, and Anton Krut. 2015. *Warum sind die Vereinbarungen von Minsk so fragil?*, Ukraine-Analysen 146. Accessed April 14, 2019. http://www.laender-analysen.de/ukraine/pdf/UkraineAnalysen146.pdf.

Jankowski, Dominik P., Tobias Bunde, and Martin Michelot. 2014. *Reassurance First: Goals for an Ambitious Weimar Triangle.* Washington, DC: Center for European Policy Analysis. Accessed March 9, 2018. http://cepa.org/index/?id=8f0ba28049c871e3c7f552a32affdbe5.

Jarábik, Balázs. 2015. *What Did Minsk II Actually Achieve?* Moscow: Carnegie Moscow Center. Accessed March 10, 2018. http://carnegie.ru/commentary/59059.

Kalb, Marvin. 2014. *Is Putin "in Another World?".* The Brookings Institution. Accessed March 15, 2018. https://www.brookings.edu/blog/up-front/2014/03/04/is-putin-in-another-world/.

Kempe, Iris. 2006. *From a European Neighbourhood Policy towards a New Ostpolitik: The Potential Impact of German Policy.* CAP Policy Analysis 6. Accessed April 14, 2019. https://www.files.ethz.ch/isn/44156/CAP-Analyse-2006-03_en.pdf.

Kempin, Ronja, and Margarete Klein. 2015. *Plädoyer für eine EU-Russland-Friedensmission in der Ukraine.* Kurz gesagt, Stiftung Wissenschaft und Politik, Berlin. Accessed March 10, 2018. https://www.swp-berlin.org/kurz-gesagt/plaedoyer-fuer-eine-eu-russland-friedensmission-in-der-ukraine/.

Kofman, Michael, and Matthew Rojansky. 2015. *U.S. and German Views on Ukraine: The Risks of Trans-Atlantic Misunderstanding.* Friedrich-Ebert-Stiftung Perspective, Berlin. Accessed April 14, 2019. https://library.fes.de/pdf-files/id/11456.pdf.

Lang, Kai-Olaf. 2008b. The Old Fears of the New Europeans. In *The Caucasus Crisis: International Perceptions and Policy Implications for Germany and Europe,* ed. Hans-Henning Schröder. Research Paper, Stiftung Wissenschaft und Politik. Universitäts- und Landesbibliothek Sachsen-Anhalt; Stiftung Wissenschaft und Politik, 30–33

Lang, Kai-Olaf, and Barbara Lipper. 2012. *The EU and Its Neighbours: A Second Chance to Marry Democratisation and Stability.* Comments, Stiftung Wissenschaft und Politik. Accessed April 14, 2019. https://www.swp-berlin.org/fileadmin/contents/products/comments/2012C02_12_lng_lpt.pdf.

Lewis, Jeffrey. 2009. The Impact of Institutional Environments on Negotiation Styles in EU Decision Making. Paper prepared for the European Union Studies Association (EUSA) Eleventh Biennial International Conference, Los Angeles, CA, April 23–25. Accessed March 2, 2019. http://aei.pitt.edu/33098/1/lewis._jeffrey.pdf.

Liik, Kadri. 2015. *The Real Problem with Mogherini's Russia,* ECFR Commentary. Accessed March 10, 2018. http://www.ecfr.eu/article/commentary_the_real_problem_with_mogherinis_russia_paper402.

————. 2018. *Winning the Normative War with Russia: An EU-Russia Power Audit.* European Council on Foreign Relations. Accessed April 14, 2019. https://www.ecfr.eu/publications/summary/winning_the_normative_war_with_russia_an_eu_russia_power_audit.

Lindner, Rainer. 2008. Die Krim als neuer "Frozen Conflict"? In *Der bewaffnete Konflikt um Südossetien und internationale Reaktionen*, ed. Heiko Pleines, Hans-Henning Schröder, and Forschungsstelle Osteuropa, 27–28. Bremen: Forschungsstelle Osteuropa.

Lippert, Barbara. 2015. *Deutsche Europapolitik zwischen Tradition und Irritation: Beobachtungen aus aktuellem Anlass*, Arbeitspapier FG EU/Europa, Stiftung Wissenschaft und Politik. Accessed April 14, 2019. https://www.swp-berlin.org/fileadmin/contents/products/arbeitspapiere/Deutsche_Europapolitik.pdf.

Lo, Bobo. 2009. *Medvedev and the New European Security Architecture.* Policy Brief, Centre for European Reform. Accessed March 12, 2019. https://www.cer.eu/sites/default/files/publications/attachments/pdf/2011/pbrief_medvedev_july09-741.pdf.

————. 2012. *21st Century Myth: Authoritarian Modernization in Russia and China.* Moscow: Carnegie Moscow Center. Accessed December 16, 2018. https://carnegieendowment.org/files/BoboLo_Shevtsova_web.pdf.

Ludlow, Peter. 2014a. *June, July and August 2014: Appointing New Leaders and Dealing with the Ukrainian Crisis.* Preliminary Evaluation, Brussels. Accessed April 14, 2019. http://www.eurocomment.eu/preliminary-evaluation-20144/.

————. 2014b. *The European Council of 20–21 March 2014: The European Semester, Energy Policy, Ukraine and Africa.* Preliminary Evaluation, Brussels. Accessed March 17, 2018. http://www.eurocomment.eu/preliminary-evaluation-20142/.

————. 2014c. *The Extraordinary European Council of 6 March 2014: The EU Stakes out Its Ground on Ukraine and the Media Do Not Listen.* Preliminary Evaluation, Brussels. Accessed March 15, 2018. http://www.eurocomment.eu/wp-content/uploads/downloads/2014/03/Preliminary-Evaluation-2014.1.pdf.

Lynch, Dov. 2006. *Why Georgia Matters.* Chaillot Paper, Institute for Security Studies 86, Paris. Accessed April 14, 2019. https://infoeuropa.eurocid.pt/files/database/000036001-000037000/000036733.pdf.

Makarychev, Andrey. 2012. *A Farewell to Meseberg?*, PONARS Eurasia. Accessed September 29, 2017. http://www.ponarseurasia.org/article/farewell-meseberg.

Malygina, Katerina. 2013. *Die Ukraine vor dem EU-Gipfel in Vilnius: Einflussversuche externer Akteure, abrupter Kurswechsel der Regierung und die Volksversammlung zugunsten der europäischen Integration.* Ukraine-Analysen 124. Accessed April 14, 2019. http://www.laender-analysen.de/ukraine/pdf/UkraineAnalysen124.pdf.

Meister, Stefan. 2011a. *A New Start for Russian-EU Security Policy?: The Weimar Triangle, Russia and the EU's Eastern Neighbourhood.* Genshagener Papiere 7. Accessed September 27, 2017. https://www.robert-schuman.eu/en/doc/actualites/genshagener-papiere-2011-7-eng.pdf.

———. 2011b. *German Eastern Policy: Is a Partnership with Poland Possible?.* DGAPanalyse kompakt 7. Accessed December 18, 2018. https://dgap.org/en/think-tank/publications/dgapanalyse-compact/german-eastern-policy.

———. 2014. *Reframing Germany's Russia Policy—An Opportunity for the EU.* Policy Brief, European Council on Foreign Relations. Accessed April 14, 2019. https://www.ecfr.eu/page/-/ECFR100_GERMANY_RUSSIA_BRIEF_AW.pdf.

———. 2015. *Warum Minsk II nicht funktionieren wird.* Ukraine-Analysen 146. Accessed March 10, 2018. http://www.laender-analysen.de/ukraine/pdf/UkraineAnalysen146.pdf.

Mendras, Marie. 2013. *Russia—France: A Strained Political Relationship.* Russian Analytical Digest 130. Accessed December 18, 2018. http://www.css.ethz.ch/content/dam/ethz/special-interest/gess/cis/center-for-securities-studies/pdfs/RAD-130-2-8.pdf.

Nünlist, Christian. 2014. Testfall Ukraine-Krise: Das Konfliktmanagement der OSZE unter Schweizer Vorsitz. In *Bulletin 2014 zur schweizerischen Sicherheitspolitik,* ed. Christian Nünlist and Oliver Thränert, 35–61. Zurich: Center for Security Studies der ETH Zürich.

Paweł, Świeboda. 2008. *The Conflict in Georgia and Its Implications for the Region—the Polish Perspective.* Heinrich Böll Stiftung. Accessed October 24, 2018. https://pl.boell.org/sites/default/files/downloads/Conflict_in_Georgia_by_Pawel_Swieboda.pdf.

Pifer, Steven. 2014. *Poroshenko Signs EU-Ukraine Association Agreement.* The Brookings Institution. Accessed March 17, 2018. https://www.brookings.edu/blog/up-front/2014/06/27/poroshenko-signs-eu-ukraine-association-agreement/.

Pleines, Heiko. 2015. *Trennlinien in der Ostukraine.* Ukraine-Analysen 146. Accessed March 10, 2018. http://www.laender-analysen.de/ukraine/pdf/UkraineAnalysen146.pdf.

Pond, Elizabeth. 2014. *Merkel's Leadership in the Ukraine Crisis.* Washington, DC: American Institute for Contemporary German Studies (AICGS). Accessed March 9, 2018. https://www.aicgs.org/publication/merkels-leadership-in-the-ukraine-crisis/.

Raik, Kristi. 2015. *No Zero-Sum Game among EU Foreign Policy Actors: Germany's Leadership in the Ukraine Crisis has Strengthened the Union.* Comment, Finnish Institute of International Affairs 8/2015, Helsinki. Accessed March 10, 2018. https://www.fiia.fi/en/publication/no-zero-sum-game-among-eu-foreign-policy-actors?read.

Referat Mittel- und Osteuropa der Friedrich-Ebert-Stiftung. 2007. *Partnership with Russia in Europe: Economic and Regional Topics for a Strategic Partnership.* Gesprächskreis Partnerschaft mit Russland in Europa. Accessed April 14, 2019. http://library.fes.de/pdf-files/id/04688.pdf.

Remler, Philip. 2013. *Negotiation Gone Bad: Russia, Germany, and Crossed Communications.* Carnegie Europe. Accessed September 27, 2017. http://carnegieeurope.eu/2013/08/21/negotiation-gone-bad-russia-germany-and-crossed-communications-pub-52712.

Richter, Wolfgang. 2017. Return to Security Cooperation in Europe: The Stabilizing Role of Conventional Arms Control. Deep Cuts Working Paper 11, Hamburg. Accessed April 14, 2019. http://deepcuts.org/images/PDF/DeepCuts_WP11_Richter.pdf.

Rinnert, David, and Florent Parmentier. 2013. *Finding Common Denominators in the Eastern Partnership Region: Towards a Strategic French-German Cooperation in the Transnistrian Conflict.* Policy Brief, The Institute for Development and Social Initiatives "Viitorul" and Friedrich Ebert Stiftung, Chisinau, Paris, Berlin. Accessed September 28, 2017. http://www.fes-moldova.org/media/pdf/Policy_Policy_Brief_2013_1.pdf.

Schröder, Hans-Henning. 2008. The Caucasus Crisis: International Perceptions and Policy Implications for Germany and Europe. Research Paper, Stiftung Wissenschaft und Politik. Accessed October 30, 2018. https://www.swp-berlin.org/fileadmin/contents/products/research_papers/2008_RP09_shh_ed_ks.pdf.

Sieg, Hans M. 2011. Der Transnistrien-Konflikt: Voraussetzungen für eine Konfliktlösung. *Südosteuropa Mitteilungen* 51 (3): 62–77.

———. 2017. *The EU's Role or Absence in "Frozen Conflicts" in Transnistria and Caucasus,* Berlin. Accessed September 29, 2017. http://nbn-resolving.de/urn:nbn:de:0168-ssoar-394784.

Smith, Michael E. 2009. European Foreign Policy as a Research Field: An Historical and Conceptual Overview. Paper prepared for delivery at the EUSA Conference Los Angeles, CA. Accessed March 2, 2019. http://citeseerx.ist.psu.edu/viewdoc/download?doi=10.1.1.523.5682&rep=rep1&type=pdf.

Socor, Vladimir. 2008a. *EU's French Presidency Rushes Partnership Talks with Moscow.* Eurasia Daily Monitor, The Jamestown Foundation 209. Accessed April 14, 2019. https://jamestown.org/program/eus-french-presidency-rushes-partnership-talks-with-moscow/.

———. 2008b. *Post-Mortems on the German Plan on Abkhazia.* Eurasia Daily Monitor, The Jamestown Foundation 140. Accessed October 21, 2018. https://jamestown.org/program/post-mortems-on-the-german-plan-on-abkhazia/.

———. 2008c. *Summit Tests EU's Capacity to Oppose Russia's Reexpansion.* Eurasia Daily Monitor, The Jamestown Foundation 165. Accessed December 16, 2018.

https://jamestown.org/program/summit-tests-eus-capacity-to-oppose-russias-reexpansion/#!.

———. 2010. *Meseberg Process: Germany Testing EU-Russia Security Cooperation Potential.* Eurasia Daily Monitor, The Jamestown Foundation 191. Accessed September 27, 2017. https://jamestown.org/program/meseberg-process-germany-testing-eu-russia-security-cooperation-potential/.

———. 2011a. *German Diplomacy Tilts toward Russia on Transnistria Negotiations.* Eurasia Daily Monitor, The Jamestown Foundation 108. Accessed September 28, 2017. https://jamestown.org/program/german-diplomacy-tilts-toward-russia-on-transnistria-negotiations/.

———. 2011b. *Moscow Signals Interest in Berlin Initiative on Transnistria.* Eurasia Daily Monitor, The Jamestown Foundation 63. Accessed September 28, 2017. https://jamestown.org/program/moscow-signals-interest-in-berlin-initiative-on-transnistria/.

———. 2016. *Surkov-Nuland Talks on Ukraine: A Nontransparent Channel (Part One).* Eurasia Daily Monitor, The Jamestown Foundation 103, Washington, DC. Accessed March 10, 2018. https://jamestown.org/program/surkov-nuland-talks-on-ukraine-a-nontransparent-channel-part-one/.

Speck, Ulrich. 2015. *German Power and the Ukraine Conflict*, Carnegie Europe, Brussels. Accessed October 30, 2015. http://carnegieeurope.eu/2015/03/26/german-power-and-ukraine-conflict.

Stewart, Susan. 2011. *Die deutsch-russische Modernisierungspartnerschaft: Skepsis angebracht.* Kurz gesagt, Stiftung Wissenschaft und Politik, Berlin. Accessed April 14, 2019. https://www.swp-berlin.org/kurz-gesagt/die-deutsch-russische-modernisierungspartnerschaft-skepsis-angebracht/.

Stiftung Wissenschaft und Politik, and The German Marshall Fund of the United States. 2013. *Neue Macht, Neue Verantwortung: Elemente einer deutschen Außen- und Sicherheitspolitik für eine Welt im Umbruch*, Berlin. Accessed September 30, 2018. https://www.swp-berlin.org/fileadmin/contents/products/projekt_papiere/DeutAussenSicherhpol_SWP_GMF_2013.pdf.

Szabo, Stephen F. 2019. *Germany: Hegemon or Free Rider?*. American Institute for Contemporary German Studies (AICGS). Accessed April 28, 2019. https://www.aicgs.org/2019/04/germany-hegemon-or-free-rider/.

Szczepański, Marcin. 2015. *Economic Impact on the EU of Sanctions over Ukraine Conflict.* Briefing, European Parliamentary Research Service, October. Accessed March 17, 2018. http://www.europarl.europa.eu/RegData/etudes/BRIE/2015/569020/EPRS_BRI(2015)569020_EN.pdf.

Thomas, Daniel C. 2008. The Negotiation of EU Foreign Policy: Normative Institutionalism and Alternative Approaches. UCD Dublin European Institute Working Paper 08-4, Dublin. Accessed March 18, 2018. https://www.ucd.ie/t4cms/WP_08-4_Daniel_Thomas.pdf.

Turkowski, Andrzej. 2011. *The Polish-German Tandem*. Washington, DC: Carnegie Endowment for International Peace. Accessed April 14, 2019. http://carnegieendowment.org/2011/11/17/polish-german-tandem/7wgo.

Ulbert, Cornelia, Thomas Risse, and Harald Müller. 2004. Arguing and Bargaining in Multilateral Negotiations. Paper presented to the Conference on "Empirical Approaches to Deliberative Politics" European University Institute, Swiss Chair. Accessed March 2, 2019. https://www.polsoz.fu-berlin.de/polwiss/forschung/international/atasp/forschung/projekte_abgeschlossen/argumentieren/ulbert_risse_mueller_2004.pdf.

Wilson, Andrew. 2010. *The Rostov Summit*. ECFR Commentary. Accessed March 8, 2018. http://www.ecfr.eu/article/commentary_the_rostov_summit.

Wolff, Stefan. 2018. *The OSCE in Moldova: From Confidence Building to Conflict Settlement?*. Accessed April 14, 2019. https://events.uta.fi/experiencesandopportunities2018/wp-content/uploads/sites/51/2018/11/Wolff_The-OSCE-in-Moldova-From-confidence-building-to-conflict-settlement.pdf.

News Articles

Abkhazia's Separatists Reject German Plan to Prevent Conflict with Georgia. 2008. *The New York Times*, July 18. Accessed October 21, 2018. https://www.nytimes.com/2008/07/18/world/europe/18iht-georgia.4.14615798.html.

Alexander, Robin, and Daniel F. Sturm. 2014. Steinmeier begleitet Lawrow nicht mal bis vor die Tür. *Die Welt*, March 9. Accessed March 13, 2019. https://www.welt.de/politik/deutschland/article125583674/Steinmeier-begleitet-Lawrow-nicht-mal-bis-vor-die-Tuer.html.

Applebaum, Anne. 2015. The Risks of Putting Germany Front and Center in Europe's Crises. *The Washington Post*, February 20. Accessed March 9, 2018. http://www.washingtonpost.com/opinions/germanys-central-role/2015/02/20/d1119cd4-b8f8-11e4-aa05-1ce812b3fdd2_story.html.

Baker, Peter. 2014. Pressure Rising as Obama Works to Rein in Russia. *The New York Times*, March 2. Accessed April 13, 2019. https://www.nytimes.com/2014/03/03/world/europe/pressure-rising-as-obama-works-to-rein-in-russia.html.

Beck, Ulrich. 2013. Germany Has Created an Accidental Empire. *Social Europe*, March 25. Accessed October 18, 2018. https://www.socialeurope.eu/germany-has-created-an-accidental-empire.

Berlin schlägt in der EU-Russlandpolitik eine "Annäherung durch Verflechtung" vor. 2006. *Frankfurter Allgemeine Zeitung*, September 4.

Beste, Ralf, Markus Feldenkirchen, and Alexander Szandar. 2008a. Germany and the Caucasus Conflict: Merkel's Most Serious Foreign Policy Crisis. *Spiegel Online*, August 18. Accessed December 16, 2018. http://www.spiegel.de/

international/world/germany-and-the-caucasus-conflict-merkel-s-most-serious-foreign-policy-crisis-a-572726.html.

Beste, Ralf, Uwe Klußmann, and Gabor Steingart. 2008b. The Cold Peace. *Spiegel Online*, September 1. Accessed March 8, 2018. http://www.spiegel.de/international/world/russia-and-the-west-the-cold-peace-a-575581-3.html.

Brown Fails to Get EU Sanctions against Russia. 2008. *The Daily Telegraph*, September 2.

Chiacu, Doina, and Arshad Mohammad. 2014. Leaked Audio Reveals Embarrassing U.S. Exchange on Ukraine, EU. *Reuters*, February 7. Accessed March 9, 2018. https://www.reuters.com/article/us-usa-ukraine-tape/leaked-audio-reveals-embarrassing-u-s-exchange-on-ukraine-eu-idUSBREA1601G20140207.

Crisis in the Caucasus: EU Considers Sanctions as Russia Looks for Friends. 2008. *Spiegel Online*, August 28. Accessed December 16, 2018. http://www.spiegel.de/international/world/crisis-in-the-caucasus-eu-considers-sanctions-as-russia-looks-for-friends-a-575041.html.

David Cameron Calls for Tough EU Sanctions on Russia. 2008. *The Guardian*, September 1.

Deal Struck to Calm Ukraine Crisis. 2014. *BBC News*, April 17. Accessed March 10, 2018. http://www.bbc.com/news/world-europe-27072351.

Dempsey, Judy. 2010. Challenging Russia to Fix a Frozen Feud. *The New York Times*, October 27. Accessed September 28, 2017. http://www.nytimes.com/2010/10/28/world/europe/28iht-letter.html.

Die deutsch-russische Modernisierungspartnerschaft. 2010. *Frankfurter Allgemeine Zeitung*, May 30. Accessed December 16, 2018. https://www.faz.net/aktuell/politik/guido-westerwelle-und-sergej-lawrow-die-deutsch-russische-modernisierungspartnerschaft-1984205.html.

Erlanger, Steven, and Katrin Bennhold. 2010. Sarkozy to Propose New Bond With Russia. *The New York Times*, October 1. Accessed September 28, 2017. http://www.nytimes.com/2010/10/02/world/europe/02france.html?_r=1.

Erlanger, Steven, and Steven Lee Myers. 2008. NATO Allies Oppose Bush on Georgia and Ukraine. *The New York Times*, April 3. Accessed October 21, 2018.https://www.nytimes.com/2008/04/03/world/europe/03nato.html.

Erler, Gernot. 2013. "In Sachen Ukraine gibt es in der EU zu viele Fehleinschätzungen": Interview mit Gernot Erler. *Internationale Politik*, December 12. Accessed March 9, 2018. https://zeitschrift-ip.dgap.org/de/ip-die-zeitschrift/themen/europaeische-union/sachen-ukraine-gibt-es-der-eu-zu-viele.

EU Considers Sanctions on Russia. 2008. *BBC News*, August 28. Accessed December 16, 2018. http://news.bbc.co.uk/2/hi/europe/7585580.stm.

EU Foreign Ministers Consider Restarting Talks with Russia. 2008. *alfa.lt*, November 11. Accessed December 16, 2018. https://www.alfa.lt/straipsnis/10235828/eu-foreign-ministers-consider-restarting-talks-with-russia.

EU Officials Warn Yerevan over "U-Turn". 2013. *RadioFreeEurope/RadioLiberty*, September 4. Accessed March 13, 2019. https://www.rferl.org/a/armenia-eu-customs-union/25095145.html.

EU will keine Sanktionen gegen Russland. 2008. *Der Tagesspiegel*, August 29. Accessed December 16, 2018. https://www.tagesspiegel.de/politik/kaukasus-konflikt-eu-will-keine-sanktionen-gegen-russland/1313272.html.

EU-Abkommen mit Ukraine endgültig geplatzt. 2013. *Wall Street Journal*, November 29. Accessed October 30, 2015. http://www.wsj.de/nachrichten/SB10001424052702304017204579226680510056584.

EU-Länder fragen nach Ursachen des Kaukasus-Konflikts. 2008. *Reuters*, September 5. Accessed December 16, 2018. https://de.reuters.com/article/eu-russland-georgien-2zf-idDEHUM56039420080905.

EU-Politik gegenüber Russland: Steinmeier will keine Sanktionen. 2008. *Frankfurter Allgemeine Zeitung*, August 28. Accessed December 16, 2018. https://www.faz.net/aktuell/politik/europaeische-union/eu-politik-gegenueber-russland-steinmeier-will-keine-sanktionen-1679457.html.

Europa sucht eine gemeinsame Haltung zum Georgien-Konflikt. 2008. *Deutschlandradio*, August 31. Accessed December 16, 2018. https://www.deutschlandradio.de/europa-sucht-eine-gemeinsame-haltung-zum-georgien-konflikt.331.de.html?dram:article_id=202409.

Filat, Vlad, and Lavinia Pitu. 2010. "Deutschland gehört zu unseren Freunden": Interview mit Vlad Filat. *Deutsche Welle*, May 14. Accessed September 28, 2017. http://p.dw.com/p/NLPx.

France and Germany Thwart Bush's Plans. 2008. *Spiegel Online*, April 3. Accessed October 21, 2018. http://www.spiegel.de/international/world/nato-expansion-defeat-france-and-germany-thwart-bush-s-plans-a-545078.html.

Frau Fix-It: A New Role for Germany in the East: Make Friends, Fix Problems. 2010. *The Economist*, November 18. Accessed April 13, 2019. http://www.economist.com/node/17522476.

French-German-Russian Summit: Sarkozy Dreams of a European Security Council. 2010. *Spiegel Online*, October 18. Accessed September 28, 2017. http://www.spiegel.de/international/europe/french-german-russian-summit-sarkozy-dreams-of-a-european-security-council-a-723664.html.

Germany Proposes Peace Plan for Abkhazia. 2008. *Spiegel Online*, July 7. Accessed October 21, 2018. http://www.spiegel.de/international/europe/calming-the-caucasus-germany-proposes-peace-plan-for-abkhazia-a-564246.html.

Germany Takes Lead in Abkhaz Diplomatic Efforts. 2008. *Civil.ge*, July 16. Accessed October 21, 2018. http://www.civil.ge/eng/article.php?id=18797.

Harte Worte aus Georgien. 2008. *ntv*, July 17. Accessed April 13, 2019. https://www.n-tv.de/politik/Harte-Worte-aus-Georgien-article13456.html.

Henderson, Barney, Arron Merat, and David Millward. 2014. Ukraine Crisis: March 6 as It Happened. *The Telegraph*, March 6. Accessed March 10, 2018. https://www.telegraph.co.uk/news/worldnews/europe/ukraine/10679802/Ukraine-Russia-crisis-live.html.

Ischinger, Wolfgang. 2015. Deutschland in der Hegemonie-Falle by Wolfgang Ischinger. *Project Syndicate*, September 14. Accessed March 10, 2018. https://www.project-syndicate.org/commentary/germany-should-support-common-eu-foreign-policy-by-wolfgang-ischinger-2015-09/german.

Kaczynski rügt deutsche Nato-Politik. 2008. *Frankfurter Allgemeine Zeitung*, April 2. Accessed October 21, 2018. http://www.faz.net/aktuell/politik/ausland/gipfeltreffen-in-bukarest-kaczynski-ruegt-deutsche-nato-politik-1541254.html.

Kimball, Spencer. 2015. Proposed US Weapons Deliveries to Ukraine Raise Fears of Further Escalation. *Deutsche Welle*, February 5. Accessed March 18, 2018. http://p.dw.com/p/1EVmN.

Kornelius, Stefan. 2010. Der Russland-Test. *Süddeutsche Zeitung*, July 16. Accessed September 28, 2017. http://www.sueddeutsche.de/politik/berlin-und-moskau-der-russland-test-1.975723.

Krumrey, Henning. 2008. Merkel zwischen Krieg und Frieden. *Focus*, August 17. Accessed March 7, 2019. https://www.focus.de/politik/ausland/kaukasus/tid-11514/georgien-merkel-zwischen-krieg-und-frieden_aid_325677.html.

Kyiv Announces First "Round Table" Talks, Without Separatists, on Steinmeier Visit. 2014. *Deutsche Welle*, May 13. Accessed March 10, 2018. http://p.dw.com/p/1Bz5U.

Lau, Jörg, and Michael Thumann. 2015. Tief im Osten, weit voraus. *Zeit Online*, December 11. Accessed April 14, 2019. https://www.zeit.de/2014/51/frank-walter-steinmeier-russland-rede.

Lawrow: Nur Kiew und Separatisten können Lösung aushandeln. 2014. *Frankfurter Allgemeine Zeitung*, November 19. Accessed March 10, 2018. http://www.faz.net/aktuell/politik/ausland/europa/ukraine-krise-sergej-lawrow-will-keine-gespraeche-mit-westen-13274570.html.

Lithuania Sends Foreign Minister to Georgia. 2008. *Reuters*, August 8. Accessed March 7, 2019. https://www.reuters.com/article/idUSL8654009.

Makhovsky, Andrei. 2014. Pro-Russian Rebels Reach Ceasefire Deal. *Reuters*, September 5. Accessed April 14, 2019. https://www.reuters.com/article/us-ukraine-crisis/ukraine-pro-russian-rebels-reach-ceasefire-deal-idUSKBN0GZ18D20140905.

Marquand, Robert. 2010. Facing a Rising China, Russia Looks to Boost Europe Ties. *The Christian Science Monitor*, October 18. Accessed September 28, 2017. https://www.csmonitor.com/World/Europe/2010/1018/Facing-a-rising-China-Russia-looks-to-boost-Europe-ties.

McElroy, Damien. 2014. Ukraine Opposition Asks EU to Intervene in Talks as Viktor Yanukovych "Wastes Time". *The Telegraph*, February 5. Accessed March 9, 2018. https://www.telegraph.co.uk/news/worldnews/europe/ukraine/10618880/Ukraine-opposition-asks-EU-to-intervene-in-talks-as-Viktor-Yanukovych-wastes-time.html.

McElroy, Damien, and Jon Swaine. 2008. Condoleezza Rice in Tbilisi to Secure Georgia Peace Plan. *The Telegraph*, August 15. Accessed December 16, 2018. https://www.telegraph.co.uk/news/worldnews/europe/georgia/2562284/Condoleezza-Rice-in-Tbilisi-to-secure-Georgia-peace-plan.html.

Merkel Backs Georgia's Bid to Join NATO in Visit to Tbilisi. 2008. *The Jerusalem Post*, August 17. Accessed December 16, 2018. https://www.jpost.com/International/Merkel-backs-Georgias-bid-to-join-NATO-in-visit-to-Tbilisi.

Merkel, Medvedev Clash Over Russia's War in Sochi Talks. 2008. *Deutsche Welle*, August 15. Accessed December 16, 2018. https://www.dw.com/en/merkel-medvedev-clash-over-russias-war-in-sochi-talks/a-3567243.

Merkel Sceptical of NATO Deployments in Eastern Europe. 2014. *Euractiv*, July 3. Accessed March 18, 2018. https://www.euractiv.com/section/europe-s-east/news/merkel-sceptical-of-nato-deployments-in-eastern-europe/.

Merkel Signals Support for Georgia's NATO Membership Bid. 2008. *Deutsche Welle*, August 17. Accessed April 13, 2019. https://www.dw.com/en/merkel-signals-support-for-georgias-nato-membership-bid/a-3570539.

Merkel: Nato-Beitritt für Ukraine zu früh. 2008. *Bild*, April 2. Accessed October 21, 2018. https://www.bild.de/newsticker-meldungen/news/02-16-merkel-nato-4166452.bild.html.

NATO demonstriert Solidarität mit Georgien. 2008. *Deutsche Welle*, August 19. Accessed December 16, 2018. https://www.dw.com/de/nato-demonstriert-solidarit%C3%A4t-mit-georgien/a-3577485.

Nato: No Map for Georgia or Ukraine, but Alliance Vows Membership. 2008. *RadioFreeEurope/RadioLiberty*, April 3. Accessed October 21, 2018. https://www.rferl.org/a/1079726.html.

Poland Joins Western World's Policy of Détente towards Russia. 2010. *Newsweek Polska*, May 24.

Rettman, Andrew. 2010a. Germany and Russia Call for New EU Security Committee. *EUobserver*, June 7. Accessed September 28, 2017. https://euobserver.com/foreign/30223.

———. 2010b. US Cables Shed Light on EU "Friends of Russia' in Georgia War". *EUobserver*, December 1. Accessed October 24, 2018. https://euobserver.com/news/31400.

Riegert, Bernd. 2015. EU Police as Peacekeepers in Ukraine?. *Deutsche Welle*, February 19. Accessed March 10, 2018. http://p.dw.com/p/1EeqH.

Rinke, Andreas. 2014. Wie Putin Berlin verlor: Moskaus Annexion der Krim hat die deutsche Russland-Politik verändert. *Internationale Politik*, pp. 33–45. Accessed March 9, 2018. https://zeitschrift-ip.dgap.org/de/ip-die-zeitschrift/archiv/jahrgang-2014/mai-juni/wie-putin-berlin-verlor.

———. 2015. Vermitteln, verhandeln, verzweifeln: Wie der Ukraine-Konflikt zur westlich-russischen Dauerkrise wurde. *Internationale Politik*, pp. 8–21. Accessed April 14, 2019. https://zeitschrift-ip.dgap.org/de/ip-die-zeitschrift/archiv/jahrgang-2015/januar-februar/vermitteln-verhandeln-verzweifeln.

Roberts, Dan. 2014. Sweeping New US and EU Sanctions Target Russia's Banks and Oil Companies. *The Guardian*, September 12. Accessed March 17, 2018. https://www.theguardian.com/world/2014/sep/12/russia-sanctions-us-eu-banks-sberbank-oil-gazprom.

Runner, Philippa. 2008a. EU Diplomats Fly out to Mediate in Russia-Georgia War. *EUobserver*, August 9. Accessed October 21, 2018. https://euobserver.com/foreign/26595.

———. 2008b. Two-Headed Poland in EU Summit Farce. *EUobserver*, October 14. Accessed April 13, 2019. https://euobserver.com/political/26926.

Russia "Ends Georgia Operation". 2008. *BBC News*, August 12. Accessed October 21, 2018. http://news.bbc.co.uk/1/hi/world/europe/7555858.stm.

Russia, Georgia Agree to Peace Plan to End Fighting. 2008. *RadioFreeEurope/RadioLiberty*, August 12. Accessed March 31, 2019. https://www.rferl.org/a/Russia_Says_Military_Action_In_Georgia_Is_Over/1190416.html.

Russia-EU Relations Need a Gas Pedal Rather Than Reset Button. 2011. *Amber Bridge*, December 13. Accessed March 9, 2018. http://ambbr.artinfo.ru:8008/newstext?id=10887&lang=eng&tid=-1&year=2011&month=12.

Schröder, Gerhard. 2001. Deutsche Russlandpolitik—europäische Ostpolitik: Gegen Stereotype, für Partnerschaft und Offenheit—eine Positionsbestimmung. *Die Zeit*, April 5. Accessed April 13, 2019. https://www.zeit.de/2001/15/Deutsche_Russlandpolitik_-_europaeische_Ostpolitik/komplettansicht.

Siddique, Haroon and others. 2014. Ukraine Crisis: Diplomacy Fails to Yield Result as Russia Stays Put in Crimea. *The Guardian*, March 5. Accessed April 13, 2019. https://www.theguardian.com/world/2014/mar/05/ukraine-crisis-russia-nato-talks-live.

Sikorski, Radosław. 2008. I Fear Germany's Power Less than Her Inactivity. *Financial Times*, November 28. Accessed April 14, 2019. https://www.ft.com/content/b753cb42-19b3-11e1-ba5d-00144feabdc0.

———. 2015. Member States Must Back Their Jointly Chosen EU Leaders. *Financial Times*, August 16. Accessed April 13, 2019. https://www.ft.com/content/92f54bb8-3791-11e5-bdbb-35e55cbae175.

Some Details of German Abkhaz Plan Reported. 2008. *Civil.ge*, July 23. Accessed October 21, 2018. http://www.civil.ge/eng/article.php?id=18830.

Steinmeier, Frank-Walter. 2009. "Im engen Schulterschluss". *Der Spiegel*, January 12. Accessed April 13, 2019. http://magazin.spiegel.de/EpubDelivery/spiegel/pdf/63546785.

Steinmeier, Frank-Walter, and Ansgar Graw. 2008. "Ein sehr fragiler Waffenstillstand". *Welt am Sonntag*, August 17. Accessed December 16, 2018. https://www.welt.de/wams_print/article2316599/Ein-sehr-fragiler-Waffenstillstand.html.

Steinmeier lehnt eine Vermittlerrolle ab. 2013. *Die Welt*, December 19.

Steinmeier mahnt zu Rücksicht auf Russland. 2008. *Die Welt*, April 2. Accessed April 13, 2019. https://www.welt.de/politik/article1861864/Steinmeier-mahnt-zu-Ruecksicht-auf-Russland.html.

Swaine, Jon. 2008. Russia and Georgia "Agree in Principle" to Nicolas Sarkozy-Backed Peace Plan. *The Telegraph*, August 13. Accessed October 21, 2018. https://www.telegraph.co.uk/news/worldnews/europe/georgia/2550129/Russia-and-Georgia-agree-in-principle-to-Nicolas-Sarkozy-backed-peace-plan.html.

Tran, Mark, Julian Borger, and Ian Traynor. 2008. EU Threatens Sanctions against Russia. *The Guardian*, August 28. Accessed December 16, 2018. https://www.theguardian.com/world/2008/aug/28/eu.russia.

Traynor, Ian. 2008. Nato Allies Divided over Ukraine and Georgia. *The Guardian*, December 2. Accessed October 21, 2018. https://www.theguardian.com/world/2008/dec/02/ukraine-georgia.

Traynor, Ian, and Luke Harding. 2008. Surrender or Else, Russia Tells Georgia. *The Guardian*, August 12. Accessed October 21, 2018. https://www.theguardian.com/world/2008/aug/12/russia.georgia1.

Trip-Wire Deterrence. 2016. *The Economist*, July 2. Accessed March 7, 2019. https://www.economist.com/europe/2016/07/02/trip-wire-deterrence.

Ukraine: Germany Calls for Second Geneva Conference. 2014. *Deutsche Welle*, May 4. Accessed March 10, 2018. http://p.dw.com/p/1BthG.

Waterfield, Bruno. 2008. Georgia Conflict: Gordon Brown Heads for Clash over Russia at EU Summit. *The Telegraph*, September 1. Accessed December 16, 2018. https://www.telegraph.co.uk/news/worldnews/europe/georgia/2661144/Gordon-Brown-heads-for-clash-over-Russia-at-EU-summit.html.

Weiland, Severin. 2008. Debatte über Russland-Sanktionen: Frankreich bremst Scharfmacher in der EU. *Spiegel Online*, August 29. Accessed December 16, 2018. http://www.spiegel.de/politik/deutschland/debatte-ueber-russland-sanktionen-frankreich-bremst-scharfmacher-in-der-eu-a-575222.html.

Westerwelle macht sich für Timoschenko stark. 2013. *Die Welt*, June 21. Accessed October 30, 2015. https://www.welt.de/politik/ausland/article117329290/Westerwelle-macht-sich-fuer-Timoschenko-stark.html.

Westerwelle, Guido, and Radosław Sikorski. 2010. Europa endet nicht an der Ostgrenze Polens. *Tagesspiegel*, November 5. Accessed September 28, 2017. https://www.tagesspiegel.de/politik/guido-westerwelle-europa-endet-nicht-an-der-ostgrenze-polens/1974462.html.

Идея независимости Приднестровья не поддерживается какой-либо международной структурой. 2011. *Interfax*, June 5. Accessed April 19, 2019. https://www.interfax.ru/russia/193205.

Лавров: РФ выступает за особый статус Приднестровья в единой Молдавии. 2011. *Ria Novosti*, March 29. Accessed April 19, 2019. https://ria.ru/20110329/358925975.html.

Index[1]

---

[1] Note: Page numbers followed by 'n' refer to notes.

© The Author(s), under exclusive license to Springer Nature Switzerland AG 2021
L. Fix, *Germany's Role in European Russia Policy*, New Perspectives in German Political Studies,
https://doi.org/10.1007/978-3-030-68226-2

225

Printed by Printforce, the Netherlands